Frommer's®

PORTABLE
Dominican Republic

2nd Edition

by Darwin Porter & Danforth Prince

D0907411

Here's what the critics say about Frommer's:

"Amazingly easy to use. Very portable, very complete."

—*Booklist*

"Detailed, accurate, and easy-to-read information for all price ranges."

—*Glamour Magazine*

WILEY

Wiley Publishing, Inc.

Published by:

WILEY PUBLISHING, INC.

111 River St.
Hoboken, NJ 07030-5774

ISBN-13: 978-0-7645-9663-6
ISBN-10: 0-7645-9663-2

Editor: John Vorwald
Production Editor: Eric T. Schroeder
Cartographer: Elizabeth Puhl
Photo Editor: Richard Fox
Production by Wiley Indianapolis Composition Services

Front cover photo: Punta Cana: beach, palm trees, and sunbathers.

For information on our other products and services or to obtain technical
support, please contact our Customer Care Department within the U.S. at
800/762-2974, outside the U.S. at 317/572-3993 or fax 317/572-4002.

Wiley also publishes its books in a variety of electronic formats. Some con-
tent that appears in print may not be available in electronic formats.

Manufactured in the United States of America

5 4 3 2 1

Contents

List of Maps

About the Authors

A team of veteran travel writers, **Darwin Porter** and **Danforth Prince,** have produced numerous titles for Frommer's, especially to warm weather destinations such as Puerto Rico, Jamaica, the Cayman Islands, the Dominican Republic, the Virgin Islands, The Bahamas, and Bermuda. Porter, a former bureau chief of *The Miami Herald*, is also a Hollywood biographer, with recent releases including *Katharine the Great* (devoted to Katharine Hepburn) and *Howard Hughes: Hell's Angel*. Prince was formerly employed by the Paris bureau of *The New York Times*, and is today the president of Blood Moon Productions and other media-related firms.

An Invitation to the Reader

In researching this book, we discovered many wonderful places—hotels, restaurants, shops, and more. We're sure you'll find others. Please tell us about them, so we can share the information with your fellow travelers in upcoming editions. If you were disappointed with a recommendation, we'd love to know that, too. Please write to:

> *Frommer's Portable Dominican Republic,* 2nd Edition
> Wiley Publishing, Inc. • 111 River St. • Hoboken, NJ 07030-5774

An Additional Note

Please be advised that travel information is subject to change at any time—and this is especially true of prices. We therefore suggest that you write or call ahead for confirmation when making your travel plans. The authors, editors, and publisher cannot be held responsible for the experiences of readers while traveling. Your safety is important to us, however, so we encourage you to stay alert and be aware of your surroundings. Keep a close eye on cameras, purses, and wallets, all favorite targets of thieves and pickpockets.

Other Great Guides for Your Trip:

Frommer's Caribbean Cruises & Ports of Call
Frommer's Caribbean Ports of Call
Frommer's Caribbean

Frommer's Star Ratings, Icons & Abbreviations

Every hotel, restaurant, and attraction listing in this guide has been ranked for quality, value, service, amenities, and special features using a **star-rating system.** In country, state, and regional guides, we also rate towns and regions to help you narrow down your choices and budget your time accordingly. Hotels and restaurants are rated on a scale of zero (recommended) to three stars (exceptional). Attractions, shopping, nightlife, towns, and regions are rated according to the following scale: zero stars (recommended), one star (highly recommended), two stars (very highly recommended), and three stars (must-see).

In addition to the star-rating system, we also use **seven feature icons** that point you to the great deals, in-the-know advice, and unique experiences that separate travelers from tourists. Throughout the book, look for:

Finds	Special finds—those places only insiders know about
Fun Fact	Fun facts—details that make travelers more informed and their trips more fun
Kids	Best bets for kids and advice for the whole family
Moments	Special moments—those experiences that memories are made of
Overrated	Places or experiences not worth your time or money
Tips	Insider tips—great ways to save time and money
Value	Great values—where to get the best deals

The following **abbreviations** are used for credit cards:

AE	American Express	DISC	Discover	V	Visa
DC	Diners Club	MC	MasterCard		

Frommers.com

Now that you have the guidebook to a great trip, visit our website at **www.frommers.com** for travel information on more than 3,000 destinations. With features updated regularly, we give you instant access to the most current trip-planning information available. At Frommers.com, you'll also find the best prices on airfares, accommodations, and car rentals—and you can even book travel online through our travel booking partners. At Frommers.com, you'll also find the following:

- Online updates to our most popular guidebooks
- Vacation sweepstakes and contest giveaways
- Newsletter highlighting the hottest travel trends
- Online travel message boards with featured travel discussions

The Best of the Dominican Republic

Sugar-white beaches, inexpensive resorts, and rich natural beauty have long attracted visitors to the Dominican Republic. But at the same time, a not-entirely-deserved reputation for high crime, poverty, and social unrest has scared away many travelers. So which is it: A poverty-stricken country rife with pickpockets and muggers, or a burgeoning destination of beautiful beach bargains?

The answer, of course, is a little of both. The people of the Dominican Republic are among the friendliest in the Caribbean, and the hospitality here seems more genuine than in more commercialized Puerto Rico. The weather is nearly perfect year-round, and the Dominican Republic's white-sand beaches are some of the Caribbean's finest. Punta Cana/Bávaro, for example, is the longest strip of white sand in the entire region.

Safety *is* still a concern here, but that shouldn't dissuade you from planning a vacation to the Dominican Republic. Crime consists primarily of theft, robberies, and muggings, and most of it is limited to Santo Domingo (although the north coast resorts around Puerto Plata and Playa Dorada are not as safe as they should be). There is little incidence of violent crime against visitors, however. Follow simple common-sense rules of safety, and you'll be fine. Lock valuables in your hotel safe, carry only a reasonable amount of cash or (better yet) one or two credit cards, and avoid dark deserted places, just as you would at home.

(*One note:* Men traveling alone here will find themselves solicited more often by prostitutes than anywhere else in the Caribbean. Prostitutes are at their most visible and aggressive in such relatively unmonitored tourist zones as Cabarete and within the bars and lounges of most of the deluxe hotels of Santo Domingo, especially the Jaragua.)

The combination of low prices and scenic tropical terrain has made the Dominican Republic one of the fastest-growing destinations in the Caribbean. Bargain-hunting Canadians, in particular, flock here in droves. Europeans arrive by the plane loads in summer. Don't expect the lavish, spectacular resorts that you'll find on Puerto Rico or Jamaica, but do expect your vacation to be that much less expensive.

Although referred to as "just a poor man's Puerto Rico," in reality the Dominican Republic has its own distinctive cuisine and cultural heritage. Its Latin flavor is a sharp contrast to the character of many nearby islands, especially the British- and French-influenced ones.

Columbus spotted its coral-edged Caribbean coastline on his first voyage to the New World and pronounced: "There is no more beautiful island in the world." The first permanent European settlement in the New World was founded here on November 7, 1493, and its ruins still remain near Montecristi in the northeast part of the island. Natives called the island Quisqueya, "Mother Earth," before the Spaniards arrived to butcher them.

Nestled amid Cuba, Jamaica, and Puerto Rico in the heart of the Caribbean archipelago, the island of Hispaniola (Little Spain) is divided between Haiti, on the westernmost third of the island, and the Dominican Republic, which has a lush landmass about the size of Vermont and New Hampshire combined. In the Dominican interior, the fertile Valley of Cibao (rich, sugar-cane country) ends its upward sweep at Pico Duarte, the highest mountain peak in the West Indies, which soars to 3,125m (10,417 ft.).

Much of what Columbus first sighted still remains in a natural, unspoiled condition. One-third of the Dominican Republic's 1,401km (870-mile) coastline is devoted to beaches. The best are in Puerto Plata and La Romana, although Puerto Plata and other beaches on the Atlantic side of the island have dangerously strong currents at times.

Political turmoil kept visitors away for many years, but even that is a thing of the past. Almost from its inception, the country was steeped in misery and bloodshed, climaxing with the infamous reign of dictator Rafael Trujillo (1930–61) and the ensuing civil wars (1960–66). But, the country has been politically stable since then, and it is building and expanding rapidly. The economic growth hasn't benefited everybody equally, though. The country is still poor, even by Caribbean standards. Every day, many Dominicans risk their lives crossing the 87km-wide (54-mile) Mona Passage, hoping to land on Puerto Rico before attempting to slip into the United States.

The greatest threat to the Dominican Republic these days comes from hurricanes, which periodically flatten entire cities. The major resorts have become adept at getting back on their feet quickly after a hurricane. Still, if a hurricane hits the country before your trip, you might want to call ahead and make sure your room is still standing.

1 The Best Beaches

- **Playa Boca Chica** This is the Riviera of Santo Domingo, lying to the capital's immediate east. With its wide white or golden sands, it is one of the choice beaches of the Caribbean Basin, and it's set against a backdrop of coconut palms. The beach is a whirlwind of activity day and night. See chapter 5.

- **Punta Cana/Bávaro Beaches** One of the world's greatest beach strips is centered at Punta Cana and Bávaro on the eastern coast of the Dominican Republic. This stretch of beachfront goes on for 32km (20 miles) and is renowned for its all-inclusive resorts, the largest concentration in the Caribbean. The beaches here are wide, filled with golden sand, gorgeous, and safe for swimming all year. See chapter 6.

- **Cayo Levantado** On the peninsula of Samaná, along the east coast of the Dominican Republic, this is an island near the mouth of Bahía de Samaná. It can easily be reached by boat. Once on this island, beach lovers will find three beautiful strips of white sand. A tropical forest covers much of this hill-studded island and, when not enjoying the beach, you can go hiking along trails that are cut through the junglelike vegetation. Cayo Levantado was known to TV watchers in the '70s as the famous Bacardi Rum island, featured in Bacardi's commercials. See chapter 7.

- **Playa Rincón** On the eastern shoreline of the Peninsula Samaná, Playa Rincón is consistently hailed by *Condé Nast Traveler* as one of the ten top beaches in the Caribbean, and we agree that it deserves such an accolade. Set at 600m (2,000 ft.) against the cliffs of Cape Cabrón, the beach is hard to reach, but once you're here you can wander a Robinson Crusoe tropical paradise of white sands. There's plenty of color in the sea—vivid turquoise, blues, and greens, and it's safe for swimming and ideal for snorkeling. See chapter 7.

- **Playa Dorada** This is the most celebrated beach along the Amber Coast and the site of the largest concentration of all-inclusive resorts in the Caribbean. The golden or white sands along its Atlantic Ocean waters—often turbulent—have been discovered, and how. Water-skiers and windsurfers alike take delight here. When not playing on a nearby 18-hole golf course, guests at all the Playa Dorada resorts have free access to the beach. See chapter 8.

- **Playa Luperón**   Less overrun than Playa Dorada, this beach lies an hour's drive west of Puerto Plata. Once here, you'll find a beach of powdery white sands set amid palm trees that provide wonderful shade. The beach is ideal for snorkeling, scuba diving, and windsurfing. See chapter 8.

2 The Best Attractions

- **Altos de Chavón,** La Romana   This is a re-creation of a 16th-century Spanish village, lying near the famous Casa de Campo resort at La Romana along the southern coastline. It is a true living museum—part artisans' colony, part tourist diversion. Its highlight is a Grecian-style amphitheater. It's also one of the best places in the Dominican Republic to shop for handicrafts. See chapter 5.

- **Zona Colonial,** Santo Domingo   Comprising nearly a dozen city blocks, this is what remains of the first European city in the Americas, and many of its monuments have been well preserved. Old Santo Domingo was the seat of Spanish power in the West Indies and was the port of that country's conquest of the Western Hemisphere. Wandering its cobblestone streets and exploring its old churches and monuments is to step back into history. At every turn, you see something historic, such as Calle Las Damas, the first paved street in the Americas. See chapter 4.

- **Alcázar de Colón,** Santo Domingo   In the Colonial Zone of the old city, this fortress was built for Columbus's son, Diego, and his wife, who was the niece of King Ferdinand of Spain. Diego ruled the colony in 1509 and made this his residence. This is also the palace-fortress where he entertained the likes of Cortés, Ponce de León, and Balboa. See chapter 4.

- **Parque Nacional Los Haïtises,** Samaná Peninsula   On the southern tier of Samaná Peninsula, this sprawling park is the second-most visited in the country, covering 208 sq. km (78 sq. miles) and spanning 24km (15 miles) west from Boca de Inferno to the head of Río Barracote. It's a mangrove swamp that's home to some 112 bird species and nearly 100 plant species. Caves of the original inhabitants, the Taíno Indians, remain to be explored. See chapter 7.

2

Planning Your Trip to the Dominican Republic

Golden- or white-sand beaches shaded by palm trees and crystalline waters teeming with rainbow-hued fish—it's all just a few hours' flight from the East Coast of the United States.

To the southeast of Cuba, the Dominican Republic shares the island of Hispaniola with the even more exotic (and dangerous) Haiti.

Spicy food, spicier merengue, and the gentle, leisurely lifestyle of the islands draw increasing thousands to the Dominican Republic every year. Its long, palm-lined *playas*—or beaches—such as Punta Cana, Boca Chica, Bávaro, and Playa Dorada have become world famous.

But the one thing that is making the beach-loving world take notice of the island is its spectacularly affordable prices, especially those charged at its all-inclusive resorts.

Frugal travelers from Canada and America, and from such European countries as Britain, Germany, Spain, Switzerland, Italy, and France, have combined forces to make the Dominican Republic the most popular country to visit in the Caribbean.

1 Regions in Brief

SANTO DOMINGO Originally called Nueva Isabela and once Ciudad Trujillo (named after the despised dictator), the capital of the Dominican Republic was founded in 1496 by none other than Bartolomé, the brother of Columbus. Today, Santo Domingo is a thriving and sprawling metropolis of some 2.5 million people.

One of the fastest-growing cities in the Caribbean, it still retains much of its Spanish flavor in its colonial zone. Other than San Juan, it also offers the largest concentration of museums in the Caribbean. What it doesn't have is a beach. So, come here for sightseeing and shopping, but for the sands head elsewhere.

BOCA CHICA & JUAN DOLIO   To the immediate east of Santo Domingo, this is the Riviera of the capital city. These twin resorts open onto one of the most beautiful beaches on the east coast, known for their powdery white sands and shallow waters, safe for swimming. Fun in the sun begins approximately 31km (19 miles) east of Santo Domingo, but only a 5-minute drive from Las Américas International Airport serving Santo Domingo. Many Europeans call the area "Playa St. Tropez," as it evokes the fun-loving port on the French Riviera. Lying immediately east of Boca Chica, the fast-rising Juan Dolio boasts even more hotels than Boca Chica, most of them all-inclusives.

CASA DE CAMPO   One of the greatest resorts in the Caribbean, Casa de Campo, lies east of Santo Domingo along the southeast coast. Offering unparalleled luxury for the Dominican Republic, this resort was built in one of the richest sugar cane–producing terrains in the Caribbean, taking about 2 hours to reach by land transport from the capital. If the allure of Casa de Campo weren't enough, the resort adjoins the biggest man-made attractions in the Dominican Republic: Altos de Chavón, the recreation of a 16th-century Spanish village that is amazingly realistic. It's part living museum, part artisans' colony. It's also a great place to go on a shopping expedition, where you can purchase many of the paintings and crafts produced on the spot, including jewelry, macramé items, and other knickknacks.

PUNTA CANA & BAVARO   Nowhere in the Caribbean is there such a concentration of resorts, most of them all-inclusives. These resort developments dominate what has come to be known as Costa del Coco or "The Coconut Coast." There are more than 32km (20 miles) of powder-white sandy beaches, among the longest stretch of such beachfront in the world. The beaches edge up to crystal-clear waters, and this coastal land is an upmarket resort, filled with government-rated four- or five-star hotels.

SAMANA   This is a peninsula in the east of the Dominican Republic that once provided a haven in the 1820s for escaped American slaves. In its national park, Los Haïtises, inscriptions from the early settlers, the Taíno Indians, have been discovered. From January to March (more or less) the humpback whales of the Atlantic Ocean come here to breed and rear their newborn calves. The peninsula stretches for 48km (30 miles), lying about 120km (75 miles) northeast of Santo Domingo. The terrain consists of lush, forested hills along with banana and coconut plantations. Since the '90s, tourism has arrived in droves, centering about Las Terrenas, the town of Samaná, and Las Galeras.

Dominican Republic

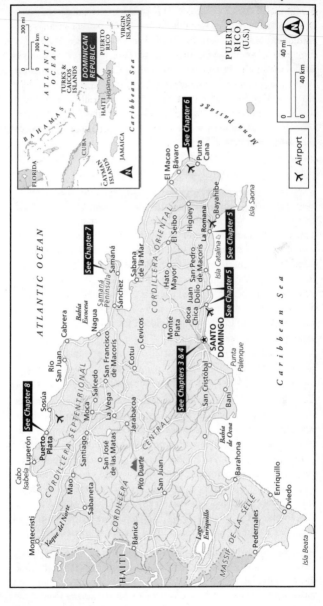

PUERTO PLATA & THE AMBER COAST   The northern shore-line of the Dominican Republic is one of the world's great beach-front playgrounds. Its center is Puerto Plata, named "port of silver" by Columbus. The Amber Coast nickname comes from the rich deposits of amber ore discovered along this coast. The waters of the Atlantic wash up on its beaches of golden sand. The tourist development here since the 1980s has been remarkable, and overbuilding is rampant. To the immediate east of Puerto Plata is Playa Dorada, the largest all-inclusive resort complex in the world, lying about halfway between the Haitian border and Samaná Peninsula. To the immediate east, in Sosúa, is the fast-rising resort of Cabarete, the windsurfing capital of the Caribbean. "It's our Malibu," is what one local told us.

2 Visitor Information

In the United States, you can contact the **Dominican Republic Tourist Information Center** at 136 E. 57th St., Suite 803, New York, NY 10022 (© **888/374-6361** or 212/588-1012); or at 248 NW 42nd Ave., Miami, FL 33126 (© **888/358-9594** or 305/444-4592; fax 305/444-4845). In Canada, try the office at 2081 Crescent St., Montréal, Quebec H39, 2B8, Canada (© **800/563-1611** or 514/ 499-1918; fax 514/499-1393); or at 35 Church St., Unit 53, Toronto, Ontario M5E 1TE (© **888/494-5050;** fax 416/361-2130). Don't expect too many specifics.

In England, there's an office at 20 Hand Court, High Holborn, WC1 (© **020/7242-7778**).

On the Web, check out www.dominicanrepublic.com.

TRAVEL AGENTS   Travel agents can save you time and money by uncovering the best package deals, airfare, and rental car rates. Most are professional, but the occasional unscrupulous agent may push deals that bag the juiciest commissions, so shop around and ask hard questions. Arm yourself with the information in this book, and don't let anyone pressure you into a vacation that's not right for you.

If you enlist a travel agent, use one that's a member of the **American Society of Travel Agents (ASTA),** 1101 King St., Suite 200, Alexandria, VA 22314 (© **703/739-2782;** www.astanet.com). Call ASTA or visit their website for a list of members in your area.

3 Entry Requirements & Customs

ENTRY REQUIREMENTS   Entry requirements can and do change, so the savvy visitor should check with the nearest Dominican embassy or consulate at least 6 weeks prior to departure. Currently, citizens of such countries as Australia, Canada, France, Germany, Ireland, Italy, Spain, Switzerland, the U.K., and the U.S. need a valid passport to enter the Dominican Republic. Upon arrival at their port of entry, they must also purchase a RD$200 ($7.15) tourist card to enter. In lieu of a passport, an original birth certificate and an additional photo-bearing document (such as a voter's registration or driver's license) is also acceptable. Passport-bearing visitors from the U.K. are exempt from purchasing the tourist card.

We recommend carrying a passport even though it may not be specifically required.

You'll certainly need identification at some point, and a passport is the best form of ID for speeding through Customs and Immigration. Driver's licenses are not acceptable as a sole form of ID.

Before leaving home, make two copies of your documents—including your passport and your driver's license, your airline ticket, and any hotel vouchers—and leave them home with someone.

CUSTOMS   Just before you leave home, check with your country's Customs or Foreign Affairs department for the latest guidelines—including information on items that are not allowed to be brought into your home country, since the rules are subject to change and often contain some surprising oddities.

WHAT YOU CAN BRING INTO THE DOMINICAN REPUBLIC   Customs allows you to bring in 1 liter of alcohol, plus 200 cigarettes and gift articles not exceeding a value of RD$2,800 ($100). Anything over that limit is subject to import taxes.

WHAT YOU CAN TAKE HOME FROM THE DOMINICAN REPUBLIC   Returning **U.S. citizens** who have been away for at least 48 hours are allowed to bring back, once every 30 days, RD$22,400 ($800) worth of merchandise duty-free. You'll be charged a flat rate of 4% duty on the next RD$28,000 ($1,000) worth of purchases. Be sure to have your receipts handy. On mailed gifts, the duty-free limit is RD$5,600 ($200). With some exceptions, you cannot bring fresh fruits and vegetables into the United States. For specifics on what you can bring back, download the invaluable free pamphlet *Know Before You Go* online at **www.cbp.gov**. (Click on "Travel," then "Know Before You Go Online Brochure.") Or contact the **U.S. Customs & Border Protection (CBP),** 1300 Pennsylvania Ave. NW, Washington, DC 20229 (© **877/287-8667**) and request the pamphlet.

For a clear summary of **Canadian** rules, write for the booklet *I Declare,* issued by the **Canada Border Services Agency** (📞 **800/ 461-9999** in Canada, or 204/983-3500; www.cbsa-asfc.gc.ca). Canada allows its citizens a C$750 exemption, and you're allowed to bring back duty-free one carton of cigarettes, one can of tobacco, 40 imperial ounces of liquor, and 50 cigars. In addition, each day you're allowed to mail gifts to Canada valued at less than C$60, provided they're unsolicited and don't contain alcohol or tobacco (write on the package "Unsolicited gift, under $60 value"). All valuables should be declared on the Y-38 form before departure from Canada, including serial numbers of valuables you already own, such as expensive foreign cameras. *Note:* The RD$21,000 ($750) exemption can only be used once a year and only after an absence of 7 days.

U.K. citizens returning from **a non-EU country** have a customs allowance of: 200 cigarettes; 50 cigars; 250 grams of smoking tobacco; 2 liters of still table wine; 1 liter of spirits or strong liqueurs (over 22% volume); 2 liters of fortified wine, sparkling wine or other liqueurs; 60cc (ml) perfume; 250 cc (ml) of toilet water; and £145 worth of all other goods, including gifts and souvenirs. People age 16 and under cannot have the tobacco or alcohol allowance. For more information, contact HM Revenue & Customs at 📞 **0845/ 010-9000** (from outside the U.K., 020/8929-0152), or consult their website at www.hmrc.gov.uk.

The duty-free allowance in **Australia** is A$400 or, for those under age 18, A$200. Citizens can bring in 250 cigarettes or 250 grams of loose tobacco, and 1.125 liters of alcohol. If you're returning with valuables you already own, such as foreign-made cameras, you should file form B263. A helpful brochure available from Australian consulates or Customs offices is *Know Before You Go.* For more information, call the **Australian Customs Service** at 📞 **1300/363- 263,** or log on to www.customs.gov.au.

The duty-free allowance for **New Zealand** is NZ$700. Citizens over age 17 can bring in 200 cigarettes, 50 cigars, or 250 grams of tobacco (or an assortment of all three if their combined weight doesn't exceed 250g); plus 4.5 liters of wine and beer, or 1.125 liters of liquor. New Zealand currency does not carry import or export restrictions. Fill out a certificate of export, listing the valuables you are taking out of the country; that way, you can bring them back without paying duty. Most questions are answered in a free pamphlet available at New Zealand consulates and Customs offices: *New Zealand Customs Guide for Travellers, Notice no. 4.* For more information, contact **New**

Zealand Customs Service, The Customhouse, 17–21 Whitmore St., Box 2218, Wellington (© **04/473-6099** or 0800/428-786; www. customs.govt.nz).

4 Money

In general the Dominican Republic is one of the most affordable destinations in the Caribbean—hence, its great popularity. Ten U.S. dollars still buys a lot on the island.

The catch is to plan a vacation way in advance. If you just show up, you'll be charged the "rack rate" (that is, bookings off the street), and some of these deals can be expensive. However, if you book at an all-inclusive resort, with a package that includes both airfare and accommodations, you can live at a rather moderate per-diem cost, even though staying at a government-rated four- or five-star hotel. Many of these package deals, offered even in winter, can amount to as little as RD$2,100 ($75) per person per day.

Even if you do arrive independently, you can often find lodgings—and rather decent ones at that—for as little as RD$980 ($35) a night in a double room. Many meals cost only RD$336 ($12) if you avoid expensive items such as lobster or steak.

Cigars are plentiful and cheap. It's always wise to stick to the national drinks such as rum or the local beer, El Presidente. If you order Scotch, a shot will be expensive because of the import taxes.

TRAVELER'S CHECKS   Traveler's checks are something of an anachronism from the days before the ATM made cash accessible at any time. These days, traveler's checks seem unnecessary. However, if you want to avoid ATM service charges, if you're staying in a remote place, or if you just want the security of knowing you can get a refund in the event that your wallet is stolen, you may want to purchase traveler's checks—provided that you don't mind showing identification every time you want to cash one.

You can get traveler's checks at almost any bank. **American Express** offers checks that usually incur a service charge ranging from 1% to 4%. You can buy American Express traveler's checks over the phone by calling © **800/221-7282;** you can also purchase checks online at www.americanexpress.com. American Express gold or platinum cardholders can avoid paying the fee by ordering over the telephone; platinum cardholders can also purchase checks fee-free in person at Amex Travel Service locations (check the website for the office nearest you).

The D.R. Peso, the U.S. and Canadian Dollars, & the British Pound

The Dominican monetary unit is the **peso (RD$),** which is made of up 100 **centavos.** Coin denominations are in 1, 5, 10, 25, and 50 centavos, and 1 peso. Bill denominations are in RD$5, RD$10, RD$20, RD$50, RD$100, RD$500, and RD$1,000.

At press time, the going exchange rate between the peso and the most frequently traded currency, the U.S. dollar, was RD$28 = US$1 (or RD$1 = 3.6 US¢). Canadian dollars and British pounds are less frequently traded and, in most cases, are accepted only at banks and at very large hotels. At this writing, the British pound traded at approximately RD$45 = 1£ (or RD$1 = 2.2 pence) and the Canadian dollar traded at RD$17 = C$1 (or RD$1 = 5.8C¢).

Remember that these rates can and will change, as reflected by a complicated roster of political and economic factors, so check the rates from time to time as a means of staying abreast of the cost of your holiday.

RD$	US$	UK£	C$	RD$	US$	UK£	C$
1	0.04	0.02	0.06	75.00	2.70	1.65	4.35
2	0.07	0.04	0.12	100.00	3.60	2.20	5.80
3	0.11	0.07	0.17	125.00	4.50	2.75	7.25
4	0.14	0.09	0.23	150.00	5.40	3.30	8.70
5	0.18	0.11	0.29	175.00	6.30	3.85	10.15
6	0.22	0.13	0.35	200.00	7.20	4.40	11.60
7	0.25	0.15	0.41	225.00	8.10	4.95	13.05
8	0.29	0.18	0.46	250.00	9.00	5.50	14.50
9	0.32	0.20	0.52	275.00	9.90	6.05	15.95
10	0.36	0.22	0.58	300.00	10.80	6.60	17.40
15	0.54	0.33	0.87	350.00	12.60	7.70	20.30
20	0.72	0.44	1.16	400.00	14.40	8.80	23.20
25	0.90	0.55	1.45	500.00	18.00	11.00	29.0
50	1.80	1.10	2.90	1000.00	36.00	22.00	58.00

Visa offers traveler's checks at Citibank branches and other financial institutions nationwide; call ✆ **800/732-1322** (www.visa.com) to find a purchase location near you. AAA members can obtain Visa

Heads Up: A Note on Pricing

Nearly all hotels in the Dominican Republic list their rates in U.S. dollars, while most restaurants and shops deal with both U.S. and Dominican Republic currencies. Accordingly, our hotel listings will reflect only U.S. dollar prices, while our restaurant, shop, and attractions listings will include Dominican peso prices followed by the U.S. dollar conversions.

checks fee-free at most AAA offices or by calling ℂ 866/339-3378. For **MasterCard** call (ℂ **800/223-9920;** www.mastercard.com).

If you carry traveler's checks, be sure to keep a record of their serial numbers (separately from the checks, of course), so you're ensured a refund in case they're lost or stolen.

ATMs   ATMs are linked to a huge network that, most likely, includes your bank at home. **Cirrus** (ℂ **800/424-7787;** www.mastercard.com) and **PLUS** (ℂ **800/843-7587;** www.visa.com) are the two most popular networks; check the back of your ATM card to see which network your bank belongs to. Use the toll-free numbers to locate ATMs in your destination; most islands now have ATMs, though they may be hard to find outside the main towns.

If you're traveling abroad, ask your bank for a list of overseas ATMs. Be sure to check the daily withdrawal limit before you depart, and ask whether you need a new personal identification number (PIN).

CREDIT CARDS   Credit cards are a safe way to carry money. They also provide a convenient record of all your expenses, and they generally offer relatively good exchange rates. You can also withdraw cash advances from your credit cards at banks or ATMs, provided you know your PIN. If you've forgotten yours, or didn't even know you had one, call the number on the back of your credit card and ask the bank to send it to you. It usually takes 5 to 7 business days, though some banks will provide the number over the phone if you tell them your mother's maiden name or some other personal information. Keep in mind that when you use your credit card abroad, most banks assess a 2% fee above the 1% fee charged by Visa or MasterCard or American Express for currency conversion on credit charges. But credit cards still may be the smart way to go when you factor in things like exorbitant ATM fees and higher traveler's check exchange rates (and service fees).

CASH   It's always a good idea to carry around some cash for small expenses, like cab rides, or for that rare occasion when a restaurant or small shop doesn't take plastic, which can happen if you're dining at a neighborhood joint or buying from a small vendor. U.S. dollars are accepted everywhere. Perhaps $100 in cash (small bills) will see you through.

5 When to Go

High season in the Dominican Republic is from mid-December to mid-April. The weather is perfect for beach conditions, in that it's usually dry, and the temperatures are moderated by cooling trade winds blowing in from the northeast. Sometimes a few days can be windy under cloudy skies, but these periods often come and go quickly.

In some ways, April is the most idyllic month, with perfect weather before the heat of summer comes in May. In spite of the heat, many Europeans prefer a summer visit. As one visitor on the beach who hails from Yorkshire told us, "After a cold winter in the north of England, I've come just for the heat."

Rainy season is from late May until late November. That doesn't mean, however, that it rains every day. Often the showers are short bursts to be followed by clear skies and plenty of sun.

If you want to know how to pack just before you go, check the Weather Channel's online 5-day forecast at **www.weather.com** for the latest information.

HURRICANES   The curse of Dominican weather, the hurricane season, lasts—officially, at least—from June 1 to November 30. But there's no cause for panic: Satellite forecasts give enough warning that precautions can be taken.

To get a weather report before you go, call the nearest branch of the **National Weather Service,** listed in your phone directory under the "U.S. Department of Commerce." You can also check the **Weather Channel** on the Web at **www.weather.com**.

Average Temperature & Rainfall in Santo Domingo

	Jan	Feb	Mar	Apr	May	June	July	Aug	Sept	Oct	Nov	Dec
Temp. (°F)	76	76	77	79	80	81	81	81	81	80	79	77
Temp. (°C)	24	24	25	26	27	27	27	27	27	27	26	25
Rainfall (in.)	2.2	1.7	1.9	3.0	7.0	6.1	6.1	6.4	6.8	6.5	4.4	2.5

Dominican Holidays

January 1	New Year's Day
January 6	Epiphany/Three Kings Day
January 21	Our Lady of Altagracia
January 26	Duarte Day
February 27	Independence Day, Carnaval
March/April	Maundy Thursday, Holy Friday, Easter Sunday
April 14	Pan-American Day
May 1	Labor Day
July 16	Foundation of Sociedad la Trinitaria
August 16	Restoration Day
September 24	Our Lady of Mercedes
October 12	Columbus Day
October 24	United Nations Day
November 1	All Saints' Day
December 25	Christmas

DOMINICAN REPUBLIC CALENDAR OF EVENTS

January

New Year's Eve No place is more fun to be in the Caribbean than Santo Domingo on New Year's Eve. Thousands of merry-makers gather along the Malecón (actually Av. George Washington) to celebrate the coming year. Along this sea-bordering boulevard, bands blast merengue and other music throughout the night. At midnight, fireworks explode and sirens go off. The party continues until daybreak.

New Year's Day The merrymaking continues on New Year's Day in the town of Bayaguana, lying northeast of Santo Domingo. Here the annual **Festivales del Santo Cristo de Bayaguana** include street dancing, singing, various folkloric activities, a procession through town, and the inevitable Mass.

Epifanía Also called Día de los Santos Reyes, this nationwide event is celebrated throughout the Dominican Republic. Every town and village marks the end of the Christmas holidays. Santo Domingo has the most interesting observances, with processions through town starring the Three Wise Men. As they sleep, children are given gifts by their parents. January 6.

Día de Duarte   Juan Pablo Duarte is hailed as the father of the Dominican Republic. Duarte executed a bloodless coup against Haiti, asserting his country's independence over their western neighbor. The date was February 27, 1844. Duarte's birthday, on January 26,1814, is celebrated with gun salutes in Santo Domingo. A carnival is staged in such cities as Santiago, Samaná, San Pedro de Macorís, and La Romana. January 26.

February

Carnaval   This is the biggest event on the Dominican calendar, and it's widely celebrated preceding and including Independence Day, February 27, which often falls around Lent. In Santo Domingo, the big event is 2 or 3 days before February 27, but festivities range around the country in all the towns and cities. Expect spectacular floats, flamboyantly costumed performers, and lots of street dancing, rum drinking, and street food. The masks worn by the participants symbolize good and evil. Some 30,000 merrymakers parade along the Malecón in Santo Domingo.

April

Semana Santa   This observance of Holy Week hardly rivals Seville's in Spain, but it's the best in the Western Hemisphere. The week surrounding Easter is marked by islandwide pageants, processions, and celebrations. Many towns and cities burn in effigy a grotesque representation of Judas Iscariot.

June

Espíritu Santo   The island's African heritage is much in evidence during this observance. Although an islandwide event, the most intriguing celebrations take place in the town of Villa Mella near Santo Domingo. The festivities are marked by the playing of African instruments such as Congo drums. First or second week of June.

Latin Music Festival   This is a mammoth 3-day event staged at Santo Domingo's Olympic Stadium. It attracts not only islanders, but also many foreign visitors and people from the other Caribbean nations, including Puerto Rico. Some of the biggest names in Latin music are featured at this event, including such past performers as Enrique Iglesias, Tito Rojas (the salsa king), and Fernando Villalona (merengue's only living legend). Jazz, salsa, merengue, reggae, and bachata players entertain the masses. Ask for the actual dates in June at the tourist office, as they vary.

July

Festival del Merengue   Slightly less raucous than Carnaval, a blast of merengue music fills the night along the Malecón in Santo Domingo the last week of July. Festivities continue into the first week of August, coinciding with the observance of the founding of Santo Domingo on August 4, 1496. Artisan fairs are just part of the agenda, along with a gastronomic festival, but it is the live merengue music that attracts participants by the thousands. The world's top merengue musicians and dancers attend this wildly crazed event.

August

Fiesta Patria de la Restauración   Restoration Day is celebrated islandwide, commemorating the regaining of Dominican Republic independence from Spain in 1863. Parades, live music, street fairs, and other events reach their crescendo in the two main cities of Santo Domingo and Santiago.

October

Puerto Plata Festival   Like the Merengue Festival, this is the major cultural event on the northern coast of the Dominican Republic, a weeklong festival that brings the best of bands— merengue, blues, jazz, and folk concerts—to Fuerte San Felipe at the end of the Malecón. Troupes from all over the island come here to perform traditional songs and dances, along with salsa, merengue steps, and African spirituals. Expect parades, costumes, and food fairs. In October, but dates vary.

Descubrimiento de América   The so-called "discovery" by Columbus of America on October 12, 1492, is no longer celebrated as a grand event in many parts of the Western Hemisphere. The explorer's arrival on an already inhabited continent brought death, destruction, and disease to much of the Caribbean. Nonetheless, because of its strong link to Spain, the festivities in Santo Domingo reach their peak with celebrations at the tomb of the explorer at Faro a Colón and at the Cathedral of Santo Domingo.

6 Travel Insurance

MEDICAL INSURANCE   Most health insurance policies cover you if you get sick away from home—but check, particularly if you're insured by an HMO. With the exception of certain HMOs and Medicare/Medicaid, your medical insurance should cover medical treatment—even hospital care—overseas. However, most out-of-country hospitals make you pay your bills up front, and send you a refund after you've returned home and filed the necessary paperwork. And, in a worst-case scenario, there's the high cost of emergency evacuation. If you require additional medical insurance, try **MEDEX Assistance** (② 410/453-6300; www.medexassist.com) or **Travel Assistance International** (② 800/821-2828; www.travel assistance.com; for general information on services, call the

company's Worldwide Assistance Services Inc. at © **800/777-8710;**
www.worldwideassistance.com).

7 Health & Safety

STAYING HEALTHY

The Dominican Republic is not the healthiest place to visit, so precautions are advised. Most visitors at some point come down with at
least a mild case of diarrhea, the *número uno* illness for D.R. travelers.

Travelers to rural areas of the island, especially the provinces bordering Haiti, are at risk for malaria. There is little risk, however, if
you stay in the major resort areas such as Playa Dorada or Punta
Cana.

Another plague, schistosomiasis, is a parasitic infection found in
fresh water in parts of the D.R. Don't go swimming in freshwater
rivers. Hepatitis B is also commonplace in the D.R.

To find out about current U.S. Department of State travel warn-
ings about the D.R. or the Caribbean in general, check http://travel.
state.gov.

STAYING SAFE

Foreigners should review their security practices and maintain a low
profile. Protests, demonstrations, and general strikes occur periodically. These disturbances have the potential to turn violent, with
participants rioting and erecting roadblocks. In the past, police have
used deadly force in response to violent protests. Although these
events are not targeted at foreigners, it is advisable to exercise caution when traveling throughout the country. In urban areas, travel
should be conducted on main routes whenever possible. Street
crowds should be avoided. U.S. citizens considering overland travel
between the Dominican Republic and Haiti should first consult the
Consular Information Sheet for Haiti as well as the Internet site of
the U.S. Embassy in Port-au-Prince at http://usembassy.state.gov
for current information about travel conditions to and in Haiti.
Additional advice about strikes and other security issues in the
Dominican Republic may be obtained from the U.S. Embassy in
Santo Domingo or by visiting the embassy's website at http://santo
domingo.usembassy.gov.

Petty street crime involving tourists does occur, and normal precautions should be taken. Visitors walking the streets should always
be aware of their surroundings to avoid becoming victims of crime.
Valuables left unattended in parked automobiles, on beaches, and in
other public places are vulnerable to theft. Cellular telephones

should be carried in a pocket, rather than on a belt or in a purse. One increasingly common method of street robbery is for a person or persons on a moped (often coasting with the engine turned off so as not to draw attention) to approach a pedestrian, grab the cell phone, purse, or backpack, and then speed away.

Passengers in private taxis (known locally as *carros públicos*) are frequently the victims of pickpocketing. In some instances, the taxi drivers themselves have been known to rob riders. At least one American passenger on a *motoconcho* (motorcycle taxi) has been robbed by the driver. Visitors to the Dominican Republic are

What to Do If You Get Sick Away from Home

Finding a good doctor in the Dominican Republic can be a problem once you leave Santo Domingo and the big resorts such as those at Playa Dorada or Punta Cana. You should be in fairly good health before venturing into the hinterlands. Most doctors, once you get one, have been educated in the United States and speak English.

If you worry about getting sick away from home, you might want to consider medical travel insurance. In most cases, however, your existing health plan will provide all the coverage you need. Be sure to carry your identification card in your wallet.

If you suffer from a chronic illness, consult your doctor before your departure. For conditions such as epilepsy, diabetes, or heart problems, wear a **MedicAlert** identification tag (© **888/633-4298**; www.medicalert.org), which will immediately alert doctors to your condition and give them access to your records through MedicAlert's 24-hour hotline.

Contact the **International Association for Medical Assistance to Travellers (IAMAT)** (© **716/754-4883** or, in Canada, © 416/652-0137; www.iamat.org) for tips on travel and health concerns in the countries you're visiting, and lists of local, English-speaking doctors. The United States **Centers for Disease Control and Prevention** (© **800 /311-3435**; www.cdc.gov) provides up-to-date information on health hazards by region or country and offers tips on food safety.

strongly advised to take only hotel taxis or taxis operated by services whose cabs are ordered in advance by phone and can subsequently be identified and tracked.

Visitors should limit their use of personal credit cards because of credit-card fraud and may wish to consider coordinating their trip with their credit-card company so that only hotel bills or other specified expenses may be charged. Credit cards should never leave the sight of the cardholder, in order to prevent the card's information from being copied for illegal use. It is advisable to pay close attention to credit-card bills following a trip to the Dominican Republic.

Automated teller machines (ATMs) are present throughout Santo Domingo and other major cities. However, as with credit cards, the use of ATMs should be minimized as a means of avoiding theft or misuse. One local scheme involves sticking photographic film or pieces of paper in the card feeder of the ATM so that an inserted card becomes jammed. Once the card owner has concluded the card is irretrievable, the thieves extract both the jamming material and the card, which they then use.

The overall level of crime tends to rise during the Christmas season, and visitors to the Dominican Republic should take extra precautions when visiting the country between November and January.

Traveling with Minors

It's always wise to have plenty of documentation when traveling with children in today's world. For changing details on entry requirements for children traveling abroad, keep up to date by going to the U.S. Department of State website: http://travel.state.gov. To prevent international child abduction, EU governments have initiated procedures at entry and exit points. These often (but not always) include requiring documentary evidence of relationship and permission for the child's travel from the parent or legal guardian not present. Having such documentation on hand, even if not required, facilitates entries and exits. All children must have their own passport. To obtain a passport, the child **must** be present—that is, in person—at the center issuing the passport. Both parents must be present as well. If not, then a notarized statement from the parents is required. Any questions parents or guardians might have can be answered by calling the **National Passport Information Center** at ℰ **877/487-2778** Monday to Friday 8am to 8pm Eastern Standard Time.

8 Specialized Travel Resources

FOR TRAVELERS WITH DISABILITIES

The Dominican Republic has done little to open up exploration of their island by persons with disabilities. Getting around the country with its potholed roads is hard enough on a healthy visitor with perfect mobility. A pole-vaulter might find it difficult walking in traffic in Santo Domingo. Your best bet is to work through a travel agent to find a resort hotel suitable for a visit by persons with disabilities. Suitable rooms and grounds are more likely to be found at Playa Dorada or Punta Cana than elsewhere.

Even so, a disability shouldn't stop anyone from traveling. There are more resources out there today than ever before.

Many travel agencies offer customized tours and itineraries for travelers with disabilities. **Flying Wheels Travel** (© 507/451-5005; www.flyingwheelstravel.com) offers escorted tours and cruises that emphasize sports and private tours in minivans with lifts. **Access-Able Travel Source** (© 303/232-2979; www.access-able.com) offers extensive access information and advice for traveling around the world with disabilities. **Accessible Journeys** (© 800/846-4537 or 610/521-0339; www.disabilitytravel.com) caters specifically to slow walkers and wheelchair travelers and their families and friends.

Avis Rent a Car has an "Avis Access" program that offers such services as a dedicated 24-hour toll-free number (© 888/879-4273) for customers with special travel needs; special car features such as swivel seats, spinner knobs, and hand controls; and accessible bus service.

Organizations that offer assistance to disabled travelers include **MossRehab** (www.mossresourcenet.org), which provides a library of accessible-travel resources online; **SATH (Society for Accessible Travel & Hospitality)** (© 212/447-7284; www.sath.org; annual membership fees: $45 adults, $30 seniors and students), which offers a wealth of travel resources for all types of disabilities and informed recommendations on destinations, access guides, travel agents, tour operators, vehicle rentals, and companion services; and the **American Foundation for the Blind (AFB)** (© 800/232-5463; www.afb.org), a referral resource for the blind or visually impaired that includes information on traveling with Seeing Eye dogs.

For more information specifically targeted to travelers with disabilities, the community website **iCan** (www.icanonline.net/channels/

travel/index.cfm) has destination guides and several regular columns on accessible travel. Also check out the quarterly magazine **Emerging Horizons** ($14.95 per year, $19.95 outside the U.S.; www.emerging horizons.com), and *Open World* magazine, published by SATH (see above; subscription: $13 per year, $21 outside the U.S.).

FOR GAY & LESBIAN TRAVELERS

Although homosexuality is not technically legal in the D.R., a staunchly Catholic country, the resorts of the island are virtual bordellos. More so than anywhere else in the Caribbean, bisexuality is rampant among the men of the D.R., and hundreds are available on a "gay-for-pay" basis. Sex tourism, even that involving minors, is on the rise in the D.R. and has even made headlines in the *New York Times*.

There isn't much of a gay bar scene outside of Santo Domingo, but cruising is evident everywhere, especially in the regular bars, on the beaches, and along the various *malecón* (seafront) promenades at night.

Some smaller hotels are especially gay friendly and openly solicit a gay or lesbian clientele. Same-sex couples seeking to share a room together should encounter no problem anywhere in the D.R. Discretion, however, is the word. Holding hands or kissing in public will be frowned upon and may invite at least verbal abuse, and there are dozens of cases of gay bashing reported yearly.

The **International Gay and Lesbian Travel Association (IGLTA)** (© **800/448-8550** or 954/776-2626; www.iglta.org) is the trade association for the gay and lesbian travel industry and offers an online directory of gay- and lesbian-friendly travel businesses; go to their website and click on "Members."

FOR SENIORS

Since everything is done for them, seniors form a large part of the patronage at the resorts of Punta Cana and Playa Dorada. Casa de Campo at La Romana is one of the most preferred destinations in the Caribbean for the senior traveler.

One of the benefits of age is that travel often costs less. Don't be shy about asking for discounts, but always carry some kind of ID, such as a driver's license, if you've kept your youthful glow. Also, mention the fact that you're a senior citizen when you first make your travel reservations; many hotels and most airlines and cruise lines offer senior discounts.

Members of the **AARP**, 601 E St. NW, Washington, DC 20049 (© **888/687-2277**; www.aarp.org), get discounts on hotels, airfares, and car rentals, plus *AARP The Magazine* and a monthly newsletter.

9 Getting There by Plane

Most visitors arrive in the Dominican Republic as part of a package deal that includes airfare. Travel agencies will inform you of the best deals, land-and-air packages that cut costs substantially. At slow periods of the year, this package deal is tantamount to a giveaway.

Most flights into the country are routed through Miami (flight time from Miami to Santo Domingo is 1¾ hr.). Flying time from New York is 4 hours, but only 30 minutes from the hub in San Juan, Puerto Rico.

Most charter flights from Canada originate out of Toronto, taking 4½ hours to reach the D.R. From many cities in western Europe, flying time to Santo Domingo ranges from 8 to 10 hours.

American Airlines (© 800/433-7300; www.aa.com) offers the most frequent service; at least a dozen flights daily from cities throughout North America to either Santo Domingo or Puerto Plata. Flights from hubs like New York, Miami, or San Juan are usually nonstop. American also offers some good package deals.

If you're heading to one of the Dominican Republic's smaller airports, your best bet is to catch a connecting flight with **American Eagle,** American's local commuter carrier. Its small planes depart every day from San Juan for airports throughout the Dominican Republic, including Santo Domingo, Puerto Plata, La Romana, and Punta Cana.

Continental Airlines (© 800/231-0856 in the U.S.; www.continental.com) has a daily flight between Newark and Santo Domingo.

US Airways (© 800/221-0133; www.usairways.com) flies daily from Philadelphia to Santo Domingo. The airline also offers flights from Charlotte, N.C., to Punta Cana on Monday, Wednesday, Friday, and Saturday.

JetBlue Airlines (© 800/JETBLUE; www.jetblue.com) flies from New York to the Dominican Republic, and **US Airways** (© 800/428-4322; www.usairways.com) also flies from New York to the island. In addition, **Delta Airlines** (© 800/221-1212; www.delta.com) flies from both New York and Miami to the Dominican Republic.

Spirit Airlines (© 800/772-7117; www.spiritair.com) flies from New York's La Guardia to Santo Domingo and also has flights from Atlantic City, Chicago, Detroit, Fort Lauderdale, Providence (R.I.), Washington, D.C., Myrtle Beach (S.C.), and San Juan.

Iberia (© 800/772-4642 in the U.S.; www.iberia.com) offers daily flights from Madrid to Santo Domingo, making a brief stop in San Juan.

Lately, several minor airlines also service the area, including **Air Atlantic** (© **800/289-4647** or 854/569-9688; www.airatlantic.com), with flights from both Miami and San Juan on Monday, Wednesday, and Friday.

Be warned: Arriving at Santo Domingo's Las Américas International Airport is confusing and chaotic. Customs officials, who tend to be rude and overworked, may give you a very thorough check. Stolen luggage is not uncommon here; beware of "porters" who offer to help with your bags. Arrival at La Unión International Airport, 37km (23 miles) east of Puerto Plata on the north coast, is generally much smoother and safer, but you should still be cautious.

10 Getting Around the Dominican Republic

Getting around the Dominican Republic is not always easy if your hotel is in a remote location. The most convenient modes of transport are shuttle flights, taxis, rental cars, *públicos* (multi-passenger taxis), and *guaguas* (public buses).

BY PLANE   The quickest and easiest way to get across a difficult landscape is on one of the shuttle flights offered by **Air Santo Domingo** (© **809/266-5222;** www.airsantodomingo.com); flying from Santo Domingo to Puerto Plata, Punta Cana, La Romana, Samaná, and Santiago, among other towns.

BY RENTAL CAR   The best way to see the Dominican Republic is to drive. *Motorists drive on the right here.* Although major highways are relatively smooth, the country's secondary roads, especially those in the east, are riddled with potholes and ruts. Roads also tend to be badly lit and poorly marked in both the city and the countryside. Drive carefully and give yourself plenty of time when traveling between island destinations. Watch out for policemen who may flag you down and accuse you (often wrongly) of some infraction. Many locals give these low-paid policemen a RD$100 (US$5) *regalo,* or gift "for your children," and are then free to go.

The high accident and theft rate in recent years has helped to raise car-rental rates here. Prices vary, so call around for last-minute quotes. Make sure you understand your insurance coverage (or lack thereof) before you leave home. Your credit-card issuer may already provide you with this type of insurance; call to find out.

For reservations and more information, call the rental companies at least a week before your departure: **Avis** (© **800/331-1212** in the U.S., or 809/535-7191; www.avis.com), **Budget** (© **800/472-3325** in the U.S., or 809/549-0351; www.budget.com), and **Hertz**

(© **800/654-3131** in the U.S., or 809/221-5333; www.hertz.com) all operate in the Dominican Republic. All three have offices at the Santo Domingo and Puerto Plata airports, as well as in downtown Santo Domingo. Avis and Hertz also have offices in La Romana and in Punta Cana.

Although the cars may not be as well maintained as the big three above, you can often get a cheaper deal at one of the local firms, notably **McAuto Rental Cars** (© **809/688-6518**). If you want a car with seat belts, you must ask. Your Canadian or American driver's license is suitable documentation, along with a valid credit card or a substantial cash deposit.

BY PUBLIC TRANSPORTATION   *Públicos* are unmetered multipassenger taxis that travel along main thoroughfares, stopping often to pick up people waving from the side of the street. A *público* is marked by a white seal on the front door. You must tell the driver your destination when you're picked up to make sure the *público* is going there. A ride is usually RD$6 (20¢).

Public buses, often in the form of minivans or panel trucks, are called *guaguas* (pronounced "*gwa*-gwas"). For about the same price, they provide the same service as *públicos,* but they're generally more crowded. Larger buses provide service outside the towns. Beware of pickpockets on board.

11 Package Deals

For value-conscious travelers, packages are the smart way to go because they can save you a ton of money. Especially in the Dominican Republic, package tours are *not* the same thing as escorted tours. You'll be on your own, but in most cases, a package will include airfare, hotel, and transportation to and from the airport—and it'll cost you less than just the hotel alone if you booked it yourself. A package deal might not be for you if you want to stay in a more intimate inn or guesthouse, but if you like resorts, read on.

You'll find an amazing array of packages. Some packages offer a better class of hotels than others. Some offer the same hotels for lower prices. Some offer flights on scheduled airlines, and others book charters. Remember to comparison shop among at least three different operators, and always compare apples to apples.

Most land-and-air packages include meals, and you'll find yourself locked into your hotel dining room every night if your meals are prepaid. Most of the all-inclusives in the D.R. break this monotony by offering a series of different restaurants, ranging from Italian to Chinese, under one roof.

If you're seeking a more varied dining experience, avoid **AP (American Plan)**, which means full board, and opt for **MAP (Modified American Plan)**, meaning breakfast and either lunch or dinner. That way, you'll at least be free for one main meal of the day and can sample a variety of an island's regional fare.

The best place to start your search is the travel section of your local Sunday newspaper. Also check the ads in national travel magazines like *Arthur Frommer's Budget Travel, National Geographic Traveler,* and *Travel Holiday.*

Liberty Travel (℃ **888/271-1584** to be connected with the agent closest to you; www.libertytravel.com) is one of the biggest packagers in the Northeast, and it usually boasts a full-page ad in Sunday papers.

Another good resource is the airlines themselves, which often package their flights together with accommodations; another good choice is **American Express Travel** (℃ **800/335-3342**; www.american express.com). Among the airline packagers, your options include **American Airlines Vacations** (℃ **800/321-2121**; www.aavacations. com) and **US Airways Vacations** (℃ **800/455-0123**; www.us airwaysvacations.com). American usually has the widest variety of offerings since it's the major carrier to the region.

The biggest hotel chains and resorts also offer package deals. If you already know where you want to stay, call the resort itself and ask if it offers land/air packages.

To save time comparing the prices and value of all the package tours out there, contact **TourScan, Inc.** (℃ **800/962-2080**; www. tourscan.com). Every season, the company computerizes the contents of travel brochures that contain about 10,000 different vacations at 1,600 hotels in the Caribbean, including the Dominican Republic. TourScan selects the best-value vacation at each hotel and condo. Two catalogs are printed each year, which list a choice of hotels. The price of a catalog (US$4) is credited toward any TourScan vacation.

Just-A-Vacation, Inc. (℃ **800/683-6313**; www.justavacation.com) also specializes in good deals for resorts.

Some of the leading North American tour operators still featuring tours include **GWV Vacations** (www.gwvvacations.com), focusing on package vacations from Boston to Puerto Plata, Punta Cana, Santo Domingo, and La Romana. This is your best bet if you live in New England.

Those wanting more than the usual hotel-and-airfare deal can book a number of adventure tours. The best of these are offered by **Iguana Mama** (© 800/849-4720; www.iguanamama.com), featuring mountain biking, hiking, canyoning, mule treks, and cultural tours.

For the active vacationer, some of the best hiking and adventure tours in the D.R. are touted by **Caribbean Bike & Adventure Tours** (© 617/792-2069) in the U.S. or 809/571-1748 in the D.R.; www.caribbeanbiketours.com).

FAST FACTS: Dominican Republic

Business Hours Most shops and businesses are open Monday to Friday from 8am to 4pm. Those serving the tourist industry are also open on Saturday. Government offices are open Monday to Friday from 7:30am to 2:30pm—that is, officially. In reality, you shouldn't bother showing up until after 9am. Most banks are open Monday to Friday, 8am to 4pm.

Currency See "Money," earlier in this chapter.

Documents See "Entry Requirements & Customs," earlier in this chapter.

Electricity The country generally uses 110-volt AC (60 cycles), so adapters and transformers are usually not necessary for U.S. appliances.

Emergencies Call © 911. See "Hospitals," below.

Embassies All embassies are in Santo Domingo, the capital. The **United States** embassy is on Calle Cesar Nicholas Penson at the corner of Leopold Navarro (© 809/221-2171). The embassy of the **United Kingdom** is located at Hotel Santo Domingo, Suite 1108 (© 809/472-7111). The embassy of **Canada** is found at Calle Capitán Eugenio de Marchena 39 (© 809/685-1136).

Hospitals Medical care is limited, especially outside Santo Domingo, and the quality of care varies widely among facilities. There is an emergency 911 service within Santo Domingo, but its reliability is questionable. Outside the capital, emergency services range from extremely limited to nonexistent. Blood supplies at both public and private hospitals are often limited, and not all facilities have blood on hand, even for emergencies. Many medical facilities throughout the country do not have staff members who speak or understand English. A private nationwide ambulance service, **Movi-med,** operates in Santo Domingo, Santiago, Puerto Plata, and La Romana; its telephone number is ℂ **809/532-0000** in Santo Domingo and ℂ **1-200-0911** outside Santo Domingo. Movi-med expects full payment at the time of transport.

Internet Access More and more this hookup is available. See individual listings in the chapters.

Language The official language is Spanish; many people also speak some English.

Liquor Laws The official drinking age in the Dominican Republic is 18, but the law is not enforced very well.

Mail A disaster! It's recommended that you not rely on D.R. postal services unless absolutely necessary. It is estimated that the chance of your letter reaching its intended destination is about 50%. If you need to send something back home or elsewhere, ask at your hotel desk. International courier services such as United Parcel Service, Federal Express, or DHL are the way to go. The hotels themselves use these services.

Medical Facilities See "Hospitals," above.

Passports **For Residents of the United States:** Whether you're applying in person or by mail, you can download passport applications from the U.S. State Department website at **http://travel.state.gov.** For general information, call the **National Passport Agency** (ℂ **877/487-2778**). To find your regional passport office, check the U.S. State Department website.

For Residents of Canada: Passport applications are available at travel agencies throughout Canada or from the central **Passport Office,** Department of Foreign Affairs and International Trade, Ottawa, ON K1A 0G3 (ℂ **800/567-6868;** www. ppt.gc.ca).

For Residents of the United Kingdom: To pick up an application for a standard 10-year passport (5-year passport for children under age 16), visit your nearest passport office, major post office, or travel agency, or contact the **United Kingdom Passport Service** at ℂ **0870/521-0410** or search its website at www.ukpa.gov.uk.

For Residents of Ireland: You can apply for a 10-year passport at the **Department of Foreign Affairs Passport Office,** Setanta Centre, Molesworth Street, Dublin 2 (ℂ **01/671-1633;**

http://foreignaffairs.gov.ie/). Those under age 18 and over 65 must apply for a €12 3-year passport. You can also apply at 1A South Mall, Cork (℃ **021/272-525**) or at most main post offices.

For Residents of Australia: You can pick up an application from your local post office or any branch of Passports Australia, but you must schedule an interview at the passport office to present your application materials. Call the **Australian Passport Information Service** at ℃ **131-232,** or visit the government website at www.passports.gov.au.

For Residents of New Zealand: You can pick up a passport application at any New Zealand Passports Office or download it from their website. Contact the **New Zealand Passports Office** at ℃ **0800/225-050** in New Zealand or 04/474-8100, or log on to www.passports.govt.nz.

Pharmacies Refer to the local listings in the individual chapters. If you're on medication, it's best to bring an adequate supply with you. Don't always count on the local pharmacy being able to fill your prescription.

Safety Refer to the section on "Staying Safe," earlier in this chapter.

Taxes A departure tax of RD$280 ($10) is assessed and must be paid in U.S. currency. The government imposes a 13% tax on hotel rooms, which is usually topped by an automatic 10% service charge, bringing the total tax to staggering heights. A 12% sales tax on food and drink is assessed.

Telephone The area code for the Dominican Republic is **809.** You place calls to or from the Dominican Republic just as you would from any other area code in North America. You can access **AT&T Direct** by dialing ℃ **800/222-0300.** You can reach **MCI** at ℃ **800/888-8000** and **Sprint** at ℃ **800/877-7746.**

Television & Radio More than seven local TV networks, all Spanish speaking, blanket the island. But most of the English-speaking TV stations in Miami are picked up as well. It's estimated that about 50% of the island's television sets can also tap into satellite programming or cable. There are some 150 radio stations, mostly featuring merengue, bachata, and the nation's national pastime: baseball.

Time Atlantic Standard Time is observed year-round. Between November and March, when it's noon in New York and Miami, it's 1pm in Santo Domingo. However, during U.S.

daylight saving time, it's the same time in the Dominican Republic and the U.S. East Coast.

Tipping Most restaurants and hotels add a 10% service charge to your check. Most people usually add 5% to 10% more, especially if the service has been good.

Water Stick to bottled water.

Weather The average temperature is 77°F (25°C). August is the warmest month and January the coolest month, although, even then, it's warm enough to swim.

3

Settling into Santo Domingo

Bartolomé Columbus, brother of Christopher, founded the city of New Isabella (later renamed Santo Domingo) on the southeastern Caribbean coast in 1496. It's the oldest city in the New World and the capital of the Dominican Republic. Santo Domingo has had a long, sometimes glorious, more often sad, history. At the peak of its power, Diego de Velázquez sailed from here to settle Cuba, Ponce de León went forth to conquer and settle Puerto Rico and Florida, and Cortés set out for Mexico. The city today still reflects its long history—French, Haitian, and especially Spanish.

Santo Domingo is one of the Caribbean's most vibrant cities, with a 12-block Colonial Zone to rival that of Old San Juan in Puerto Rico. Come here to walk in the footsteps of Cortés, Ponce de León, and, of course, Columbus himself. Allow at least a day to capture some of the highlights of the old city, such as its Alcázar (a palace built for Columbus's son, Diego).

Santo Domingo is also one of the grand shopping bazaars of the Caribbean, with such "hot" items as hand-wrapped cigars for sale virtually everywhere, along with local handicrafts. Jewelry made of larimar or amber is also much sought after. From gambling to merengue, Santo Domingo is also one of the liveliest cities in the Caribbean after dark. Be careful, however. Most of the Dominican Republic's crime is concentrated in Santo Domingo. Keep valuables in your hotel safe, carry a minimum of cash with you, don't wear flashy jewelry, and, if in doubt, take a cab.

1 Orientation

ARRIVING

Most flights arrive at **Aeropuerto Internacional Las Américas** (© **809/549-0219**), lying 13km (8 miles) east of the city center. This is not a good introduction to the Dominican Republic. Customs officials are often hostile. Once you've survived them, you have to face an array of hustlers waiting to steal your money, grab your luggage (and disappear with it), or else hawk dubious deals on everything from hotel rooms, gypsy cabbies, or cheap car rentals. Not only that, but if you're a single man traveling alone, you might be offered a woman for the duration of your trip. If you express no interest, a boy might be offered instead.

Expect a lot of hassle and aggression. It's better to have everything reserved in advance, including your hotel and your car rental, before you face these touts trying to separate you from your money.

At the exit to the baggage reclaim area, you'll see a branch of **Banco de Reservas,** where you can change your currency into Dominican pesos.

If you don't rent a car, you'll need to take a taxi. The local taxi union is powerful enough to prevent bus service from operating here. Taxis, available 24 hours, cost RD$500 ($18) and up to take you into town. Always negotiate and agree on the fare before getting in.

If you're flying from somewhere within the Dominican Republic, perhaps Puerto Plata or La Romana, chances are your plane will land at the smaller **Aeropuerto Herrera,** Avenida Luperón (© **809/ 567-3900**), on the west side of Santo Domingo. A taxi from Herrera to a hotel in the center of Santo Domingo costs from RD$200 ($7.20). Always negotiate and agree upon the fare before getting in.

Motorists who arrive from one of the popular resorts will find it easy to access the central city. If you're coming from the north on Autopista Duarte, the highway becomes Avenida Kennedy at Luperón, which will take you into the heart of Santo Domingo. If you're driving from a resort in the east, follow the signposts marked CENTRO CIUDAD until you come to the Puente Duarte, a bridge over the Río Ozama. The road at this point becomes Avenida 27 de Febrero. Follow this road to the intersection with Calle 30 de Marzo, at which point you turn left and head for the Zona Colonial, or Colonial Zone.

Chances are you won't be arriving from elsewhere in the Dominican Republic by bus, although the major towns and cities of the D.R. maintain bus links with Santo Domingo. Buses let passengers off at the terminal at Avenida 27 de Febrero and Navarro (© **809/221-4422**), at Av. Máximo Gómez 61 (© **809/221-4422**), behind the Plaza Central, or at the terminal at Guarocuya 4 (© **809/531-0383**), across the street from Centro Olímpico. Taxis are found at all bus terminals to take you to your hotel within the city itself.

VISITOR INFORMATION

A not-very-helpful staff mans the city's main tourist office at the **Secretaría de Estado de Turismo,** Edificios Gubernamentales, avenidas México and 30 de Marzo (© **809/221-4660;** fax 809/ 682-3806; www.dominicana.com.do). Hours are Monday to Friday 8:30am to 3pm. Much of the information dispensed here—such as it is—is hopelessly out-of-date.

MAPS

A good map of Santo Domingo is imperative for getting around, and vital if you plan to traverse the country by car. The best ones are published by **Mapas Triunfo** (© **809/566-0959**). A map simply called *Dominican Republic* has a detailed street map of Santo Domingo and a good road map of the country. This map is sold all over the city in gift shops and bookstores and even at newspaper and magazine kiosks.

CITY LAYOUT

To get your bearings, you need to know that no one refers to the city's main artery as **Avenida George Washington.** This is a palm-lined boardwalk open to the sea. The *Guinness Book of World Records* calls it "The Planet's Largest Disco" because of all the clubs found here. Locals call it the **Malecón** (meaning sea wall), and it hugs the edge of the Caribbean for a total distance of 7.9km (5 miles). This is one of the dozen or so major boulevards of the city, and the most important one. Parading along this boulevard at night (beware of pickpockets) is the major nighttime activity of both locals and visitors.

Forget about street addresses. Presumably, buildings are assigned a number, but locals rarely use them. The way to find an address is to tie in a building you're seeking with either a landmark or else the major cross street.

Chances are your hotel will be along the Malecón. For sightseeing, however, most interest focuses on the **Zona Colonial (Colonial Zone),** the heart of the centuries-old city where Sir Francis Drake, and even Columbus, once walked.

Running parallel to the Malecón, but inland from the Caribbean, is **Avenida Independencia.** This wide boulevard cuts through the Gazcue sector of town, coming to an end at **Parque Independencia** and its nearby Palacio Nacional, lying just west of Zona Colonial. Parque Independencia is "ground zero" for the denizens of Santo Domingo.

The city's most attractive district is **Gazcue,** lying to the west of Zona Colonial and north of the Malecón. This is a middle-class neighborhood with tree-shaded sidewalks. It centers on Plaza de la Cultura. A number of museums are here, and chances are you'll be visiting, if not living in a hotel in the district.

Río Ozama separates the western or right bank of Santo Domingo from the left or eastern bank. Lying directly off the Avenida España, the two districts here are **Villa Duarte** and **Sans Souci,** with most interest focusing on the controversial **Columbus Lighthouse,** which locals call simply **El Faro.** This lighthouse towers over the western end of **Parque Mirador del Este,** a stretch of woodland spanning the length of the barrios east of the river.

The city's outer barrios won't concern the average visitor. These include **Villa Mella** to the north, a dreary sector of thatch huts and concrete structures locals call home. Villa Mella is different from the rest of the districts in that most of its population was largely descended from slaves from the Congo, and some of the old Congolese culture still lives on in music, religion, and language.

A barrio of more interest to the average visitor is **Arroyo Hondo,** lying to the immediate northwest and the site of the much-visited **Jardín Botánico,** or botanical gardens. Closer to the city's heart, the area begins with some upper-crust villas in the south. By the time it reaches its northern tier, this architecture has given way to shacks. Further east of the botanical gardens lies the **Parque Zoológico (zoo).**

GETTING AROUND
BY PUBLIC TRANSPORTATION

From sunup to sundown, public buses serve Santo Domingo. A ride from one end to the other costs no more than RD $5 (US20¢). These often overcrowded buses go up and down all the major arteries, such as the Malecón. To catch a bus, all you have to do is stand by the road and hail one down (as opposed to going to a more orderly and signposted bus stop).

BY TAXI

Taxis aren't metered, and determining the fare in advance (which you should do) may be difficult if you and your driver have a language problem. You can easily hail a taxi at the airport and at most major hotels. *Warning:* Don't get into an unmarked street taxi. Many visitors, particularly in Santo Domingo, have been assaulted and robbed by doing just that. The minimum fare within Santo Domingo is RD$80 ($2.85). In Santo Domingo, the most reliable taxi company is **Tecni-Taxi** (℃ **809/567-2010**). In Puerto Plata, call **Tecni-Taxi** at ℃ **809/320-7621.**

WALKING

This is virtually the only way to get around such districts as Zona Colonial, site of the major attractions. Do so during the day and avoid night walks, where you may be the victim of a mugging. Even during the day, you can expect to be hassled by hustlers calling themselves "guides" and offering tours. Many of them are hard to get rid of and will continue to follow you even if you turn down their services.

FAST FACTS: Santo Domingo

American Express The regional office is at Banco Dominicano del Progreso, Av. Kennedy 3 (© 809/563-3233), open Monday to Friday 8:30am to 3pm and Saturday 9am to 1pm.

Currency Exchange All banks will exchange your currency and all maintain ATMs. Two of the most central and convenient are Banco BHD, Ave. 27 de Febrero (© 809/243-3232); and Banco de Reservas, Avenida Duarte and Mella (© 809/960-2000).

Internet Access Internet cafes aren't plentiful. The best and most convenient one is **The Chat Room,** Dr. César Dargan, Esq. 27 (© 809/412-7369), open Monday to Friday 8:30am to 11pm, Saturday 9am to 6pm. The cost is RD$50 ($1.80) per hour, RD$30 ($1.10) per half hour.

Mail Chances are if you use regular mail in the Dominican Republic, your cards and letters will arrive at their destination long after you've returned home. Many Dominican residents mailing money back to their homeland have their letters stolen and the money removed. If you must use the postal service (and we recommend that you don't), the main office— and the most convenient—is Instituto Postal Dominicano, Parque Colón in the Zona Colonial (© 809/534-5838); open Monday to Friday 8am to 5pm, Saturday 9am to noon. If you've got to ship something home, try the more reliable **Federal Express,** Avenida de los Proceres, corner of Camino del Oeste (© 809/565-3636); open Monday to Friday 8:30am to 5:30pm and Saturday 8:30am to 12:30pm.

Medical Services The best hospital in Santo Domingo, and the one recommended by the U.S. Embassy, is **Clínica Abreu,** Calle Beller 42 (© 809/688-4411). Most of its English-speaking doctors trained in the United States. It is always open.

Newspapers There are four major dailies, including *El Siglo,* which publishes a good deal of useful information for visitors, including a listing of international flight schedules. One of the best listings of local events, cultural or otherwise, is found in *Hoy*'s "Revista" section. The same data also appears in *Listin Diario*'s "La Vida" section. The afternoon daily, *Ultima Hora*, also carries helpful listings, such as a movie schedule.

Pharmacies **Carol,** Ricart 24 (© **809/562-6767**), and **San Judas Tadeo,** Av. Independencia 57 (© **809/685-8165**) are open 24 hours.

Safety Exercise extreme caution when walking around Santo Domingo at night, and keep your guard up during the day as well. Violent crime against tourists is not commonplace, but muggings are. Avoid the overcrowded barrios at all cost. They are some of the worst slums in the Caribbean, and crime is rampant. One of the worst sections is on the west bank of the Río Ozama just north of Puente Duarte, the bridge. Another section that's riddled with crime is on the east side of Avenida Máximo Gómez north of the Río Isabela. The safest zones are the Zona Colonial or the Malecón, even though these sections are rife with pickpockets and muggers.

Telephone The area code for the Dominican Republic is **809.** You place calls to or from the Dominican Republic just as you would from any other area code in North America. You can access **AT&T Direct** by dialing © **800/222-0300.** You can reach **MCI** at © **800/888-8000** and **Sprint** at © **800/877-7746.**

Travel Agencies In addition to American Express (see above), there are a number of travel agencies which can handle your arrangements if you're venturing out of Santo Domingo and into the country. The best ones include **Colonial Tour & Travel,** Calle Arzobispo Meriño 209 (© **809/688-5285**); open Monday to Friday 8:30am to 1:30pm and 2:30 to 5:30pm, Saturday 8:30am to 1:30pm. Another good agency is **Turis Centro,** Av. George Washington 101 (© **809/688-6607**); open Monday to Friday 8:30am to 5pm, Saturday 8:30am to noon. Also giving good service is **Giada Tours & Travel,** inside Hostal Duque de Wellington, Av. Independencia 304 (© **809/686-6994**); open Monday to Friday 9am to 5pm and Saturday 9am to noon.

2 Where to Stay

Most hotels in the city (unlike some of the beach resorts) accept only bookings on the European Plan (no meals) and, also unlike the resorts, charge the same rates year-round. If you want nightclubs, action, and lots of restaurant choices, do what most visitors do and stay in a hotel on or near the Malecón, opening onto the Caribbean. If you're a history buff interested mainly in sightseeing, stay in one of the historic old buildings in the Zona Colonial (Colonial Zone), a good area for sightseeing.

Because Santo Domingo can be dangerous at night, some security-conscious guests prefer to stay at one of the larger hotels that combines casino action, night clubs, a choice of restaurants, and bars all under one roof. After a night of gambling, dining, drinking, or clubbing, all you have to do is take the elevator upstairs.

Note: Nearly all hotels in the Dominican Republic deal in U.S. currency. Accordingly, our hotel listings reflect the U.S. price rates.

EXPENSIVE

Barceló Gran Hotel Lina ⟨⟨   Rising nine floors in the heart of the capital in a sterile cinder-block design, the Lina offers a wide range of amenities. All the units contain refrigerators, and at least a third overlook the Caribbean. Bedrooms are comfortable and many are quite spacious, but the decor is the standard motel style. The best rooms, on the eighth and ninth floors, have balconies. The tiled bathrooms have spacious marble vanities and shower/tub combinations.

The hotel boasts one of the best-known restaurants in the Caribbean, the Lina Restaurant (see "Where to Dine," later in this chapter).

Avs. Máximo Gómez and 27 de Febrero, Santo Domingo, Dominican Republic. ⓒ 800/942-2461 in the U.S., or 809/563-5000. Fax 809/686-5521. www.barcelo. com. 217 units. Year-round US$126 double; US$155–US$190 suite. Extra person US$34. Rates include breakfast. AE, DC, MC, V. **Amenities:** 2 restaurants; 2 bars; pool; health club; Jacuzzi; sauna; 24-hr. room service; babysitting; laundry service; dry cleaning; casino; snack bar. *In room:* A/C, TV, minibar, hair dryer, iron/ironing board, safe.

Francés Sofitel ⟨⟨   A favorite small hotel in the old city, this intimate inn lies within a stone-fronted town house dating from the 16th century. Arches surround an Iberian-style fountain, and columns reach up to the second-floor patios, with palms and tropical plants surrounding the rooms. You'll think you've arrived in Seville. A gracefully winding stone staircase leads to the high-ceilinged and thick-walled bedrooms outfitted in a somber, rather dark colonial style. Accommodations are simple but tasteful, with rugs resting on tile floors; each has a somewhat cramped but tidily kept bathroom with shower and tub.

Where to Stay in Santo Domingo

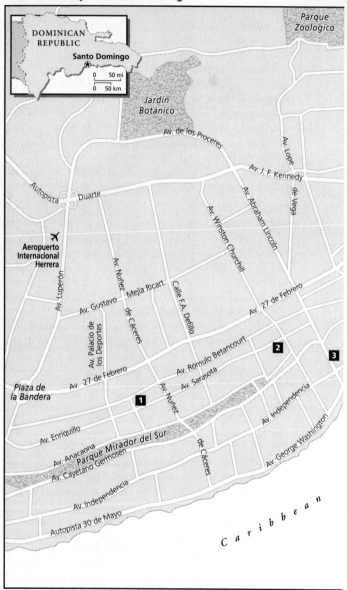

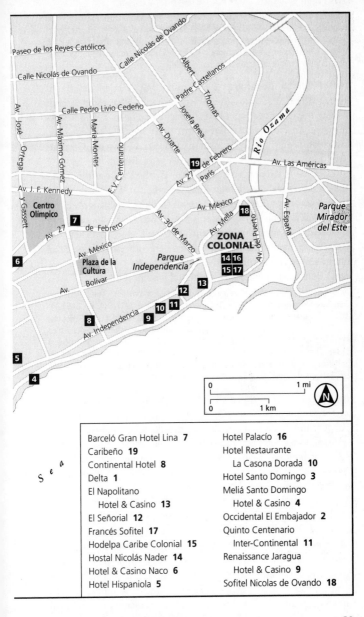

Paseo de los Reyes Católicos
Calle Nicolás de Ovando
Calle Nicolás de Ovando
Calle Pedro Livio Cedeño
Calle Nicolás de Ovando
Albert
Padre Castellanos
Thomas
Josefa Brea
Av. Duarte
Río Ozama
Av. Las Américas
Av. José
Ortega
Av. Máximo Gómez
María Montes
E.V. Centenario
de Febrero
Av. J. F. Kennedy
y Gassett
Centro
Olímpico
7
de Febrero
Av. 27
Av. 27
Paris
Av. México
19
18
Av. España
Parque
Mirador
del Este
6
Av. México
Av. 30 de Marzo
Av. Mella
Av. del Puerto
ZONA
COLONIAL
Plaza de la
Cultura
Parque
Independencia
14 **16**
15 **17**
Av.
Bolívar
12 **13**
8
10 **11**
Av. Independencia
9
5
4

0 — 1 mi
0 — 1 km
N

S e a

Barceló Gran Hotel Lina **7**
Caribeño **19**
Continental Hotel **8**
Delta **1**
El Napolitano
  Hotel & Casino **13**
El Señorial **12**
Francés Sofitel **17**
Hodelpa Caribe Colonial **15**
Hostal Nicolás Nader **14**
Hotel & Casino Naco **6**
Hotel Hispaniola **5**

Hotel Palacio **16**
Hotel Restaurante
  La Casona Dorada **10**
Hotel Santo Domingo **3**
Meliá Santo Domingo
  Hotel & Casino **4**
Occidental El Embajador **2**
Quinto Centenario
  Inter-Continental **11**
Renaissance Jaragua
  Hotel & Casino **9**
Sofitel Nicolas de Ovando **18**

Calle las Mercedes (corner of Calle Arzobispo Meriño), Santo Domingo, Dominican Republic. ✆ **809/685-9331.** Fax 809/685-1289. www.sofitel.com. 19 units. Year-round US$170 double. Rates include breakfast. AE, MC, V. **Amenities:** Restaurant; 2 bars; limited room service; laundry service; dry cleaning. *In room:* A/C, TV, dataport, minibar, hair dryer, iron/ironing board, safe.

Hotel Santo Domingo ✲✲✲

Run by Premier Resorts & Hotels, the Hotel Santo Domingo is tastefully extravagant without having the glitzy overtones of the Jaragua (see below). Those seeking local character in a home-grown hotel should check in here. This waterfront hotel sits on 6 tropical hectares (15 acres), 15 minutes from the downtown area, in the La Feria district.

Oscar de la Renta helped design the interior. Most of the rooms have views of the sea, though some face the garden. Accommodations have bright floral carpets, tasteful Caribbean fabrics, and mirrored closets along with firm double beds. Bathrooms are tiled with shower/tub combinations and adequate shelf space. The superior Excel Club rooms offer seaview balconies and other amenities. Excel guests also have access to a private lounge.

The cuisine is among the finest hotel food in the capital.

Ave. Independencia (at the corner of Ave. Abraham Lincoln), Santo Domingo, Dominican Republic. ✆ **800/877-3643** in the U.S., or 809/221-1511. Fax 809/535-4050. www.hotelsantodomingo.com.do. 220 units. Year-round US$160 double; US$195 Excel Club double; US$300 executive suite. Rates include American-style breakfast. AE, MC, V. **Amenities:** Restaurant; 2 bars; Olympic-size outdoor pool; 3 lit tennis courts; health club; sauna; business center; salon; limited room service; babysitting; laundry service; dry cleaning. *In room:* A/C, TV, dataport (in some), minibar, coffeemaker, hair dryer, safe.

Meliá Santo Domingo Hotel & Casino ✲✲

Though still not in the same league as the Quinto Centenario or the Renaissance Jaragua, this hotel is much improved following extensive renovations, and now competes successfully for the upmarket traveler. The 12-story building is in a classic style, not very innovative, but exceedingly comfortable and inviting. The location is about a 35-minute drive from the airport, about a 5-minute taxi ride from the city center, and 1.9km (1¼ miles) from the Colonial Zone. Accommodations range from midsize to spacious, each newly furnished in a tasteful and comfortable style. All the rooms have private marble bathrooms with a combination tub/shower, and most of the units offer a "lookout balcony" with a view of the Caribbean. The public areas here are exceptional for the city, with a terrace bar lit by street lamps, a lobby restaurant specializing in lunch and dinner buffets, and a contemporary grill attracting a more upmarket clientele. An evening crowd of patrons pours in for casino action, and there's live Dominican music coming from the bar.

Av. George Washington 365, Santo Domingo, Dominican Republic. © **809/221-6666**. Fax 809/687-8150. www.solmelia.com. 245 units. Year-round US$160 double; US$180 triple; US$285 suite. Children 11 and under stay free in parent's room. AE, DC, DISC, MC, V. **Amenities:** 2 restaurants; bar; pool; health club; sauna; 24-hr. room service; babysitting; laundry service; dry cleaning; casino. *In room:* A/C, TV, minibar, coffeemaker, hair dryer, iron/ironing board, safe.

Occidental El Embajador ⊕ No hotel in Santo Domingo evokes the heyday of the dictator Trujillo in the 1950s more than this plush choice. Called "the Goat" because of his sexual excesses, Trujillo once maintained a luxury penthouse in this concrete-and-glass deluxe hotel built 15km (9¼ miles) southwest of the city center. After several renovations, the seven-story structure is as fine today as it ever was.

The hotel is complete with a pool from the golden days of Hollywood and a landscaped drive-up entrance. All guest rooms have been gracefully renewed, with elegant fabrics and marble-lined bathrooms that feature tub/shower combos. For the most part, the rooms are the most spacious in Santo Domingo, and many have walk-in closets, making living here exceedingly comfortable. Those seeking an ocean view won't be disappointed, as the rooms open onto balconies overlooking the sea.

Av. Sarasota 65, Santo Domingo, Dominican Republic. © **809/221-2131**. Fax 809/532-5306. www.occidental-hoteles.com. 286 units. Year-round US$130–US$175 double; US$250–US$385 suite. Children US$25–US$40 3–11 years old. Children 2 and under stay free in parent's room. AE, DC, DISC, MC, V. **Amenities:** 2 restaurants; bar; outdoor pool; tennis court; health club; 24- hr. room service; babysitting; laundry service; dry cleaning; casino. *In room:* A/C, TV, dataport, minibar, hair dryer, iron/ironing board, safe.

Quinto Centenario Inter-Continental ⊕ This hotel was inaugurated in 1992 to mark the 500th anniversary of the landing of Columbus. The hotel doesn't compare favorably with other Inter-Continentals around the world. Yet there is much to recommend it, including its location on the Malecón, bordering the water. The best public area is the rooftop restaurant opening onto dramatic nighttime vistas of Santo Domingo. The bedrooms are the hotel's best feature, decorated handsomely with Caribbean styling and comfortable, tasteful appointments. They range from midsize to spacious, and come with roomy private bathrooms with tub and shower.

Av. George Washington, NRO 218, Santo Domingo, Dominican Republic. © **809/221-0000**. Fax 809/221-2020. www.ichotelsgroup.com. 196 units. Year-round US$125 double; US$145 triple; US$165 suite. Children 12 and under stay free in parent's room. AE, DC, DISC, MC, V. **Amenities:** 2 restaurants; 2 bars; outdoor pool; sauna; health club; 24-hr. room service; babysitting; laundry service; dry cleaning, nonsmoking rooms. *In room:* A/C, TV, dataport, minibar, coffeemaker, hair dryer, iron/ironing board, safe.

Renaissance Jaragua Hotel & Casino 🌟🌟

A Las Vegas–style palace, this 10-story hotel lies on the 6-hectare (15-acre) site of the old Jaragua (ha-*ra*-gwa) Hotel, which was popular in Trujillo's day. Open since 1988, it's a splashy, pink-colored waterfront palace that doesn't have the dignity and class of the Hotel Santo Domingo. For example, the casino and bars are often rife with prostitutes plying their trade. Located off the Malecón and convenient to the city's major attractions and shops, the hotel consists of two separate buildings: the 10-story Jaragua Tower and the two-level Jaragua Gardens Estate. Jaragua boasts the largest casino in the Caribbean, a 1,000-seat Vegas-style showroom, a cabaret theater, and a disco. The luxurious rooms, the largest in Santo Domingo, feature multiple phones, refrigerators, and marble bathrooms with large makeup mirrors and shower/tub combos.

The Jaragua features some of the best hotel dining in the city. You can enjoy tasty Dominican barbecue and some of Santo Domingo's best steaks.

Ave. George Washington 367, Santo Domingo, Dominican Republic. ☎ 800/ HOTELS-1 in the U.S. and Canada, or 809/221-2222. Fax 809/686-0528. www.renaissancehotels.com. 300 units. Year-round US$140–US$169 double; US$309 junior suite; US$500–US$750 suite. AE, DC, MC, V. **Amenities:** Restaurant; 2 bars; outdoor pool; tennis center with 4 lit clay courts and a pro shop; health club; spa; salon; 24-hr. room service; babysitting; laundry service; dry cleaning; nonsmoking rooms; casino; disco;. *In room:* A/C, TV, dataport, kitchenettes (in some), minibar, fridge, hair dryer, iron/ironing board, safe.

Sofitel Nicolas de Ovando 🌟🌟

In the heart of the colonial city, this 16th-century mansion has been restored and reopened as a hotel with all the modern amenities. The hotel is named after one of Santo Domingo's earliest governors and stands next door to the Alcázar de Colón, where Diego, son of Columbus, lived. For those seeking comfort among antiquity, this is an even better bet than the smaller Francés Sofitel (see above), another restoration. On the premises is a restaurant with a terrace facing a courtyard and two bars with a view of the pool. All the bedrooms are well furnished and handsomely maintained. The choice of accommodations ranges from standard doubles to spacious suites, which can also be used as family units. The classic architecture of the original mansion has been respected, although the property has been vastly enlarged.

Calle Las Damas, Santo Domingo, Dominican Republic. © **809/685-9955**. Fax 809/ 686-6590. www.sofitel.com. 104 units. Year-round US$238 double; US$427 junior suite; US$622 suite. Rates include breakfast. AE, DC, MC, V. **Amenities:** Restaurant; 2 bars; outdoor pool; health club; 24-hr. room service; laundry service; dry cleaning; nonsmoking rooms; limited mobility rooms; disco. *In room:* A/C, TV, dataport, mini-bar, hair dryer, iron/ironing board, safe.

MODERATE

Delta   In spite of this hotel's inconvenient location on the west side of town—a 45-minute drive to a good beach—it always seems full of satisfied American clients, attracted to its affordable prices and nice, well-maintained bedrooms. There's an abundance of energy about the place, but the look is rather basic. Okay, it's not the Ritz, but prices aren't as high as the Ritz's, either. Rising eight floors, the Delta is a traditional choice in a building dating from the late 1980s.

Av. Sarasota 53, Santo Domingo, Dominican Republic. © **809/535-0800**. Fax 809/ 535-6448. www.hoteldelta.com.do. 141 units. Year-round US$87 double; US$132 suite. Children 8 and under stay free in parent's room. AE, DC, MC, V. **Amenities:** Restaurant; bar; outdoor pool; limited room service; babysitting; laundry service; dry cleaning. *In room:* A/C, TV, dataport, kitchenette, hair dryer, safe.

El Napolitano Hotel & Casino ★ *Value*   This is a comfortable and safe haven—and a great bargain—for those who want to stay on the Malecón, right by the water. The hotel has been popular with the Dominicans themselves since it opened its seven floors back in the 1970s. The look is traditional in all the bedrooms, which are comfortable but simple. Most bedrooms are midsize and well maintained, each with a modern bathroom with a tub/shower combo. All accommodations open onto the sea, and there's a pool on the second floor. The hotel chef specializes in lobster and other seafood dishes, and there's plenty to do at night if you like disco or casino action, maybe both. If you prefer crowds, lots of action, and informality, El Napolitano may be for you.

Av. George Washington 101, Santo Domingo, Dominican Republic. © **809/687-1131**. Fax 809/686-0255. www.hotelnapolitano.net. 72 units. Year-round US$84 double. Children 12 and under stay free in parent's room. AE, DC, DISC, MC, V. **Amenities:** 2 restaurants; bar; outdoor pool; 24-hr. room service; laundry service; dry cleaning; casino; disco. *In room:* A/C, TV, dataport, safe.

Hodelpa Caribe Colonial ★ *Finds*   This boutique hotel in the Colonial Zone attracts both businesspeople and vacationers to its handsomely decorated precincts. A four-story structure, it is warm and inviting with Art Deco–styled rooms. If you don't mind not being on the water, you'll find the handsomely furnished rooms here extremely comfortable. Many of the city's best cafes, restaurants, attractions, and nightlife lie right outside your door. There's a special all-white honeymoon suite and fabric-draped beds are a standard feature. The suites are an especially good deal and have extras like a kitchenette, walk-in closet, balcony with chaise lounges, and bathroom with Jacuzzi. A well-prepared Dominican cuisine is served in the main restaurant, with lots of tropical favorites, and there is also a rooftop sun deck.

Isabel La Católica 159, Zona Colonial, Santo Domingo, Dominican Republic. ℂ **809/688-7799.** Fax 809/685-8128. www.hodelpa.com. 54 units. Year-round US$90–US$100 double; US$170 suite. Rates include breakfast. Children 11 and under stay free in parent's room. AE, MC, V. Free parking. **Amenities:** Restaurant; bar; limited room service; laundry service; dry cleaning. *In room:* A/C, TV, kitchenette, minibar, hair dryer, iron/ironing board, safe.

Hostal Nicolás Nader ℛ *Finds*   This is a small, almost luxurious little hotel that's a bit more comfortable than its competitor, the Palacio. Like the Palacio, the Nicolás Nader is also from the colonial era and was also the home of a former D.R. president, Ulises Heureaux. This 19th-century building has been sensitively restored. Many people in the area drop in during the day to check out the little art gallery in the courtyard or to patronize the on-site restaurant and bar. The bedrooms range from midsize to spacious, and each is comfortably furnished and comes with a bathroom with a tub/shower combo. The white paint in all the rooms gives the limestone-built mansion a real tropical flavor. You get quite a lot for your money here.

Calle General Luperón 151 at Calle Duarte, Santo Domingo, Dominican Republic. ℂ **809/687-6674.** Fax 809/687-7887. nicolasnader@verizon.net.do. 10 units. Year-round US$80 double. Children 8 and under stay free in parent's room. AE, MC, V. **Amenities:** Bar. *In room:* A/C, TV.

Hotel & Casino Naco ℛ *Value*   Very close to the ocean-bordering Malecón, this three-story hotel has been a favorite since the 1970s. After a 45-minute taxi ride from the airport, you can cocoon here in the comforts and facilities of a fine but hardly dramatic big-city hotel. Most bedrooms are midsize and are handsomely furnished, each with a well-maintained private bathroom with tub and shower. Nightlife centers on its casino, and there is a good restaurant serving international dishes for those who don't want to risk the often dangerous streets of Santo Domingo at night. In its affordable price range, this hotel is better equipped than most of its competitors.

Av. Tiradentes 22, Santo Domingo, Dominican Republic. ℂ **809/562-3100.** Fax 809/544-0957. www.hotelnaco.net. 106 units. Year-round US$88 double; US$93 triple; US$110 suite. Children 11 and under stay free in parent's room. AE, DC, DISC, MC, V. **Amenities:** Restaurant; bar; outdoor pool; sauna; limited room service; babysitting; laundry service; casino. *In room:* A/C, TV, kitchenette, safe.

Hotel Hispaniola ℜ   This is a reincarnated version of the old Trujillo-era Hotel Pax which once housed the exiled president of Argentina, Juan Perón (yes, the husband of the now-more-famous Evita). Standing on its own landscaped grounds, the hotel is still going strong, located across from the far superior Hotel Santo Domingo. Built in 1956, the five-floor hotel can no longer pretend to be the city's best, but it still looks good, having stayed abreast of the times with any number of renovations. Bedrooms are midsize to spacious for the most part, with comfortable furnishings and private bathrooms, each with tub/shower combos. Private balconies are attached to most accommodations. There's a full array of facilities here, including a spa and a casino next door, and you can also use the facilities of the Santo Domingo, as both are operated by Premier Resorts & Hotels.

Av. Independencia, at the corner of Abraham Lincoln, Santo Domingo, Dominican Republic. ℒ 809/221-7111. Fax 809/535-0876. www.hotelhispaniola.com. 165 units. Year-round US$80 double; US$134 triple. Children 5–11 US$12.60 extra. Children 4 and under stay free in parent's room. Rates include breakfast. AE, MC, V. **Amenities:** 2 restaurants; bar; outdoor pool; 24-hr. room service; babysitting; laundry service; dry cleaning. *In room:* A/C, TV, minibar, hair dryer, iron/ironing board, safe.

Hotel Palacio (Value)   History buffs often opt to stay here, since the hotel is in the heart of the historic zone, only 2 blocks from the cathedral. The Palacio is also popular with business travelers. Built in the 1600s, it was the family home of a former president of the Dominican Republic, Buenaventura Báez, and still retains its original iron balconies and high ceilings. Not all rooms are the same size; if you want a more spacious unit, just ask. The shower-only bathrooms tend to be small.

Calle Duarte 106 (at Calle Solomé Ureña), Santo Domingo, Dominican Republic. ℒ 809/682-4730. Fax 809/687-5535. www.hotel-palacio.com. 34 units. Year-round US$79–US$109 double; US$125–US$129 suite. Children 12 and under stay free in parent's room. AE, MC, V. **Amenities:** Bar; breakfast room; health club; rooftop Jacuzzi; limited room service; laundry service. *In room:* A/C, TV, dataport, minibar, hair dryer, safe.

INEXPENSIVE

Caribeño   Next door to a government building, this nine-floor structure dates from the 1980s but has seen improvements and rejuvenations since. Most of the rooms, painted in lime, range from small to midsize and are simply though comfortably furnished, with tiny bathrooms with a tub/shower combination. Noise might be a factor in some of the rooms, and the place is utterly without much style. But very few customers complain when it comes time to pay the bill.

Avs. 27 de Febrero and Duarte, Santo Domingo, Dominican Republic. ℂ **809/685-3167.** Fax 809/685-3391. hotelcaribeno@hotmail.com. 106 units. Year-round US$38 double; US$40 triple. Children 11 and under stay free in parent's room. AE, DC, DISC, MC, V. **Amenities:** Restaurant; bar; outdoor pool; 24-hr. room service; babysitting; laundry service; dry cleaning. *In room:* A/C, TV, minibar, safe.

Continental Hotel A government-rated three-star hotel, the Continental offers rooms with either ocean views or vistas of cityscapes. The location is 1.9km (1¼ miles) from the center, about a 30-minute drive from the airport, and a 40-minute drive to a good beach. The building is from the late 1970s, offering midsize bedrooms that are comfortably but simply decorated, each with a bathroom with a tub/shower combo. Although the place doesn't have a lot of style, it does have a dance club, a cocktail lounge, and a restaurant serving international food.

Av. Máximo Gómez 16, Santo Domingo, Dominican Republic. ℂ **809/689-1151.** Fax 809/687-8397. www.hotelbook.com. 84 units. Year-round US$60–US$75 double; US$$75–US$104 suite. Children 11 and under stay free in parent's room. AE, DC, MC, V. **Amenities:** Restaurant; bar; outdoor pool; 24-hr. room service; laundry service; dry cleaning; disco. *In room:* A/C, TV, coffeemaker, iron/ironing board, safe.

El Señorial *Kids* This is typical of the little modern inns that dot the city of Santo Domingo, short on glamour but long on comfort and cleanliness. One of the city's better bargains, El Señorial offers a warm, welcoming atmosphere. Lying close to the commercial center, it is near art galleries, pubs, dance clubs, museums, and cinemas, and within an easy commute of good beaches and casinos. The four-story, white-painted building, a hotel since the early '80s, stands in front of María Eugenia parquet. The comfortable but simply furnished bedrooms come with modern plumbing, plus tub/shower combos in all bathrooms. Many rooms come with three beds (an additional roll-away can be added) for families, although most standard doubles have a "matrimonial" (double) bed or twins.

Presidente Vicini Burgos 58, Santo Domingo, Dominican Republic. ℂ **809/687-4359.** Fax 809/687-0600. 22 units. Year-round US$45–US$65 double. Rates include breakfast. Children 11 and under stay free in parent's room. AE, DC, DISC, MC, V. Free parking. **Amenities:** Restaurant; bar. *In room:* A/C, TV, fridge (in some), hair dryer.

Hotel Restaurante La Casona Dorada *Value* This 19th-century building was another property that belonged to former president

Buenaventura Báez, whose family also owned what is now the Hotel Palacio. A mansion successfully converted to receive paying guests, the hotel lies on tranquil grounds set back from the street at the corner of Calle Osvaldo Báez; it's a 5-minute ride to the Colonial Zone or a 30-minute ride to the beaches. Opened in 1993, the hotel caters to visitors and business clients and is gay friendly. The small bedrooms are traditionally and comfortably decorated and are well maintained, each with a modern bathroom with tub and shower. The restaurant and bar on site are popular gathering places even among locals, and the swimming pool is a social mecca, especially in summer.

Av. Independencia 255 at the corner of Osvaldo Báez, Santo Domingo, Dominican Republic. (**809/221-3535**. Fax 809/221-3622. casona.dorada@codetel.net.do. 51 units. Year-round US$50 double. Children US$5 extra. AE, MC, V. **Amenities:** Restaurant; bar; outdoor pool; 24-hr. room service; laundry service; dry cleaning. *In room:* A/C, TV.

3 Where to Dine

Most of Santo Domingo's restaurants stretch along the seaside, bordering Avenida George Washington, popularly known as the Malecón. Some of the best restaurants are in hotels. It's safest to take a taxi when dining out at night.

In most restaurants, casual dress is fine, although shorts are frowned upon at the fancier, more expensive spots. Many Dominicans prefer to dress up when dining out, especially in the capital.

EXPENSIVE

David Crockett ♠♠ STEAKHOUSE   The name is corny, suggesting a retro fad of the '50s, but this super-expensive restaurant serves the finest steaks in the Dominican Republic. For those who like red meat, it draws the true carnivore. As we heard one American woman telling the waiter, "Just brush it over the grill lightly, sugar." Huge portions of porterhouse, rib-eye, or even Kobe beef will rest on your plate. Should you want some other meat, the chefs are skilled at turning out a perfectly cooked rack of lamb, aromatic with herbs and infused with garlic. Naturally, the decor is country-and-western style.

Gustavo Meliá Ricart 34. (**809/547-2999**. Main courses RD$1,000–RD$2,000 ($36–$72). AE, MC, V. Daily noon–midnight.

El Mesón de la Cava ♠ DOMINICAN/INTERNATIONAL At first we thought this was a gimmicky club—you descend a perilous iron stairway into an actual cave with stalactites and stalagmites—but the cuisine is among the finest in the capital. The

Where to Dine in Santo Domingo

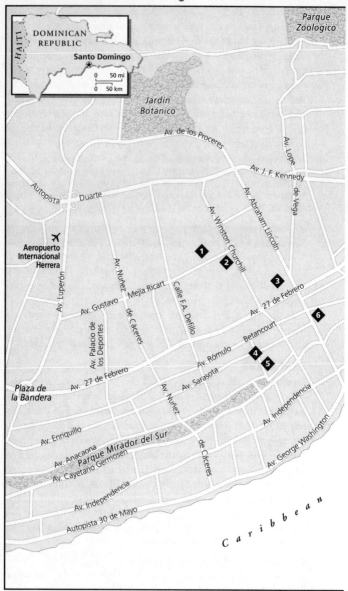

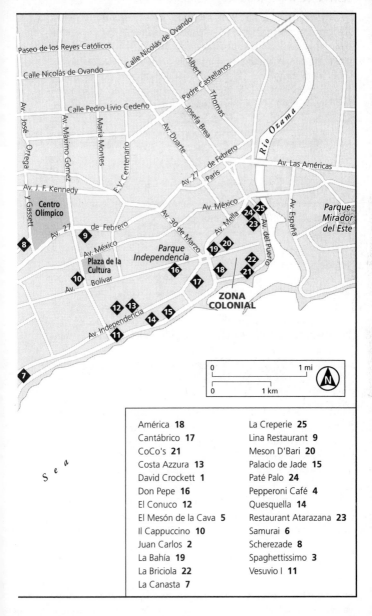

Paseo de los Reyes Católicos
Calle Nicolás de Ovando
Calle Nicolás de Ovando
Calle Pedro Livio Cedeño
Padre Castellanos
Albert Thomas
Josefa Brea
Río Ozama
Av. José Ortega y Gassett
Av. Máximo Gómez
Maria Montes
E.V. Centenario
Av. Duarte
Av. 27 de Febrero
Paris
Av. Las Américas
Av. J. F. Kennedy
Centro Olímpico
Av. 27 de Febrero
Av. México
Av. Mella
Av. España
Parque Mirador del Este
Av. 30 de Marzo
Av. México
Parque Independencia
Av. del Puerto
ZONA COLONIAL
Av. Bolívar
Av. Independencia

8 **9** **10** **12** **13** **14** **15** **11** **16** **17** **18** **19** **20** **21** **22** **23** **24** **25** **7**

0 _____ 1 mi
0 _____ 1 km

S e a

América **18**	La Creperie **25**
Cantábrico **17**	Lina Restaurant **9**
CoCo's **21**	Meson D'Bari **20**
Costa Azzura **13**	Palacio de Jade **15**
David Crockett **1**	Paté Palo **24**
Don Pepe **16**	Pepperoni Café **4**
El Conuco **12**	Quesquella **14**
El Mesón de la Cava **5**	Restaurant Atarazana **23**
Il Cappuccino **10**	Samurai **6**
Juan Carlos **2**	Scherezade **8**
La Bahía **19**	Spaghettissimo **3**
La Briciola **22**	Vesuvio I **11**
La Canasta **7**	

quality ingredients are well prepared and beautifully flavored. Recorded merengue, Latin jazz, blues, and salsa give the place a festive ambience. Launch your repast with the small shrimp sautéed in a delicate sauce of garlic or white wine, perhaps a mixed seafood or "sexy" conch gratinée. The gazpacho is also an excellent beginning, as is the bubbling *sopa de pescado* (red snapper chowder). Follow it up with the grilled Caribbean rock lobster or the double French lamb chops, which are perfectly, tenderly done.

Mirador del Sur 1. © 809/533-2818. Reservations required. Main courses RD$145–RD$1,300 ($5.20–$46). AE, DC, MC, V. Daily noon–midnight.

MODERATE

América SPANISH/INTERNATIONAL   Two blocks from Parque Independencia, this is one of the most centrally located of all the restaurants in Santo Domingo. The building itself is a dull 1950s structure. The waiters are very attentive, taking care of your needs and advising on specialties or wines as requested. The place is informal, drawing young couples on dates, families, visitors, and locals with its satisfying, filling, and savory cuisine. We like to launch our meals with a bowl of the seafood soup. The fresh fish filet, grilled to your specifications and served with fresh vegetables, is an excellent choice, as is the savory platter of paella studded with shellfish. The tender and well-flavored grilled filet of beef is a perennial local favorite.

Arzobispo Hotel, esquina San Tome 201. © 809/682-7194. Reservations not required. Main courses RD$150–RD$975 ($5.40–$35). AE, DC, DISC, MC, V. Daily 11am–midnight.

Cantábrico SPANISH/SEAFOOD   Very close to the Colonial Zone, this eatery evokes a Spanish *tasca,* or tavern. Now moving into its third decade, it is an informal crowd-pleaser, drawing many city families as well as visitors. One specialty is *zarzuela,* seafood in a broth seasoned with lots of garlic, another is "El Filete Especial Cantabrico" (beef filet). The chefs also do a most satisfying paella with lots of shrimp, and, like the chefs in the Spanish city of Segovia, they turn out a tender, well-flavored platter of roast suckling pig. Flavorful grilled meats are also a cornerstone of this kitchen.

Av. Independencia 54. © 809/687-5101. Main courses RD$355–RD$990 ($13–$36). AE, DC, MC, V. Daily 11am–midnight.

Juan Carlos SEAFOOD/INTERNATIONAL   Once a simple eatery for local workers, today Juan Carlos is a more formal

Spanish-style restaurant, with a traditional decor similar to something you'd find in Old Madrid. Despite the change, it retains the
warmth of a mom-and-pop place. The chefs do a good job roast-
ing lamb, flavoring it with fresh herbs and garlic, and serving it
with rice; and black rice (flavored with squid ink) is another
favorite. But nothing beats their selection of grilled seafood, done
to your specifications and based on the fresh catch of the day.
Paella is as much beloved in Santo Domingo as it is in Valencia,
the Spanish city of its origin. The version served here—in a huge
portion—bespeaks of years of training. Most dishes appear at the
lower end of the price scale.

Gustavo Mejía Ricart 7. ℂ 809/562-6444. Reservations recommended. Main
courses RD$270–RD$790 ($9.70–$28). AE, DC, DISC, MC, V. Sun–Fri noon–3pm and
7pm–midnight; Sat 7pm–midnight.

Don Pepe ℛ SPANISH/SEAFOOD   Treat yourself to at least
one lavish meal here during your stay in Santo Domingo. The fish,
including Caribbean lobster, arrives fresh daily and is displayed
extravagantly on ice, awaiting your selection. We usually gravitate to
the giant crab, but any of the fresh seafood grilled to your specifications is the way to go here. Begin, perhaps, with a freshly made
Caldo Gallego, a Galician broth with sausages, greens, and potatoes.
Plump and sweet red peppers are delectably stuffed with seafood,
and the imported salmon arrives with a salsa verde, a green sauce
made with fresh herbs. To end a perfect meal, dig into the offerings
of the dessert tray, an array of smooth flans, delectable cheesecakes,
and crème caramel.

Av. Pasteur 41 at Santiago. ℂ 809/686-8481. Reservations required. Main courses
RD$300–RD$995 ($11–$36). AE, DC, DISC, MC, V. Mon–Fri 11:30am–3:30pm and
7pm–midnight; Sat–Sun 11:30am–midnight. Closed Dec 24, 25.

La Briciola ℛℛ ITALIAN/INTERNATIONAL   This place has a
touch of class, offering an elegant setting in two restored colonial
palaces from the 16th century. Tables are romantically candlelit at
night. In the Colonial Zone, it stands in front of Plazoleta Park. The
menu reflects a commitment to prime ingredients and a determina-
tion not to let style overrule substance. The dishes here hardly test
the creative culinary limits, but are tried-and-true favorites, beginning with a variety of pastas and sauces—all made fresh daily. Our
favorite is the linguini with seafood, but we've also enjoyed a nicely
grilled T-bone steak. This is also a good place at which to order fresh
fish. Dominican rice accompanies all the meat and fish courses. A
piano bar overlooks a courtyard.

Calle Arzobispo Meriño 152-A. ✆ **809/688-5055.** Reservations required. Main courses RD$300–RD$500 ($11–$18). AE, DC, DISC, MC, V. Mon–Sat 6pm–2am. Closed Dec 24–25, 31, and Jan 1.

La Bahía ✵ *Finds* SEAFOOD/INTERNATIONAL   This unassuming place on the Malecón serves some of the best and freshest seafood in the Dominican Republic. One predawn morning as we passed by, fishermen were waiting outside to sell the chef their latest catch. Rarely in the Caribbean will you find a restaurant with such a wide range of seafood dishes. To start, you might try ceviche (seafood marinated in lime juice) or lobster cocktail. Soups usually contain big chunks of lobster as well as shrimp. Our favorite specialties include kingfish in coconut sauce, sea bass Ukrainian style, baked red snapper, and a savory kettle of seafood in the pot. The chef also works magic with conch. Desserts are superfluous. The restaurant stays open until the last customer departs.

Ave. George Washington 1. ✆ **809/682-4022.** Main courses RD$325–RD$725 ($12–$26). AE, MC, V. Daily 11am–2am.

Lina Restaurant ✵✵ INTERNATIONAL/SPANISH   This is one of the most prestigious restaurants in the Caribbean. Spanish-born Lina Aguado originally came to Santo Domingo as the personal chef of the dictator Trujillo, whom she served until opening her own restaurant. Today, four master chefs, whom Dona Lina entrusted with her secret recipes, rule the kitchen of this modern hotel restaurant. The cuisine is international, with an emphasis on Spanish dishes, and the service is first rate. Try the paella Valenciana, the finest in the Dominican Republic. We think the sea bass flambé with brandy is just as good, and few can resist the mixed seafood medley doused with Pernod and cooked casserole-style. Lina's cuisine even wins the approval of some hard-to-please Madrileños we know, who are a bit contemptuous of Spanish food served outside Spain.

In the Barcelo Gran Hotel Lina. Máximo Gómez and 27 de Febrero avs. ✆ **809/563-5000,** ext. 7250. Reservations recommended. Main courses RD$245–RD$1,000 ($8.75–$36). AE, DC, DISC, MC, V. Daily noon–4pm and 6:30pm–midnight.

Pepperoni Café ✵ *Finds* FUSION   A real dining discovery, this is a hip, fun rendezvous, with a rustic decor and exotic paintings. The menu boasts beautifully prepared treats based on the use of high-quality ingredients. The pasta might be Thai, with stir-fried vegetables, or else penne with fresh mushrooms, rock shrimp, prosciutto, and Parmesan. A small part of the menu is dedicated to fresh sushi and sashimi. The salads are among the best in town—varied and fresh—including a Southwest chicken salad with grilled poultry, avocado, bacon, and a lime dressing. Starters range from Peking pork spring rolls to a Thai-influenced tuna ceviche. Don't miss such house specialties as spicy tuna tartar, Mai Thai Crab (with coconut and curry), or braised short beef ribs with garlic whipped potatoes.

Plaza Universitaria Av., Sarasota 25. ℂ **809/508-1330**. Reservations recommended. Main courses RD$295–RD$685 ($11–$25). AE, DC, MC, V. Sun–Thurs noon–midnight; Fri–Sat noon–1am.

Quesquella ⋇ INTERNATIONAL   The food and service at this deluxe hotel are among the best in the capital, and this dining room is one of the finest places to go. It's also a safe bet if you're strolling along the Malecón at night. The chefs strive for great flavor, especially in their imported beef. We've enjoyed the taste, texture, and tenderness of both their T-bone steak and their filet mignon. You could also opt for that 1950s Eisenhower-era steak-and-lobster combination. The chefs graciously let you specify the way you'd like your fish; most discerning diners order it grilled with fresh herbs. That retro classic lobster thermidor is still served here with flourish. As one of the chefs said, "If it were a great dish way back when, why change it?"

Av. George Washington 367, Hotel Renaissance Jaragua. ℂ **809/221-2222**. Main courses RD$280–RD$450 (US$14–US$23). AE, DC, DISC, MC, V. Daily 6am–3pm and 6pm–midnight.

Vesuvio I ⋇ ITALIAN   Along the Malecón, the most famous Italian restaurant in the Dominican Republic draws crowds of visitors and local businesspeople in spite of its fading decor. What to order? That's always a problem, as the Neapolitan owners, the Bonarelli family, have worked since 1954 to perfect and enlarge the menu. As they claim: "We like to catch it ourselves, cook it from scratch, or even grow it if that's possible." Their homemade soups are excellent. Fresh red snapper, sea bass, and oysters are prepared in enticing ways. Specialties include Dominican crayfish *a la Vesuvio* (topped with garlic and bacon). Recent menu additions feature *pappardelle al Bosque* (noodles with porcini mushrooms, rosemary, and garlic), and black tallarini with shrimp *a la crema*.

The owner claims to be the pioneer of pizza in the Dominican Republic. At **Pizzeria Vesuvio** next door (ℂ **809/221-3000**), he makes a unique .9m-long (3-ft.) version! Also look for **Vesuvio II** at Ave. Tiradentes 17 (ℂ **809/562-6060**).

Ave. George Washington 521. ℂ **809/221-3333**. Reservations recommended Fri–Sat. Main courses RD$300–RD$700 ($11–$25). AE, MC, V. Daily noon–2am.

Palacio de Jade CANTONESE/MONGOLIAN   Authentic flavors from faraway China aromatically fill the rooms at this choice restaurant, which is a good change of pace from regular Dominican fare. The chefs work their magic with Peking duck, a dish that's almost impossible to duplicate in a home kitchen. The preparations are often minimal but the results are maximal, as exemplified by the chicken with lettuce or the shrimp in a black-bean sauce. Expect spicy, beautifully presented compositions that balance flavor with texture. The only downside are some of the sounds emerging from the private karaoke rooms.

José María Heredia 6. ℂ **809/686-3226.** Main courses RD$100–RD$950 ($3.60–$34). AE, MC, V. Daily noon–midnight.

Restaurant Atarazana INTERNATIONAL/CREOLE   Although it's clear that not much money was spent on the decor, and most of the furnishings look as though they came from someone's outdoor garden patio, the food is so good and affordable it makes dining here worthwhile. Now deep into its fourth decade, this informal restaurant is in a restored colonial building. Lobster is a specialty and is particularly good grilled. The various catches of the day can also be grilled to your specification or served in a peppery sauce. One of the chef's finest dishes, and one of our favorites, is sea bass stuffed with shrimp and served in a white wine sauce with vegetables and rice. Other well-executed dishes include filet of beef stuffed with cheese and served in a savory sauce, and fresh shrimp in a creamy white sauce.

Atarazana 5. ℂ **809/689-2900.** Reservations recommended. Main courses RD$225–RD$600 ($8.10–$22). AE, DC, DISC, MC, V. Mon–Sat noon–midnight.

Samurai 🍴 ⓚⓘⓓⓢ SUSHI/JAPANESE   A bit unusual in Santo Domingo, this 11-table restaurant is the best sushi bar in town. There's an open view of the kitchen so that you can see what the chefs are up to. Some diners sit Japanese style on the floor. The service is swift, efficient, and charming. It's rare that you get such an interesting assortment of sushi at such an inexpensive restaurant, but there's a full array here, plus sashimi platters, shabu shabu, and sake to wash everything down. The grilled seafood with rum is perhaps more West Indian than Japanese, but the delightful clam soup will take you on a trip to the Far East. We suggest you finish off with the fried ice cream for dessert.

Av. Abraham Lincoln 902. ℂ **809/541-0944.** Reservations recommended. Main courses RD$359–RD$765 ($13–$28). AE, DC, DISC, MC, V. Mon–Sat noon–3pm and 6:30pm–midnight; Sun noon–4pm and 7–11pm. Closed Dec 25 and 31.

Scheherezade INTERNATIONAL/MEDITERRANEAN   Arabian nights live again in this mock mosque with faux Moroccan decor, waiters in embroidered vests and fezzes, and the occasional belly dancer. For Santo Domingo, this restaurant is a real change of pace. Since there are two bars, many guests drop in just for drinks. Expect a selection of extremely fresh salads and flaky flatbread. Your best bets are the grilled seafood and lamb. The Italian-style pastas are rather standard. The desserts are truly superb, especially the delightful orange soufflé.

Roberto Pastoria 226. © 809/227-2323. Main courses RD$250–RD$900 ($9–$32). AE, DC, DISC, MC, V. Daily noon–1am.

Spaghettissimo ✿ ITALIAN/INTERNATIONAL   The name aside, there's a lot more served here than spaghetti. The food is quite good, and the place often fills up with regulars who dive into the generous portions and are drawn by the affordable prices and the charming owner, Frederic Gollong. You can begin with a selection from the antipasto buffet. The various risottos are usually good, and almost daily the chefs bake big tempting plates of creamy lasagna with a savory tomato sauce and lots of cheese. Steaks and both fresh and local fish are also served.

This air-conditioned, 123-seat restaurant lies right off the Malecón and attracts an equal mixture of locals and visitors. It is especially popular on Tuesday and Thursday evenings, when live Italian or South American music fills the candlelit garden.

Manuel de Jesus Troncoso 13. © **809/547-2650.** Main courses RD$145–RD$995 ($5.20–$36). AE, MC, V. Daily noon–3pm and 7pm–midnight. Closed Dec 25 and Jan 1.

INEXPENSIVE

CoCo's ✿ *Finds* BRITISH/CONTINENTAL   British food—and delicious at that—is about the last cuisine you'd expect to find in the Dominican Republic. But that's what is served here, the creation of English expats, whose chefs are also adept at turning out continental favorites. This rather formal bistro lies behind the cathedral in the heart of the Colonial Zone. One of the most traditional and attractive restaurants in the district, it evokes, in some ways, a tastefully decorated English tearoom, reflecting the personal style of its owners, Colin Hercok and Christopher Gwillym. Many residents of the area like to drop in for a pint at the publike bar before dining here. The most popular dish on the menu is breast of chicken in a delightful ginger-and-mango sauce. The kitchen turns out the best cod and chips in the old town, or you might opt for the filet steak Chasseur and (most definitely) the veal-and-mushroom pie.

Padre Billini 53. ℂ **809/687-9624.** Main courses RD$195–RD$320 ($7–$12). AE, DC, MC, V. Tues–Sun noon–2:30pm and 6:30pm–midnight.

El Conuco ℛ DOMINICAN   Come to "the countryside" (its English name) for the best-tasting and most authentic Dominican dishes in the capital. La Bahía (see below) may have better seafood, but otherwise this place is superb, if a bit corny. The waiters in costume will even dance a wicked merengue with you. Few restaurants have been as successful at commercializing the charms of rural Dominican life, and as such, it has attracted many of the country's sports and pop-music stars. You'll find it within an upscale residential neighborhood near the Malecón, close to the Jaragua Resort. Inside, you'll find hammocks, domino tables, colorful weavings, and thatch-covered *bôhios* (beach huts). Familiar menu items here include six kinds of steak, and chicken merengue, prepared with red wine, onions, and mushrooms. If you're adventurous, try the cow's foot stew. A specialty here is the Dominican flag, a traditional platter whose various colors derive from artfully arranged portions of white rice, beans, meat, fried bananas, and salad.

Calle Casimiro de Moya 152, Gazcue. ℂ **809/686-0129.** Reservations recommended. Main courses RD$90–RD$300 ($3.20–$11); lunch buffet RD$175 ($6.25); dinner buffet RD$310 ($11). AE, DC, MC, V. Daily noon–2am.

Il Cappuccino ITALIAN   When Il Cappuccino is crowded, it can be a bit loud, but the terrific pasta dishes more than compensate. Linguini is a specialty, and it is served with a number of sauces. Our all-time favorite is *estrella de mar,* pasta stuffed with king crab. Another specialty is fresh fish—the selection is based on the catch of the day—grilled to your specifications. The desserts are a bit ordinary, but all things considered this is a good choice. It's near the National Theater.

Av. Máximo Gómez 60. ℂ **809/689-8600.** Main courses RD$130–RD$350 ($4.70–$13). AE, DC, DISC, MC, V. Daily noon–3pm and 8–11pm.

Costa Azurra ITALIAN/INTERNATIONAL   This eatery isn't as formal or fancy as Vesuvio I, but it serves some of the same fine food at slightly cheaper prices. Costa Azurra resembles an Italian trattoria with checkered tablecloths and is patronized by an informal, convivial crowd eating heartily and enjoying both the company and the food. Everything is properly sauced and full of flavor, but it doesn't get much better than the spaghetti marinara. Many dishes have a hint of Creole flavors, making use of such ingredients as fresh tomatoes and sweet peppers. It opens early enough for breakfast if your hotel doesn't serve one. The antipasti, soups, and salads are made fresh daily.

Av. Independencia 1107. 🕐 **809/682-3373**. Reservations not required. Main courses RD$180–RD$300 ($6.50–$11). No credit cards.

La Canasta *Value* CREOLE   Within a previously recommended first-class hotel, this is one of the best places in the city for a late-night snack. Many local couples conclude their evenings here devouring the Dominican chicken, which is deep fried and served in small pieces. Other favorite island recipes include the seafood in Creole sauce; *sancocho,* a typical stew with a variety of meats and yucca; and *mondongo,* tripe cooked with tomatoes and sweet peppers. You might start with a satisfying shrimp soup and follow with a beef stew. Cuban sandwiches, a chef's salad, and everything from filet mignon to fish sticks round out the menu.

Av. George Washington 365, Meliá Santo Domingo. 🕐 **809/221-6666.** Reservations not required. Main courses RD$495–RD$825 ($18–$30). AE, DC, DISC, MC, V. Daily 24 hours a day.

La Creperie *Kids* CREPES   The best crepes in all the Dominican Republic are served here. In the Colonial Zone, in the vicinity of the Atarazana, this eatery offers two different types of crepes, both the savory and traditional French variety and some marvelously tasty dessert crepes. Ham and cheese is, of course, the classic, but you can also order many other varieties, including one made with smoked salmon, asparagus points, and a creamy white sauce. Should you not be in the mood for crepes, you can order other dishes as well, including grilled salmon or grilled lobster. Many patrons come here just for the dessert crepes, including a real surprise, a crepe made with homemade orange marmalade. If you want to be completely "illicit," you can order a crepe with grated coconut and chocolate which is wicked enough to get you expelled from the Garden of Eden. Their ice creams are to die for, especially the mango.

Atazara 11 🕐 **809/221-4734**. Reservations not required. Main courses RD$185–RD$930 ($6.65–$33). AE, DC, DISC, MC, V. Mon and Wed–Thurs 10:30am–12:30am, Fri–Sun 10:30am–1am. Closed Dec 25 and 31.

Meson D'Bari CREOLE   In the Colonial Zone in what used to be a private family home, this restaurant has both ambience and good food. Paintings by Dominican artists—the art is for sale—decorate the walls of this handsomely restored building. Dishes are rich and satisfying, and beautifully rendered, and the waiters are supremely attentive. *Filete a la criolla* (filet of beef served Creole style) landed on our plate on our last visit. Beef also appears in a number of other ways, including with a freshly made mushroom sauce. A savory crab stew is another choice item to order, as is the grilled fish, based on the catch of the day. A daily special is also offered, perhaps *chivo guisado* (stewed goat).

C/Hostos 302, corner of Salome Ureña. (✆ **809/687-4091**. Main courses RD$285 ($10). AE, DC, MC, V. Daily noon–midnight.

Paté Palo *(Finds)* INTERNATIONAL   Part of Paté Palo's charm derives from its location, overlooking Plaza Colón, the graceful arcades of the Alcazar de Colón, and amiable clusters of Dominican families who promenade with their children every night at dusk. During the 1500s, the building was a bistro under the supervision of a mysterious Dutch buccaneer known as Peg-Leg (Paté Palo), who's credited with establishing the first tavern in the New World.

In the late 1990s, another Dutchman and his four partners transformed the place into a gregarious and engaging bistro that, on weekends, is one of the most crowded and popular singles bars in the country. Tables are thick-topped wooden affairs, set either on the plaza outside or within the antique walls of the dark and shadowy interior. The food is some of the best in the capital, and is usually accompanied by live guitar music every Thursday to Sunday from 6 to 10pm. Having dined here many times, we feel at home with the menu and can most recommend the sautéed shrimp in coconut curry sauce. On festive occasions, ask for the brochette of mixed meats; the meat has been marinated in fresh spices and herbs and is artfully flambéed at your table. The sea bass with white wine sauce is perfectly prepared, although the fancy continental dishes such as charbroiled steak with onion sauce and a grilled rack of lamb might be more suited for the cold Alps.

La Atarazana 25, Zona Colonial. (✆ **809/687-8089**. Burgers and salads RD$385–RD$425 ($14–$15). Main courses RD$450–RD$1,100 ($16–$40). AE, MC, V. Daily noon to 1am.

Exploring Santo Domingo

Santo Domingo—a treasure trove of historic, sometimes crumbling buildings—is undergoing a major government-sponsored restoration. The old town, or Zona Colonial, is still partially enclosed by remnants of its original city wall. The narrow streets, old stone buildings, and forts are like nothing else in the Caribbean, except perhaps Old San Juan. The only thing missing is the clank of the conquistadors' armor.

Old and modern Santo Domingo meet at the **Parque Independencia,** a big city square whose most prominent feature is its **Altar de la Patria,** a national pantheon dedicated to the nation's heroes, Duarte, Sánchez, and Mella, who are all buried here. These men led the country's fight for freedom from Haiti in 1844. As in provincial Spanish cities, the square is a popular family gathering place on Sunday afternoon. At the entrance to the plaza is **El Conde Gate,** named for the count (El Conde) de Penalva, the governor who resisted the forces of Admiral Penn, the leader of a British invasion. It was also the site of the March for Independence in 1844, and holds a special place in the hearts of Dominicans.

In the shadow of the Alcázar de Colón, **La Atarazana** is a fully restored section of one of the New World's finest arsenals. It extends for a city block, holding within it a catacomb of shops, art galleries, boutiques, and some good regional and international restaurants.

Just behind river moorings is the oldest street in the New World, **Calle Las Damas (Street of the Ladies),** named not because it was the red-light district, but for the elegant ladies of the viceregal court who used to promenade here in the evening. It's lined with colonial buildings.

Try to see the **Puerta de la Misericordia** (Calle Palo Hincado just north of Calle Arzobispo Portes). Part of the original city wall, this "Gate of Mercy" was once a refuge for colonists fleeing hurricanes and earthquakes.

You'll see a microcosm of Dominican life as you head east along **Calle El Conde** from Parque Independencia to Columbus Square (Plaza de Colón), which has a large bronze statue honoring the discoverer (or to be more politically correct, the explorer of an already inhabited land). The statue was created in 1882 by a French sculptor.

As impressive as the old town or Zona Colonial is, monuments are not the total allure of Santo Domingo, as you'll soon discover in this chapter. Following a day of shopping for handicrafts, or perhaps jewelry fashioned from amber or larimar—a semiprecious ocean-blue gemstone found only in a remote mountain in the southwestern region of the country—the sound of merengue will lure you to the bars, dance clubs, and casinos of the capital after dark.

1 Fortresses & a Cathedral

If you like views more than you do wandering around dusty relics, head for the **Fuerte de Santa Bárbara (Fort of Santa Barbara)** standing at the corner of Juan Parra and Avenida Mella. When it was constructed in the 1570s, it was one of Santo Domingo's principal points of defense. As formidable as it was, it fell to Sir Francis Drake—locals call him "the pirate"—and his two dozen ships, who took the fort in 1586. Today the place is a complete ruin, but worth a visit for its small garden and little square. The view of Santo Domingo from here is panoramic.

Alcázar de Colón 🏵🏵   The most outstanding structure in the old city is the Alcázar, a palace built for Columbus's son, Diego, and his wife, who was also niece to Ferdinand, king of Spain. Diego became the colony's governor in 1509, and Santo Domingo rose as the hub of Spanish commerce and culture in America. For more than 60 years, this coral limestone structure on the bluffs of the Ozama River was the center of the Spanish court, entertaining such distinguished visitors as Cortés, Ponce de León, and Balboa. The nearly two dozen rooms and open-air loggias are decorated with paintings and period tapestries, as well as 16th-century antiques. A walk downhill from the Alcázar leads to the impressive **Puerto de San Diego,** which dates from 1571 when it was built as the main gate into Santo Domingo. Some of the original wall can be seen by this gate, which once guarded against attacks coming from the river.

Calle La Atarazana (at the foot of Calle Las Damas). 📞 **809/682-4250,** ext. 232. Admission US$1.75. Mon–Sat 9am–5pm; Sun 9am–4pm.

Catedral Primada de América 🏵🏵   The oldest cathedral in the Americas was begun in 1514 and completed in 1540. With a gold coral limestone facade, the church combines elements of both Gothic

What to See & Do in Santo Domingo

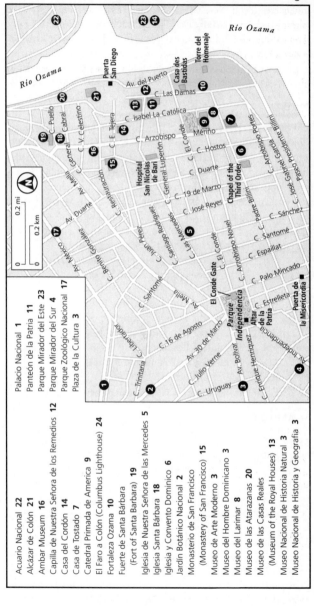

Acuario Nacional **22**
Alcázar de Colón **21**
Ambar Museum **16**
Capilla de Nuestra Señora de los Remedios **12**
Casa del Cordón **14**
Casa de Tostado **7**
Catedral Primada de America **9**
El Faro a Colón (Columbus Lighthouse) **24**
Fortaleza Ozama **10**
Fuerte de Santa Bárbara
  (Fort of Santa Barbara) **19**
Iglesia de Nuestra Señora de las Mercedes **5**
Iglesia Santa Bárbara **18**
Iglesia y Convento Dominico **6**
Jardín Botánico Nacional **2**
Monasterio de San Francisco
  (Monastery of San Francisco) **15**
Museo de Arte Moderno **3**
Museo del Hombre Dominicano **3**
Museo del Larimar **8**
Museo de las Atarazanas **20**
Museo de las Casas Reales
  (Museum of the Royal Houses) **13**
Museo Nacional de Historia Natural **3**
Museo Nacional de Historia y Geografía **3**

Palacio Nacional **1**
Panteón de la Patria **11**
Parque Mirador del Este **23**
Parque Mirador del Sur **4**
Parque Zoológico Nacional **17**
Plaza de la Cultura **3**

61

and baroque, with some lavish Plateresque styles as exemplified by the high altar chiseled out of silver. The cathedral was the center for a celebration of the 500th anniversary of the European discovery of America in 1992.

In between Calle Arzobispo Meriño and Isabel La Católica (on the south side of Columbus Sq.). © 809/682-3848. Admission RD$30 ($1.10). Cathedral Mon–Sat 9am–4pm; masses Sun noon and 5pm, Mon and Wed–Sat 5pm; treasury Mon–Sat 9am–4pm.

El Faro a Colón (Columbus Lighthouse) 🏛 Built in the shape of a cross, the towering 206m-tall (688-ft.) El Faro a Colón monument is both a sightseeing attraction and a cultural center. In the heart of the structure is a chapel containing the Columbus tomb, and, some say, his mortal remains. The "bones" of Columbus were moved here from the Cathedral of Santa María la Menor. (Other locations, including the Cathedral of Seville, also claim to possess the explorer's remains.) The most outstanding and unique feature is the lighting system composed of 149 searchlights and a 70-kilowatt beam that circles out for nearly 71km (44 miles). When illuminated, the lights project a gigantic cross in the sky that can be seen as far away as Puerto Rico.

Although the concept of the memorial is 140 years old, the first stones were not laid until 1986, following the design submitted in 1929 by J. L. Gleave, the winner of the worldwide contest held to choose the architect. The monumental lighthouse was inaugurated on October 6, 1992, the day Columbus's "remains" were transferred from the cathedral.

Av. España (on the water side of Los Tres Ojos, near the airport in the Sans Souci district). © 809/591-1492. Admission RD$30 ($1.05) adults, RD$5 (20¢) children 11 and under. Tues–Sun 9am–5pm.

Fortaleza Ozama On the southern side of old town's most famous street, this fortress was constructed in 1502, but much was changed and altered over the centuries. It lies on a steep hill over the mouth of the Río Ozama, and, from this point, the Spanish launched conquests of Jamaica, Peru, Mexico, Cuba, and Colombia. Still standing today, it remains the oldest colonial military building in the New World, a position it held until the American invasion of 1965, when it was decommissioned and opened to the public. Among the walled buildings here stands the Torre del Homenaje (Tower of Homage), evoking a Spanish castle with walls 2m (6½ ft.) thick and a crenellated tower. If you climb to the roof, you'll be rewarded with 360-degree **view of the city** 🏛🏛🏛.

Other attractions include the excavated ruins of a fort from 1502; the intact wall of Fort Santiago, the first line of defense; and an old arsenal where gunpowder was once stored. In the courtyard beyond the main gate there is a statue of González Oviedo, author of the first *History of the Indies.* He also commanded the fort from 1533 to 1557.

Calle Las Damas. ℂ **809/686-0222.** Admission RD$15 (55¢). Mon–Sat 9am–7pm; Sun 9am–3pm.

2 The Leading Museums

Amber World Museum   The Dominican Republic is the home of the finest amber in the world. This museum provides a fascinating glimpse into the world of amber. Amber, of course, is hardened tree resin. The resin often trapped and preserved mosquitoes, flies, spiders, ants, and even lizards and frogs, for millennium upon millennium. In addition to displaying amber that preserves animals and insects from long ago, the museum also displays a beautiful collection of amber jewelry and other artifacts. Audiovisual displays show amber being mined and made into jewelry. Amber comes in a variety of colors, ranging from deep red to a light yellow, even a blue or the extremely rare smoky green.

Calle Arzobispo Meriño 452. ℂ **809/682-3309.** Admission RD$50 ($1.80). Mon–Sat 8:30am–6pm; Sun 9am–2pm.

The Larimar Museum   On the ground floor is an elegant shop selling larimar and amber jewelry at prices that are negotiable. Upstairs is a museum devoted to the rare larimar, a blue pectolite mined only in the Dominican Republic. Exhibits explain everything from the mining of the stone to how it is used, most often appearing in jewelry. You also learn how nature created larimar, with its distinctive volcanic blue color, and where it is found.

Isabel la Católica 54. ℂ **809/689-6605.** www.larimarmuseum.com. Free admission. Mon–Sat 8:30am–6pm; Sun 9am–1pm.

Museo de las Atarazanas   This is a rarely visited but worthy museum filled with some unexpected treasures, including some of the rescued booty from the 1500s wreck of *Concepción,* the Spanish galleon that was sunk during a hurricane while sailing off the coast of Bahía de Samaná. Divers have spent 4 centuries trying to rescue all the loot that went down to a sea burial, and some of the treasure is exhibited here, including bars of silver, gold coins, ancient china, and shards of pottery. Many other relics rescued from shipwrecks off the Dominican coast are on display, including belt buckles, pipes, brandy bottles, and pewter plates. The building housing the museum was once a customs house and later a storage house.

Calle Colón 4. ⓒ **809/682-5834**. Admission RD$20 (70¢). Daily 9am–5pm.

Museo de las Casas Reales (Museum of the Royal Houses) ⭐ *Kids*   Through artifacts, tapestries, maps, and re-created halls, including a courtroom, this museum traces Santo Domingo's history from 1492 to 1821. Gilded furniture, arms and armor, and other colonial artifacts make it the most interesting museum of Old Santo Domingo. It contains replicas of the *Niña,* the *Pinta,* and the *Santa Maria,* and one exhibit is said to hold some of Columbus's ashes. In addition to pre-Columbian art, you can see the main artifacts of two galleons sunk in 1724 on their way from Spain to Mexico, along with remnants of another 18th-century Spanish ship, the *Concepción.*

Calle Las Damas (at corner Las Mercedes). ⓒ **809/682-4202**. Admission RD$30 ($1.05), children under 12 free. Tues–Sun 9am–5pm.

Plaza de la Cultura ⭐⭐   Once the personal property of the dictator Trujillo, this modern complex of buildings, known as the Plaza de la Cultura, houses four museums. These ultramodern buildings stand in a parklike setting, and you occupy the better part of your day if you choose to visit everything.

Museo de Arte Moderno ⭐   Four floors here are dedicated to 20th-century Dominican art, with the permanent collection on the second and third floors and the temporary exhibits on the first and fourth. Temporary exhibitions of art might be devoted to the Caribbean or else international in origin. Visitors expecting to see Dominican art as primitive as that which Haiti made famous are in for a surprise. Many Dominican artists vie with some of the best modern artists in the world, painting in a variety of styles. Some island artists have gone on to world acclaim, including Cándido Bidó, known for stylized idealizations of *campesino,* or peasant life. Bidó's works are characterized by exaggerated lips and hollowed-out eyes. All six of the Bidó works on display are on the second floor, including his best known, *El Paseo a las 10am,* depicting a woman in a sun hat with a handful of flowers.

Many island artists were obviously influenced by big names elsewhere—thus, you might encounter an Andy Warhol rip-off or a painting derivative of Diego Rivera's brand of social realism. Other Dominicans, however, produce very original and imaginative art. The greatest art is that of Spanish expat Vela Zanetti, including his

La Vida de los Campesinos series. Zanetti's work is found in many public buildings, including the United Nations' Security Council chambers in New York.

Av. Pedro Henríquez Ureña and Máximo Gomes, Plaza de la Cultura. ℂ **809/685-2153**. Admission RD$20 (70¢), students RD$5 (20¢). Tues–Sun 10am–6pm.

Museo del Hombre Dominicano 👀 If you have to skip all the other museums at the Plaza de la Cultura, try to spare an hour to an hour and a half to explore these exhibits, the finest collection in the Caribbean of the artifacts of the pre-Columbian peoples, including the Taíno Indians. This is, in fact, the most important collection in the world of the Taínos, who greeted Columbus in 1492, little knowing the horrible fate that awaited them, including disease, slavery, and ultimately death at the hands of these strange visitors from another world.

Thousands of magnificently sculpted ceramic, bone, and shell works are on display, along with grinding stones, carved necklaces, axes, and pottery. One section is devoted to the conquest of the West Indies, focusing on the pain suffered by the slaves under the domination of the Spanish. The life of the peasant is brilliantly depicted, including a typical country house that has been reconstructed in the museum. The exhibits are a pastiche of African, Taíno, and Spanish cultures, all of which went to influence Dominican life today. There's a little bit of everything here, even the "throne car" the pope rode through the streets of Santo Domingo on a 1979 visit. One very festive section depicts carnival costumes from around the island.

Av. Pedro Henríquez Ureña, Plaza de la Cultura. ℂ **809/687-3622** or 809/687-3623. Admission RD$20 (70¢). Tues–Sun 10am–5pm.

Museo Nacional de Historia y Geografía Near the National Library, this museum displays many personal belongings of Rafael Trujillo, one of the most notorious Caribbean dictators of the 20th century, including items of clothing, military uniforms, even his briefcases and medals he was awarded from such countries as Spain and Argentina, both of which knew a lot about dictators themselves. Many of his personal documents are on exhibit, as well as personal items such as his comb, his razor, and his wallet. Also on display, along with portraits of El Benefactor (as Trujillo liked to call himself), you'll see one of the bullet-riddled cars that was part of the presidential motorcade when Trujillo was assassinated. You get a look at the pancake makeup kit Trujillo used to hide his Haitian ancestry. There are also exhibits relating the story of the American occupation of the island; artifacts of the conquistadors, the early colonists under Spanish rule; and exhibits depicting the Haitian invasion of the Dominican Republic, as well as other highlights of the nation's history. One wing concentrates on re-creating the legend of General Ulises Heureaux, the D.R.'s most important dictator of the 19th century.

Av. Pedro Henríquez Ureña, Plaza de la Cultura. (*) **809/686-6668.** Admission RD$5 (20¢). Tues–Sun 9:30am–4:30pm.

3 Most Historic Churches

The **Monasterio de San Francisco (Monastery of San Francisco)** is but a mere ruin, but romantically lit at night. It was built between 1512 and 1544. That any part of it is still standing is a miracle; it was destroyed by earthquakes, pillaged by Sir Francis Drake and his men, and bombarded by French artillery. To get here, go along Calle Hostos and across Calle Emiliano Tejere; continue up the hill, and about midway along you'll see the ruins.

Capilla de Nuestra Señora de los Remedios   You'll recognize this chapel in the Colonial Zone by its attractive triple-arched belfry atop a brick-built facade. The Chapel of Our Lady of the Remedies was constructed in the Gothic style in the 1500s by Francisco de Avila, an alderman. It was not intended for public use but built as a private chapel and family mausoleum for the Ovando and Dávila families, two of the most prominent in the city back then. In time, people of the old town did attend Mass here under a barrel-vaulted ceiling. When city officials pronounced the building dangerous in 1884, it was torn down and rebuilt.

Calle Las Damas esq. Mercedes. (*) **809/686-8657.** Free admission, donations appreciated. When there is an art exhibit, fee of RD$200 ($7.20). Mon–Fri 8am–2:30pm.

Iglesia de Nuestra Señora de las Mercedes   This is one of the most historic churches of Santo Domingo, although the staff overseeing it today aren't the city's brightest bulbs. It may or may not be open at the time of your visit. Constructed back in the 1530s, the Church of Our Lady of Mercy was once sacked by Sir Francis Drake and his "pirates." The building suffered major disasters in the wake of Drake, including hurricanes and earthquakes. Still standing, it is of interest today because of its mahogany altar carved in the shape of a demon serpent. The cloister adjacent to the church is more or less in its original condition. During the Haitian rule of the island, some 6,000 Africans were held here before being shipped off to Puerto Plata and Samaná.

Corner of Las Mercedes y José Reyes. © 809/682-3744. Free admission, donations appreciated. Open to public daily 4–6:15pm. Mon–Sat mass 5:30pm; Sun masses 9:30am, 11am, and 7pm.

Iglesia Santa Bárbara   Completed in 1574, this is a combination church and fortress, the only one of its kind in the country. This impressive whitewashed building honors the saint of the military. The capital crowning the baroque building is ridiculously tiny for such a structure, and its towers are of different height and design, a curious hodgepodge. Two of its three arches were reconstructed without windows, the third framing a massively sturdy door. This architecture followed in the wake of attacks by Sir Francis Drake's men but might also have been to protect the building against hurricanes. There is little of interest inside, so you may be in and out the door in 10 minutes or so.

Isabel la Católica, corner of Gabino Coello. © 809/682-3307. Free admission, donations appreciated. Open to the public 5–7pm. Sun masses 7:30am, 9am, and 6pm. Mon–Sat mass 6pm.

Iglesia y Convento Domínico   Founded in 1510, this is one of the oldest churches and convents in the West Indies. In the Colonial Zone, it lies just south of El Conde. This was the site of the New World's first university, San Tomé de Aquino, before it folded and moved on. Impressive pillars frame the stone facade, and blue Mudéjar tiling, evocative of Spain, runs along the top of the portal. Vine ornamentation—which the Spaniards call "Isabelline" style—surrounds the circular window at the core of the church. Saturday and Sunday hours, especially Saturday hours, are severely limited.

Across the plaza, at the corner of Avenida Duarte and Padre Billini, stands **Capilla de la Tercera Orden Domínica,** or the Chapel of the Third Dominican Order. Constructed in 1729, this is the only colonial monument in the city to reach the 21st century intact. Today, it is the office of the archbishop of Santo Domingo. Although you can stop to admire its impressive baroque facade, you're not allowed to peek inside.

Calle Padre Bellini and Av. Duarte. © 809/682-3780. Free admission. Office open Mon–Fri 8am–noon and 3–7:30pm. Open to public during mass hours Sun 8am, 11am, 7:30pm, Mon–Sat 6pm.

4 Other Attractions & Curiosities

Acuario Nacional (*Kids*)   This is the grandest aquarium in the Caribbean, a project funded during the Balaguer administration that caused great controversy, opponents claiming "the people's money" could be better spent elsewhere, perhaps on public schools, hospitals, and housing. Nonetheless, *el presidente* wanted a grand aquarium and continued to press for funds.

Misspent money or not, the results are spectacular. At one point you can take an underwater corridor under a Plexiglas tank, watching sharks, barracuda, and other ferocious-looking big fish glide by over your head. The exhibits are in Spanish only so you may not know the English names of some of the weirder denizens of the deep. You'll surely recognize a manatee. Lesser known might be the endangered slider turtle, part of a breeding project of the aquarium hoping to save this species from extinction.

Av. España 75. (*C*) **809/766-1709.** Admission RD$15 (55¢) adults, RD$10 (35¢) children under 11. Tues–Sun 9:30am–5:30pm.

Casa del Cordón (*Finds*)   Near the Alcázar de Colón, the Cord House was named for the cord of the Franciscan order, which is carved above the door. Francisco de Garay, who came to Hispaniola with Columbus, built the casa from 1503 to 1504, which makes it the oldest stone house in the western hemisphere. It once lodged the first Royal Audience of the New World, which performed as the Supreme Court of Justice for the island and the rest of the West Indies. On another occasion, in January 1586, the noble ladies of Santo Domingo gathered here to donate their jewelry as ransom demanded by Sir Francis Drake in return for his promise to leave the city. The restoration of this historical manor was financed by the Banco Popular Dominicano, where its executive offices are found.

Calles Emiliano Tejera and Isabel la Católica. No phone. Free admission. Mon–Fri 9am–5pm.

Casa de Tostado   The beautiful Gothic geminate (double) window in the Casa de Tostado is the only one existing today in the New World. The house was first owned by the scribe Francisco Tostado, and then was inherited by his son of the same name, a professor, writer, and poet who, in 1586, was the victim of a shot fired during Drake's bombardment of Santo Domingo. The Casa de Tostado, which at one time was the archbishop's palace, now houses the **Museo de la Familia Dominicana,** which focuses on life in the 19th century in a well-to-do household.

Calle Arzobispo Meriño, corner of Padre Billini. ☎ **809/688-6918.** Admission RD$20 (70¢). Mon–Sat 9am–4pm.

Palacio Nacional   You may or may not be granted entrance to the seat of government of the Dominican Republic. Instead of calling on your own, it might be better to have your hotel do it for you. If you do get an invitation extended, show up in the finest garb you brought along. The mammoth palace near the Zona Colonial was built of roseate marble extracted from the Peninsula of Samaná. The architect was an Italian, Guido D'Alessandro, who inaugurated the palace in 1947 in the neoclassical style. It is magnificently furnished with gilt mirrors, crystal chandeliers, and art from some of the nation's most prominent painters. The most dramatic salon is the Room of the Caryatids, with 44 sculpted and clothed women rising like columns in a miniature Hall of Versailles with Baccarat chandeliers and French mirrors. Filled with government offices, the building stretches for nearly a block.

Corner of avs. México and 30 de Marzo. ☎ **809/695-8000.** Free admission. By appointment only.

Panteón de la Patria   When this structure was built in 1747, it was a church for the Jesuits. Later it was a warehouse and then a theater before the dictator, Rafael Trujillo, seized it in the days when Santo Domingo was called Ciudad Trujillo. No doubt dreaming of imperial glory, he wanted to make the building a shrine to some of the country's most illustrious citizens, including perhaps a memorial to himself. He did not succeed in his dream. Instead of a monument honoring Trujillo, you get a chapel preserving the ashes of the martyrs of June 14, 1959, who tried in vain to overthrow the dreaded tyrant. In addition, the ashes or remains of many of the nation's most illustrious personages are enshrined here. Trujillo had bodies re-interred. Some figures ended up buried next to their political enemies, as was the case with Pedro Santana, the 19th-century dictator, who rests—perhaps not so peacefully—with a string of *caudillos* who fought bitterly to overthrow each other as *el presidente*. The Spanish dictator, Franco, donated the mammoth central chandelier. Many of the metal crosses, or so the rumor mill has it, were once Nazi swastikas. The rather sterile structure is constructed of mammoth limestone blocks behind a neoclassical facade, its entrance constantly guarded by an armed soldier.

Calle Las Damas, corner of Mercedes. ☎ **809/685-4466.** Free admission. Tues–Sun 8am–5pm.

5 Gardens, Parks & a Zoo

Jardín Botánico Nacional ⚜   In the northern sector of Santo Domingo, these Botanical Gardens are the biggest in all of Latin America, containing flowers and lush vegetation from around the island. You can wander at leisure or else take a RD$20 (70¢) shuttle to get around the park, taking in a wealth of luxuriant planting, including ferns, palms, orchids, and bromeliads. The Japanese Garden is a special highlight, as are a floor clock and the Great Ravine. If you don't have time to escape to the Dominican countryside, this is your best chance for a preview.

Av. República de Colombia. © **809/385-0860.** Admission RD$20 (70¢) adults, RD$10 (35¢) children 9 and under. Daily 8am–5pm.

Parque Mirador del Este   This sprawling city park ("Eastern Lookout Park" in English) lies across the Río Ozama from the Zona Colonial. Most foreigners come here to see the controversial monument to Christopher Columbus (see "El Faro a Colón," p. 62). But, if time permits, you can linger for 2 hours or so and explore the park more fully.

The park is riddled with caves—really, limestone sinkholes—created eons ago. The most famous and most explored of these is **Los Tres Ojos (The Three Eyes),** which can be reached by taking a long staircase carved into the side of this cave. Here, three lagoons are set in these scenic caverns, studded with lots of stalactites and stalagmites. One lagoon is 12m (40 ft.) deep, another 6m (20 ft.) deep. A third lagoon—known as "Ladies Bath"—is only 1.5m (5 ft.) deep. A Dominican Tarzan will sometimes dive off the walls of the cavern into the deepest lagoon. You can explore the caverns on walkways. Admission is RD$20 (70¢), and visits are possible daily from 9am to 5pm.

Popular with joggers and cyclists, the park is also peopled with some of the most aggressive souvenir hawkers in the Dominican Republic. To see the park's natural attractions, anticipate lots of hassle to buy postcards, jewelry, or whatever.

Along Av. Mirador del Este. Daily 24 hr.

Parque Mirador del Sur   "Southern Lookout Park" (its English name) lies in the southwestern sector of Santo Domingo. The young professional set of the city can be seen here in the early morning in their jogging suits. They also roller skate and bicycle through the park. Later in the day an older crowd visits the park. After school, it is often filled with mothers and their children. The park was created on a large limestone ridge that is studded with caves, many the size of a football field, although some hardly have room for a mongoose and its offspring. When you get thirsty, you'll find any number of food stands or juice bars. Baseball is the national sport of the Dominican Republic, and you'll note several baseball diamonds scattered about. The park is closed to cars daily from 6 to 9am and 4 to 8pm.

Av. Mirador del Sur. Free admission. Daily 24 hr.

Parque Zoológico Nacional ⚓ *Kids*   This is one of the largest zoos in Latin America, but attracts few visitors as it lies in a hard-to-reach northwest corridor in a poor section of narrow, winding streets. It's best to go by taxi to avoid getting lost. These 128 hectares (320 acres) are home to both native and exotic animals and birds. An aquatic bird lake, a crocodile pond, a snake exhibit, and the huge "African Plain," where fauna from that continent roam, make this a fascinating place to visit. There's also a beautiful pond filled with graceful flamingo and a tiger compound without bars. The zoo has a souvenir shop, snack bar, and rest areas.

Av. Los Arroyos. ✆ **809/562-3149.** Fax 809/562-2070. Admission RD$30 ($1.10). Tues–Sun 9am–5pm.

ORGANIZED TOURS   Prieto Tours, Avenida Francia 125 (✆ **809/685-0102**), one of the capital's leading tour operators, offers a 3-hour tour of the **Colonial Zone,** leaving most mornings at 9am and again at 3pm if there's sufficient demand; it costs RD$700 ($25). A 6-hour tour visits the Colonial Zone, the **Columbus Lighthouse,** the **Aquarium,** and the city's modern neighborhoods; the RD$1,400 ($50) fee includes lunch and entrance to several well-known museums and monuments. About an hour of the tour is devoted to shopping.

6 Beaches & Other Outdoor Pursuits

BEACHES   The Dominican Republic has some great beaches, but they aren't in Santo Domingo. The principal beach resort near the capital is at **Boca Chica,** less than 3.2km (2 miles) east of the airport and about 31km (19 miles) from the center of Santo Domingo. Here you'll find clear, shallow blue water, a white-sand beach, and a natural coral reef. The east side of the beach, known as "St. Tropez," is popular with Europeans. In recent years, the backdrop of the beach has become rather tacky, with an array of pizza and fast-food stands, beach cottages, chaise longues, watersports concessions, and plastic beach tables.

Moments *Un, Dos, Tres* **Strikes—You're Out**

Dominicans were crazy about baseball long before their countryman Sammy Sosa set the United States on fire with his home run race against Mark McGwire. Almost every Major League baseball team has at least one player from the Dominican Republic on its roster these days. Pedro Martinez, Manny Ramirez, and Alphonso Soriano are just a few of the all-star team of players who hail from the Dominican Republic.

If you're here between October and January, you might want to catch a game in the Dominican Republic's Professional Winter League. The **Liga de Beisbol** stadium (© **809/ 567-6371**) is in Santo Domingo; check local newspapers for game times, or ask at your hotel. There are also games at the Tetelo Vargas Stadium in San Pedro de Macoris, known to die-hard sports fans as the "land of shortstops" for the multitude of infielders that call this tiny town home.

Slightly better maintained is the narrow white-sand beach of **Playa Juan Dolio** or **Playa Esmeralda,** a 20-minute drive east of Boca Chica. Several resorts have recently located here. The beach used to be fairly uncrowded, but with all the hotels now lining it, it's likely to be as crowded as Boca Chica any day of the week.

If a holiday on the beach is what you're seeking in the Dominican Republic, consider checking into one of the beach-bordering properties at the resorts of Boca Chica, Juan Dolio, or La Romana and commuting to Santo Domingo just for shopping or attractions. For a complete review of what's available, see chapter 5.

HORSE RACING   Santo Domingo's racetrack, **Galapagos Hipódromo V Centenario,** on Avenida Las Américas, km 14.5 (© **809/ 687-6060**), schedules races Tuesday, Thursday, and Saturday at 2pm. You can spend the day here and have lunch at the track's restaurant. Admission is free.

TENNIS   You can often play on the courts at the major resorts if you ask your hotel desk to call in advance for you and make arrangements.

7 Best Shopping Buys

The best buys in Santo Domingo are handcrafted native items, especially amber jewelry. **Amber,** petrified tree resin that has fossilized over millions of years, is the national gem. Look for pieces of amber with objects like insects or spiders trapped inside. Colors range from a bright yellow to black, but most of the gems are golden in hue. Fine-quality amber jewelry, along with lots of plastic fakes, is sold throughout the country.

A semiprecious stone of light blue (sometimes a dark-blue color), **larimar** is the Dominican turquoise. It often makes striking jewelry, and is sometimes mounted with wild boar's teeth.

Ever since the Dominicans presented John F. Kennedy with what became his favorite rocker, visitors have wanted to take home a **rocking chair.** These rockers are often sold unassembled, for easy shipping. Other good buys include Dominican rum, hand-knit articles, macramé, ceramics, and crafts in native mahogany.

BEST SHOPPING AREAS

The best shopping streets are **El Conde,** the oldest and most traditional shop-flanked avenue, and **Avenida Mella.** In the colonial section, **La Atarazana** is filled with galleries and gift and jewelry stores, charging inflated prices. Duty-free shops are found at the airport, in the capital at the **Centro de los Héroes,** and at both the Hotel Santo Domingo and the Hotel Embajador.

Head first for the National Market, **El Mercado Modelo** ☆☆☆, Avenida Mella, filled with stall after stall of crafts, spices, and produce. The market lies in a decaying two-story structure near Calle Santomé, just north of the Colonial Zone, and is open daily from 9am to 6pm. The merchants will be most eager to sell, and you can easily get lost in the crush. Remember to bargain. You'll see a lot of tortoiseshell work here, but exercise caution, since many species, especially the hawksbill turtle, are on the endangered-species list and could be impounded by U.S. Customs if discovered in your luggage. Also for sale here are rockers, mahogany, sandals, baskets, hats, and clay braziers for grilling fish. That's not all. Expect to find everything from musical instruments to love potions, even voodoo objects. *Warning:* Pickpockets, regrettably, are rampant.

Tips You Call That a Bargain?

Always haggle over the price of handicrafts in the Dominican Republic, particularly in the open-air markets. No stall-keeper expects you to pay the first price asked. Remember the Spanish words for too expensive: *muy caro.*

SHOPPING A TO Z
AMBER & LARIMAR

Ambar Marie   This is a trustworthy source for amber. Look for the beautiful necklaces, as well as the earrings and pins; you can even design your own setting here. Although some of the displays are not for sale, in an adjoining salon you can watch craftspeople at work, polishing and shaping raw bits of ancient amber for sale. Open 8am to noon and 2 to 5pm. Caonabo 9, Gazcue. ✆ 809/682-7539.

Ambar Nacional   This is another reliable source for stunning amber, as well as coral. This is also one of the best sources for purchasing larimar jewelry. In general, prices here are a bit less expensive than those at the more prestigious Ambar Marie. Open Monday to Saturday from 8am to 6pm, Sunday from 8am to noon. Calle Restauración 110. ✆ 809/686-5700.

The Swiss Mine   In front of the cathedral, this prestigious store is one of the finest places in Santo Domingo to purchase amber or larimar jewelry. It is also one of the most convenient outlets. The design work on the jewelry here is the most impressive and imaginative in the city. Prices, it is estimated, are about a third less than what they'd be in such cities as Miami. Open Monday to Saturday from 9am to 6pm, Sunday times are irregular. El Conde 101. ✆ 809/221-1897.

CIGARS

Cigar King   The store is aptly named. Cigars are a big-selling item in Santo Domingo. The best selection of cigars in the colonial city is found here. Its selection of Dominican and Cuban cigars in a temperature-controlled room is wide ranging. However, those Cuban stogies have to be smoked locally, as they are not allowed into the United States. Open Monday to Saturday from 9am to 6:30pm. Calle Condo 208, Baguero Building. ✆ 809/686-4987.

Santo Domingo Cigar Club   This is a good outlet for all types of tobacco products, featuring both Cuban and Dominican-made cigars. In the lobby of the Renaissance Jaragua Hotel, this is a good place to sit, smoke, and read magazines. Open Monday to Saturday from 9am to 10pm. Av. George Washington 367. ✆ 809/221-1483.

DEPARTMENT STORE

La Sirena   This is one of Santo Domingo's leading department stores. Although it exists mainly for the city's residents, visitors are always casing the joint for low prices on any number of items, ranging from cut-rate clothing to innumerable household items. You can also pick up Dominican crafts here cheaply. Open Monday to Saturday from 8:30am to 8pm, Sunday from 9am to 2pm. Av. Mella 258. ✆ 809/221-3232.

HANDICRAFTS & GIFTS

Columbus Plaza (Decla, S.A.) One of the largest supermarket-style gift and artifacts store in the country, this emporium is well organized and imaginative, with a helpful English-speaking staff. It sprawls over three floors of a modern building divided into boutiques specializing in amber, larimar, gold and silver jewelry, cigars, paintings and sculpture, plus craft items. Open Monday to Saturday from 9:30am to 6pm, Sunday from 11am to 2pm. Calle Arzobispo Meriño 204. ✆ 809/689-0565.

Tu Espacio In the Espacio Hotel, this is one of the better outlets dispensing Dominican souvenirs and handicrafts. The outlet also sells home furnishings made of cedar or rattan. A limited selection of art and antiques is also for sale. Open Monday to Friday from 9:30am to 5pm, Saturday from 9am to 2:30pm. Calle Cervantes 102, corner of Lea de Castro. ✆ 809/685-2627.

HOME FURNISHINGS

Nuebo Patronized by some of the capital's most socially conscious, this upmarket outlet sells a carefully chosen assortment of art objects, lamps, and furnishings, including the kind of four-poster beds that tend to be showcased in fashion layouts. With some persuasion, anything you buy here can be shipped. Open Monday to Friday from 8:30am to 6:30pm, Saturday from 8:30am to 6pm. Fantino Falco 36, Naco. ✆ 809/562-3333.

Von Some visitors furnish new rooms in their homes with a selection of the handcrafted mahogany furnishings sold here. Many of the furnishings are also made of cedar and pine. Designs are original and very contemporary. Von ships in the furnishings directly from its factory. Open Monday to Friday from 9am to 7pm, Saturday from 10am to 6pm. Calle Virato Fiallo 16, Sánchez Julieta. ✆ 809/566-1433.

PAINTINGS & SCULPTURE

Galería de Arte Nader In the center of the most historical section of town, you'll find so many Latin paintings here that they're sometimes stacked in rows against the walls. The works of the country's best-known painters and most promising newcomers are displayed here. There is also a lot of tourist junk, shipped in by the truckload from Haiti. In the ancient courtyard in back, you can get a glimpse of how things looked in the Spanish colonies hundreds of years ago. Open Monday to Friday from 9am to 7pm, Saturday from 9am to 1pm. Rafael Augusto Sánchez 22. ② 809/544-0878.

Galería El Greco   This is a good showcase for Dominican painters, both newly emerging and more established. In business for some 4 decades, this is one of the more reliable galleries in town, and it also features an array of art from neighboring Haiti. Open Monday to Friday from 8am to noon and 2 to 6pm, Saturday from 8am to noon. Av. Tiradentes 16. ② 809/562-5921.

Lyle O. Reitzel Art Contemporáneo   This first-rate gallery displays only the finest work of island artists, with some work by international painters as well. The exhibits tend to focus on well-known artists' work, such as the very dark paintings of José García Cordero, a Dominican living in Paris. Open Monday to Friday from 9am to 1pm and 3:30 to 8pm, Saturday from 10:30am to 2pm. Plaza Andalucía II. ② 809/227-8361.

8 Santo Domingo After Dark

CLASSICAL MUSIC & DANCE

Teatro Nacional, Plaza de la Cultura (② **809/687-3191**), is the major cultural venue of the Dominican Republic. The 1,600-seat theater is the home to opera, ballet, and symphonic performances. The various presentations are announced in the newspapers, and tickets can be purchased at the box office daily from 9:30am to 12:30pm and 3:30 to 6:30pm. Ticket prices vary, depending on the event, but usually range from RD$60 to RD$240 ($3–$12).

DANCE CLUBS

Local young people flock to the dance clubs in droves after dinner. Even the hotel discos cater to locals as well as tourists. Great dancers abound, so go and watch even if you're not as light on your feet as you wish.

La Guácara Taína   This is the best *discoteca* in the country, drawing equal numbers of locals and visitors. Set in an underground cave within a verdant park, the specialty is merengue, salsa, and other forms of Latin music. There are three bars, two dance floors, and banquettes and chairs nestled into the rocky walls. The cover is RD$250 ($8.95) (includes one drink). Open Tuesday to Sunday from 9pm; closing time varies. Avenida Mirador del Sur, in Parque Mirador del Sur (② 809/533-1051).

Fantasy Disco   One of the capital's most popular discos is about a block inland from the Malecón. Once you get past the vigilant security staff, you'll find lots of intimate nooks and crannies, a small dance floor, and one of the country's best-chosen medleys of nonstop merengue music. Entrance is free, and beer costs RD$77 to RD$98 ($2.75–$3.50) a bottle. The place is open daily from 6pm 'til 4am. Avenida Heroes de Luperón 29, La Feria (© 809/535-5581).

Jet Set   As one of the capital's most formal and elaborate nightclubs, Jet Set admits couples only, and nobody who is too rowdy. Most of the tables and chairs slope down toward an amphitheater-style dance floor, giving the place the feel of a bullfighting arena. The collection of live orchestras that play here are better than anywhere else in town. Entrance costs between RD$280 and RD$1,162 ($10–$41.50), depending on the artist. The Jet Set takes off at 9pm and flies until the early morning. Centro Comercial El Portal, Avenida Independencia (© 809/533-9707).

Bachata Rosa   In the Colonial Zone, Bachata Rosa takes its name from a popular song on the island. In fact, Juan Luis Guerra, the Dominican merengue megastar who made the song a hit, is part owner. Currently, this is the island's best dance club, with action taking place on two floors. This club draws a heavier concentration of locals than of visitors. There's also a typical restaurant here serving local specialties. Daily 8pm to 4am. No cover. La Atarazana 9 (© 809/688-0969).

El Napolitano Disco   This place attracts some of the wealthiest of the young Dominicans along with a mixture of visitors who like to dance the night away along the Malecón. It's elegantly decorated and a dress-up place. Music is recorded merengue, salsa, reggae, and other music. An RD$50 ($1.80) cover is imposed Thursday to Saturday. Otherwise the club is free and open daily 6pm to 4am. Avenida George Washington 101 (© 809/687-1131).

Hotel Santo Domingo Disco   Of the hotel discos, this is the most elegant, attracting a much older crowd (35–45 years old) than the other recommended dance clubs. It's a big space with marble tables, plus colors and decoration provided by Oscar de la Renta himself. The music beat is usually merengue and salsa, with live bands brought in on Wednesday. There's no cover, but you must consume RD$200 ($7.20) in beverages. Open Monday to Thursday 5pm to 1am, Friday to Saturday 5pm to 3am. Avenida Abraham Lincoln at Avenida Independencia (© 809/221-1511).

ROLLING THE DICE

Santo Domingo has several major casinos. We view gambling here as a very minor attraction and find the odds pretty much against you. If gambling is your raison d'être, you'd do better to plan a holiday in Puerto Rico. In addition to the casinos listed below, you'll find one at the **Hispaniola Hotel,** Avenida Independencia (© **809/535-9292**), open daily noon to 5am.

Renaissance Jaragua Hotel & Casino   The most glamorous casino in the country is fittingly housed in the capital's poshest hotel. You can't miss the brightly flashing sign; it's the most dazzling light along the Malecón. You can wager on blackjack, baccarat, roulette, and slot machines in either Dominican pesos or U.S. dollars. Open daily 4pm to 4am. Avenida George Washington 367 (© **809/221-2222**).

Casino Diamante   This is one of the most stylish choices; its bilingual staff will help you play blackjack, craps, baccarat, and keno, among other games. There's also a piano bar. Open daily noon to 6am. In the Meliá Santo Domingo Hotel & Casino, Avenida George Washington 361 (© **809/682-2102**).

Casino Hispaniola   Come here, and you'll experience Santo Domingo's most elegant casino. Against a setting of beautiful rugs, woods, and paintings, you can play such games as roulette, blackjack, baccarat, poker, and sometimes bingo. Guests from Hotel Santo Domingo and Hotel Hispaniola have access to the casino. Open daily 4pm to 5am. Avenida Independencia (© **809/535-9292**).

El Napolitano Casino   While this place is a bit downscale as far as hotels go, the action is more frantic than at the Casino Hispaniola. Blackjack, poker, mini-baccarat and roulette are just some of the games of chance offered here. Open daily 4pm to 6am. Avenida George Washington 101 (© **809/687-1131**).

Hotel and Casino Naco   Although not as well known as some of the other casinos, Casino Naco is nonetheless elegant. It offers all the same games of chance as the other casinos and is especially popular with roulette players. Open daily from 4pm to 4am. Avenida Tiradentes 22 (© **809/562-3100**).

PIANO LOUNGES & BARS

K-Ramba   K-Ramba lies in the Zona Colonial, and is especially popular late at night. Owned by an Austrian expat, the bar features rock 'n' roll, merengue, and sometimes pop. Many visitors are attracted to the area, as it's one of the safer bars at night in this historic district. Snacks and freshly made salads are also served. Open Monday to Saturday 6pm to 3am. Calle Isabel la Católica (☎ **809/ 688-3587**).

Marrakesh Bar & Café   Lying within the precincts of the city's most elegant hotel, the Hotel Santo Domingo (see chapter 3), Marrakesh serves some of the best cocktails in town, and there's never a cover. Every Monday is jazz night, and Tuesday to Friday from 6 to 9pm, it's piano music. Live music of some sort is also presented on Tuesday and Thursday. On other nights, the atmosphere is more subdued. The bar is known for presenting the best lounge acts in town, and the age range is from 30 to 60. The bar is open 4pm to midnight. Avenida Abraham Lincoln at Avenida Independencia (☎ **809/221- 1511**).

Mesón D'Bari   This is an atmospheric bar known for its sound-track of old-time bachata, merengue, and typical music from Cuba known as *son*. In the Colonial Zone, it is a big bar with wooden furniture and floors set on two different levels, the walls decorated with Dominican art. Patrons range in age from their early 20s to their 70s. No cover. Open daily noon to midnight. Calle Hostos 302, corner of Salome Urena, Ciudad Colonial (☎ **809/687-4091**).

Punto y Corcho   This is the city's best wine bar. It can seat 100 patrons, most of whom fall into the 30 to 50 age range. For entertainment, you can hear pop, jazz, and salsa, and sometimes the music is live. The range of wine is one of the most varied in the city, outside of the first-class hotels. A selection of Chilean, French, Italian, and Spanish wines await your choice. Open Monday to Friday 10am to 11pm and Saturday 10am to 6pm. Avenida Abraham Lincoln at the corner of Gustavo Mejia Ricart (☎ **809/683-0533**).

GAY & LESBIAN
Most gay bars in Santo Domingo have the life span of sickly butterflies. **Aire Club,** Calle de las Mercedes 313 (☎ **809/689-4163**), is the most reliable and the most enduring. The setting is a restored house from the colonial era, with a garden. The dance floor is packed by 11pm, mostly with men dancing to the hits of the '70s and '80s. Lesbians also show up here. Open Friday and Saturday 11pm to 6am. Cover charge on Friday is RD$150 ($5.40), Saturday RD$200 ($7.20). There is also a bar on the first floor called **Punto SDQ,** open daily from 6pm to 2am with no cover charge.

5

Beach Resorts East of Santo Domingo

Once you leave Santo Domingo, heading east along Highway 3, you quickly approach what is virtually the Dominican Republic Riviera centered on the resorts of Boca Chica and Juan Dolio. This is the land where the citizens of Santo Domingo themselves go to cool off in the fiery summer months.

Boca Chica itself became the virtual summer retreat of the wealthy residents of the city during the Trujillo era before developing into the mass vacation resort it is today. To Boca Chica's immediate east, Juan Dolio is a wide beach-bordering string of tourist developments that started to grow up in the 1980s. Don't expect a lot in facilities and attractions except at the hotels themselves, most of which are all-inclusives, attracting a lot of patronage from Western Europe, especially France and Spain. Although Americans and Canadians are also lured in great numbers to these resorts, most of the clients book in on low-cost package deals instead of paying the "rack rates" quoted to everybody.

The eastward trek continues through San Pedro de Macoris, ringed with sugar plantations, until La Romana is reached. We prefer La Romana to either Juan Dolio or Boca Chica, primarily because of its deluxe Casa de Campo (see listing later in this chapter).

At La Romana is found Altos de Chavón, an artists' community built in the style of a 16th-century Mediterranean village. This is the greatest man-made attraction of the Dominican Republic, and is worth a visit even if you have to rush down from Santo Domingo and view the sight in a day before returning to the capital in the evening.

1 Boca Chica

31km (19 miles) E of Santo Domingo

This is the Santo Domingo Riviera, dubbed "Playa St. Tropez" by the more fanciful. A favorite stamping ground for the French and Canadians, it also draws massive hordes of city dwellers on weekends.

Lying only a 5-minute drive east of Las Américas International Airport, it grew as a port in the 1930s because of a sugar mill. It wasn't until the 1960s, during the Trujillo era, that it began to develop as a beach resort, when wealthy Dominicans came here to build vacation villas. A decline came about in the 1970s with the rise of such competitive resorts as Puerto Plata and Punta Cana.

The sands are wide and golden, opening onto a shallow lagoon protected by a reef. Meaning "little mouth," Boca Chica Beach is shaped like a bay, and is often called "the largest natural swimming pool" in the West Indies. This mirrorlike body of water has no crashing surf, so it's ideal for a swim and is a special favorite with families with young children.

In recent years the beach has become known for prostitution of both young boys and young girls, with tourists flying in from all over the world to form sexual liaisons. Every now and then, the so-called "tourist police" have a major roundup of these hookers and hustlers, but they seem to appear on the streets and at the beach the next day.

In back of the beach is a winding, rather narrow street filled with small shops whose vendors hawk souvenirs, along with bars (both hooker and otherwise) and lots of seafood eateries. This street is closed to traffic at night, when tables and chairs spill out of the cafes and restaurants and the atmosphere becomes quite festive.

ESSENTIALS

VISITOR INFORMATION   In spite of all the thousands upon thousands of tourists descending on Boca Chica, the government has yet to open a tourist office here. The information that's available at the tourist center in Santo Domingo is so limited as to be almost worthless.

GETTING THERE   If you're motoring, take Highway 3 east of Santo Domingo. Independently operated express buses leave during the day from Santo Domingo on the north side of Parque Central, costing RD$45 ($1.60) one way to Boca Chica. You can also flag down any *guagua* or midsize bus heading east.

CITY LAYOUT   Everything is centered in an area of 10-by-15 blocks stretched out between Highway 3 and Bahía de Andrés, the shallow bay that borders the resort. If you're traveling on Highway 3, you can take a trio of avenues to the heart of the resort: Caracol, Juan Bautista Vicini, or Avenida 24 de Julio. The major street that cuts across Boca Chica is shop- and bar-lined Avenida Duarte. Another smaller artery, Avenida Abraham Núñez, is centered on

Parque Central, where seemingly everybody gathers. This artery is closest to the sea.

GETTING AROUND   Most visitors simply walk around Boca Chica because of its small size. Locals or visitors who don't want to walk often avail themselves of a *motoconcho,* or motorcycle taxi. The fares are to be negotiated, but they are usually cheap. These *motoconchos* abound all over town and are driven by young men. Given the obvious danger, we don't recommend them. Should you not want to take our advice, you'll find many near Parque Central in the heart of town or cruising along bustling Avenida Duarte. If you want a tour of the area, call **Si Tratuboza,** Av. Duarte 30 (© 809/523-4797), which offers 24-hour service. For example, a driver will take you into Santo Domingo for shopping or sightseeing, a total of 3 hours costing RD$1,540 ($55).

FAST FACTS

For money transfer and other services, go to **Western Union,** Calle Duarte 65 (© **809/523-4625**), open daily 8am to 5pm. To call the local **police,** dial © **809/523-4152.** There is a 24-hour medical clinic at Boca Chica: **Central de Especialidades Médicas,** Mella 47 (© **809/523-5546**). The most central pharmacy is **Farmacia Boca Chica,** Av. Duarte 17 (© **809/523-4708**), open daily 8:30am to 9pm, and Sunday 8:30am to 7pm. To exchange money, go to **Banco Popular,** Av. Duarte 51 (© **809/544-8921**), which doesn't have an ATM.

WHERE TO STAY

Dominican Bay   For years known as *the* Boca Chica Resort, this all-inclusive is the most famous at Boca Chica. Set on well-maintained grounds, it takes up almost a town block and has been much expanded and improved. Although it's one of the best resorts at the beach, its major drawback—at least to some visitors—is its location 18m (60 ft.) from the beach. Bedrooms are midsize and comfortably furnished, each equipped with a private bathroom with a combination tub and shower. The cuisine is better here than that served at Don Juan.

Calle Juan Bautista Vicini, esq. 20 de Diciembre, Boca Chica, Dominican Republic. © **809/412-2001.** Fax 809/412-0687. www.hotetur.com. 436 units. Year-round US$68–US$79 per person. Children 11 and under stay free with parents, ages 12–17 50% discount. Rates are all inclusive. AE, DC, MC, V. Free parking. **Amenities:** 4 restaurants; 4 bars; 4 pools; 3 tennis courts; water sports equipment; 24-hr. room service; laundry service; nightly entertainment. *In room:* A/C, TV, minibar, safe.

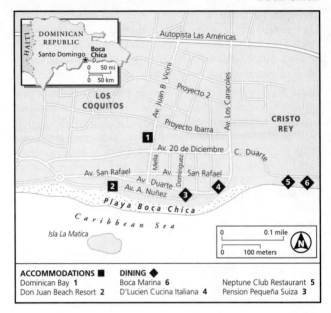

ACCOMMODATIONS ■ **DINING** ◆

Dominican Bay **1**

Don Juan Beach Resort **2**

Boca Marina **6**

D'Lucien Cucina Italiana **4**

Neptune Club Restaurant **5**

Pension Pequeña Suiza **3**

Don Juan Beach Resort   Built in 1989, this resort is a multilevel structure that opens onto fine golden sands. It is the best resort for those who want to pursue an active watersports program, including diving, water-skiing, catamaran sailing, snorkeling, and paddle-boating. Many groups from France can be seen around the pool or strolling through the public rooms. The balconied bedrooms, though reasonably comfortable, are not state of the art, reflecting the wear and tear that comes with group check-ins. The public grounds and areas could also be better maintained. That said, the place is popular, and, because the staff is always arranging for such activities as horseback riding and sunset cruises, guests often enjoy a vacation here if they're not too demanding. There is also a disco with a tropical setting called La Tambora. One of the downsides of staying here, though, is that you're booked in with all meals included. Buffets dominate the culinary agenda, and they're not always of the best quality.

Calle Abraham Núñez, Boca Chica, Dominican Republic. ℂ **809/523-4511.** Fax 809/523-6422. www.caei.com/djbr. 223 units. Year-round US$160–US$270 double. Rates are all-inclusive. Children 2–12 50% discount. AE, MC, V. Free parking. **Amenities:** 2 restaurants; 4 bars; 2 pools; health club; babysitting; nightly entertainment. *In room:* A/C, TV, dataport, hair dryer, safe.

WHERE TO DINE

At least for lunch, consider eating at the beach after ordering your meal from one of the many food shacks found here. A freshly cooked seafood lunch on the beach is the way to go, as you sample such tasty local treats as *lambí criolla* (Creole-styled conch).

Boca Marina SEAFOOD   One of the most enduring, most popular, and most festive places to dine in Boca Chica, this restaurant lies at the eastern end of the resort. Wooden tables are placed out in the open air but shaded by canvas. Some of the tables are actually built out over the Caribbean Sea itself. You're cooled by the trade winds as you peruse the menu of some of the freshest seafood served in the area. The long bar here is also a popular rendezvous point. Established in the late '90s, the restaurant is known for its lobster thermidor. You can also order such delights as fried fish filet with fresh shrimp, or grilled calamari in a zesty sauce. *Langostinos* are always sizzling on the grill as well.

Calle Duarte 12A. (℡ 809/523-6750. Main courses RD$80–RD$695 ($2.90–$25) .AE, DC, MC, V. Daily 10am–midnight.

D'Lucien Cucina Italiana ℛ SEAFOOD/ITALIAN   Somehow, and we don't know how, the cooks here are able to locate good ingredients needed to fashion a tasty cuisine. Established in the mid '90s, this casual beachlike shack stands in the center of the resort, attracting many guests booked in on all-inclusive terms at their hotel but wanting more variety in their cuisine. We recently started out with the seafood salad, finding it freshly made and studded with tasty morsels such as shrimp. Few can resist the grilled lobster, which is done to perfection here and not allowed to dry out. The chefs also make homemade pasta with fresh seafood that's quite succulent. Spaghetti comes with a selection of a dozen different sauces, and you can also order ravioli and tortellini. Vegetarian dishes are also featured, along with thin-crust pizzas and perfectly grilled steaks.

Av. Duarte 1. (℡ 809/523-5878. Main courses RD$80–RD$460 ($2.90–$17). AE, DC, MC, V. Daily 4pm–1am. Closed Dec 24.

Neptune Club Restaurant ℛ SEAFOOD   Lying west of the Boca Marina, a five minute drive from Aeropuerto Internacional Las Américas, this is the local dive for seafood. All the fish dishes are well prepared and some with imagination, such as the rarely offered Peruvian fish chowder made with milk. *Parrillada del mar,* or the platter of grilled seafood, is a beloved signature dish and justifiably the most requested. Neptune's chefs also turn out the resort's best paella, studded with fresh morsels of seafood. Another house specialty is the seafood casserole. We'd walk more than a mile for the lobster lasagna and the spaghetti with seafood. Established in the 1980s, the restaurant offers tables that extend out over the surf, one of the best places to be in Boca Chica on a starry night. Often, even with a reservation, you will have to wait for a table.

Calle Duarte 12. ✆ **809/523-4703**. Reservations required. Main courses RD$400–RD$1,200 ($14–$43). AE, DC, MC, V. Sun–Thurs 10am–11pm; Fri–Sat 10am–midnight. Closed Dec 24.

Pensión Pequeña Suiza ⍟ *Finds* ITALIAN/DOMINICAN/ SWISS/SEAFOOD   You wouldn't think of heading here for a night of dining, but this little pension or boardinghouse—opened in the late '90s—prepares one of the finest cuisines in town, with a careful choice of first-rate ingredients. In honor of its namesake, Switzerland, the kitchen specializes in fondues, an unusual cheese dish for the Dominican Republic. The seafood fondue is especially recommendable. You're given several choices of fondues. Of course, you can also order any number of other good-tasting dishes such as homemade pastas, grilled seafood, and—our favorite—the grilled catch of the day, which can also be fried for you. The offerings also include everything from antipasti to cappuccino. Round off your meal with a good cup of their home-brewed coffee.

Calle Duarte 58. ✆ **809/523-4619**. Main courses RD$380–RD$1,200 ($14–$43). MC, V. Daily 9am–midnight.

PLAYA BOCA CHICA ⍟⍟⍟

This is the town's only attraction and, presumably if this beach didn't exist, there would be no Boca Chica. Long a favorite of Santo Domingo's city dwellers before its discovery by foreigners, Playa Boca Chica is one of the grand beaches of the Caribbean, very wide with white or golden sands set against a backdrop of coconut palms with the inevitable beach bars, restaurants, and fast-food stands. The beach is fronted by the amazingly shallow Bahía Andrés. Unlike the north coast, with its turbulent waters, this is the most tranquil beach in the country.

The beach is a whirlwind of activity day and night, with an international crowd staking a claim on a "place in the sun." They are not always allowed to rest in peace, as vendors ply the beach hawking fruit or souvenirs. As mariachi bands entertain (wanting a tip, of course), young boys seek out gay tourists (and the occasional woman), and young girls ply their trade with older men desiring sex with a teenager.

Lying only 9m (30 ft.) from the shore is a little uninhibited island covered with shrub that you can wade over to. But once you get here, there's nothing to see.

The general public enters the beach on Avenida Duarte. Near the main entrance here you'll see a number of wooden hovels hawking fried fish and *yani queque,* the pizza-size rounds of flavored batter. If you're seeking less crowded conditions, you can walk west along the beach as the tourist facilities gradually disappear. The drawback here is that the waters this far west are often muddy.

GOLF   Near the beach at Boca Chica with four tee positions, **San Andrés Caribe Golf Club,** Km 27, Las Américas Highway, Boca Chica (© **809/545-1278**), opened in 1993 with 9 holes. It is open daily from 8am to 6:30pm. The course is par 36, reaching 3,281 yards. Greens fees are RD$476 ($17), with caddies, club rentals, and carts costing extra.

SCUBA DIVING & OTHER OUTDOOR PURSUITS   For divers, the chief attraction in the area is **La Caleta National Marine Park** ✿, lying 23km (14 miles) to the east of Santo Domingo and close to the airport, and 12km (7½ miles) west of Boca Chica. At only 41 square km (16 sq. miles), this is the smallest of the country's national parks, but the most frequented because of its closeness to both Santo Domingo and Boca Chica.

The park was created in 1984, the same year that the salvage ship *Hickory* was scuttled to create an added attraction for divers. The ship is 38m (127 ft.) long, and in its heyday was used for the recovery of Spanish galleons sunk off the coast of Bahía de Samaná in the east. Many sea creatures make the *Hickory* their home, and its shallow waters allow divers to spend much time there studying the marine life.

For the snorkeler or diver, the best outfitter is **Treasure Divers** at the Don Juan Beach Resort, Calle Abraham Núñez 4 (© **809/523-5320**), a beachside outlet offering an array of aquatic sports. They offer day sails to offshore Catalina Island for a day of snorkeling, costing RD$1,960 ($70) per person and leaving at 7am. The trip includes lunch and beverages, returning to shore at 6:30pm. Paddleboats can also be rented here, costing RD$280 ($10) per person for both guests and nonguests of the hotel. The center also features 3-day diving packages for RD$2,800 ($100) per person, RD$3,192 ($114) including gear. Day 1, for example, includes a morning and an afternoon dive, followed by a night dive. Some of these dives take place in La Caleta National Marine Park, where you can view the sunken vessel, *Hickory.*

SHOPPING   We suggest you confine your serious shopping to Santo Domingo. However, we did discover an intriguing little jewelry store: **Lary 6D,** at the Coral Hamaca Beach Hotel, Calle Duarte 1 (*©* **809/523-4611**). It sells jewelry made with semiprecious stones, along with a selection of amber and both white and yellow gold items.

BOCA CHICA AFTER DARK

Many people like to enjoy the beach at night, but the only part that's safe is the strip east of Don Juan Beach Resort. Here revelers sip rum punches and listen to merengue until around midnight. Muggings elsewhere on the beach are commonplace, especially of those who go for moonlit strolls.

Much of the beach at night is a hot cruising ground, with young men bargaining with older gays over the cost of their "services." Hooker bars are plentiful along Avenida Duarte, as men pursue for-sale *chicas.* In fact, one local paper referred to the street at night as a "gringo brothel."

Many of the after-dark diversions center around **Las Olas** at Coral Hamaca Beach Hotel & Casino, Calle Duarte, corner of Corales (*©* **809/523-4611**). The dance club here is the most formal—and the safest—at the resort. Sometimes the music is live, at other times recorded, but expect a lot of merengue and salsa, enjoyed by patrons from 18 to their early 30s. The dance club is open to guests of this all-inclusive hotel. But for a nonguest to gain entrance, he or she must purchase a night pass for RD$450 ($16). The pass is a good deal in that it entitles you to a lavish dinner, plus all the liquor or beer you want for the evening.

The Coral Hamaca is also the site of the major **casino** in the area, which is open daily from 5pm to 4am. Guests pay no cover to enter. The usual games of chance include poker, blackjack, roulette, and other games. You're provided with a welcome drink. Patrons must be 18 years of age to enter.

Another option is to purchase a RD$1,100 ($40) night pass into the all-inclusive precincts of **Don Juan Beach Resort,** Calle Abraham Núñez (*©* **809/523-4511**). The pass entitles you to a dinner, a show (if any is presented), and all your drinks. It's valid daily from 11pm to 2am. The on-site dance club, and scene of most of the action, is La Yola Disco Club.

2 Juan Dolio

10km (6¼ miles) E of Boca Chica, 50km (31 miles) E of Santo Domingo

Unlike Boca Chica (see above), Juan Dolio is more of a sprawling strip of tourist development along the beach opening onto the Caribbean Sea. Except for a few fishing huts, the development didn't exist until the 1980s, when builders eyed the great beaches here and moved east from Boca Chica. Today these resorts, mainly all-inclusives along with other developments, stretch out for some 5km (3 miles).

The competition from the emerging resorts of Punta Cana and Playa Dorada have dealt a severe blow to Juan Dolio, yet it struggles on—at least the better-financed businesses.

Be careful in your selection of a hotel as, chances are, you will spend much of your time at the resort and along its beachfront. In lieu of the meager attractions of Juan Dolio itself, the resort of your choice becomes much more important than it would be in a more developed resort with more diversity.

Highway 3 runs along the northern tier of Juan Dolio coming in from Santo Domingo to the west. Most of the development lies south of this highway, fronting the Caribbean. Two minor roads lie south of Highway 3, including Carretera Vieja (or old highway) and Carretera Local (or local highway). These are more lanes than roads and filled with milling throngs of beach-goers and souvenir hawkers.

ESSENTIALS

VISITOR INFORMATION   Even though Juan Dolio is one of the Caribbean's biggest tourist developments, the government still hasn't opened a tourist office here. You can stop in at the tourist office before leaving Santo Domingo, but don't expect to obtain much information there.

GETTING THERE   Most arrivals are at the Santo Domingo international airport, where a taxi can be found waiting to take you to a hotel for a cost of RD$600 (US$30). Of course, the drivers will ask a lot more, but you can negotiate. Many cab rides are shared.

If you want to go by bus from Santo Domingo, you can go to Parque Enriquillo and search out the little bus station at the south-eastern corner of the park. Several independently operated buses depart from here on the half hour (schedules are a bit erratic) for Juan Dolio, carrying passengers for just RD30 (US$1.50) for a one-way trip. It's a bumpy ride and is not suitable for passengers with a lot of luggage.

If you're in Boca Chica (see above), go to the Highway 3 and hail any of the eastbound *guaguas* (midsize buses). Locals use this form of transport, and rides—depending on where you're going—are very cheap.

GETTING AROUND   Most visitors walk where they want to go in Juan Dolio, and the frontage road opening onto the Caribbean is mainly for passengers anyway. In lieu of that, you can hail one of the *motoconchos* or else a car taxi to get around. Fares are always inexpensive, but must be negotiated and agreed upon in advance.

FAST FACTS

Don't expect the services of a town. Boca Chica (see above) is more developed and likely to have what you want in the way of services. Most hotels, at least at the big resorts, will exchange either U.S. or Canadian dollars into pesos. If you need to mail something, ask at your reception desk. The staff there will most often turn your mail over to a local carrier when he passes through. Only the first-class all-inclusives sell postage stamps. Most hotels provide laundry service.

WHERE TO STAY
THE ALL-INCLUSIVES

Barceló Capella Beach Resort $\mathcal{R}\mathcal{R}$ *Kids*   The Barceló chain dominates Juan Dolio, and this all-inclusive five-star, government-rated hotels, is its finest property. Right at the Villas de Mar beach, set against lush landscaping, it is a mammoth resort with some 1,000 beds. The hotel is lavish and complete unto itself; indeed, many patrons head here from the airport and never leave until it's time to go home.

All the buildings in the sprawling complex are less than five floors, and the architectural styles range from Moorish to Victorian, with white latticework, graceful pillars, and red-tile roofs. Even the least desirable units—called standard—are comfortably furnished and well maintained. Because there's so little difference in price, we'd opt for one of the superior or deluxe accommodations, or one of the "executive club rooms" or suites. The deluxe rooms with spacious sitting areas and two queen-size beds are regrettably farther from the sands. As compensation for their reduced size, the standard units in the front wing with one king-sized bed are closer to the beach.

Honeymooners often book one of the special suites with a king-size bed and a Jacuzzi. All the modern bathrooms come with a tub/shower combination.

The restaurants here, including everything from lavish buffets to a first-class French cuisine, are the best in Juan Dolio. This is an excellent venue for children, as two pools are set aside for them and day and nighttime entertainment programs are specially geared for them. There's also a kids' club on the beach.

Playa de Villas del Mar, San Pedro de Macoris, Dominican Republic. ℂ **809/526-1080.** Fax 809/526-1088. www.barcelo.com. 500 units. Year-round US$120–US$140 double; US$136–US$156 junior suite. Children 2–12 US$24–US$35 extra. AE, DC, MC, V. Free parking. **Amenities:** 4 restaurants; 4 bars; 3 pools; 2 tennis courts; health club; sauna; watersports equipment; children's center; car-rental desk; business center; salon; 24-hr. room service; massage; babysitting; laundry service; dry cleaning; nightly entertainment. *In room:* A/C, TV, minibar, fridge, coffeemaker, hair dryer, safe.

Barceló Colonia Tropical ⚲   This is the smallest and most intimate of the Barceló properties strung along Juan Dolio's beachfront, and we prefer it for that reason. You get more personalized attention in this two-story building surrounded by palm trees and gardens. The complex was built in the closing year of the 20th century, and it's decorated with tropical pastels. Bedrooms range from midsize to spacious, and each comes with a neatly tiled bathroom with tub/shower combo. When checking in, you're asked if you want one king-size bed or two queen-size beds. Many guests request one of the 32 studios with a kitchenette; three of the suites also come with kitchens. Clients who check in here can use the superior facilities at the Barceló Capella Beach Resort. The food is better here than at the standard Barceló restaurant, although the Colonia Tropical can't offer the vast variety of cuisine of the megaresorts.

Playa de Villas del Mar, San Pedro de Macoris, Dominican Republic. ℂ **809/526-1660.** Fax 809/221-0483. www.barcelo.com. 40 units. Year-round US$73–US$92 double; US$186–US$275 suite. Children 2–12 US$37 extra. AE, DC, MC, V. Free parking. **Amenities:** Restaurant; bar; outdoor pool; watersports equipment; limited room service; babysitting; laundry service. *In room:* A/C, TV, kitchenette, minibar, fridge, coffeemaker, hair dryer, safe.

Coral Costa Caribe Beach Hotel & Casino ⚲⚲ *Kids*   If you're fleeing from some snowswept northern clime, and are dreaming of a wide sandy beach with the fronds of palm trees blowing in the trade winds, this cliché of a tropical resort is very much a reality here. Coral Costa Caribe is one of the best of the all-inclusives scattered along the vast beachfront of sprawling Juan Dolio. It caters to every client from high-rollers with its casino, to families with children with facilities such as a day-care center.

Accommodations rated superior or deluxe open onto sea or garden views, and junior suites or grander suites are available both on

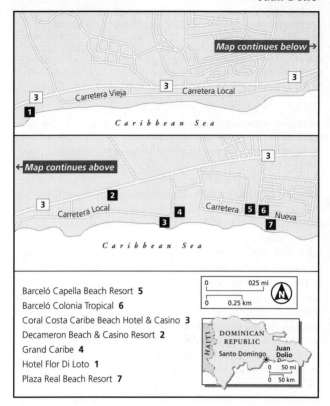

Barceló Capella Beach Resort **5**
Barceló Colonia Tropical **6**
Coral Costa Caribe Beach Hotel & Casino **3**
Decameron Beach & Casino Resort **2**
Grand Caribe **4**
Hotel Flor Di Loto **1**
Plaza Real Beach Resort **7**

the beach side and at the modern business and convention center. Sometimes conferences take over one of these all-inclusives. The bedrooms are comfortably decorated though a bit minimalist in styling, and are midsize for the most part, with well-maintained, tiled bathrooms with tub/shower combinations.

The food is much better than the standardized fare offered at nearby all-inclusives. Guests can opt for a three-meal-a-day buffet on the terraced restaurant, or else dine more exclusively in one of the specialty a la carte dining rooms. Featuring watersports on the beach, the resort has one of the most activity-filled agendas of any of the megaresorts—yes, even aerobics. The hotel lies just a short distance from the 18-hole Guavaberry Golf Course.

Autopista Blvd, San Pedro de Macoris, Dominican Republic. ℂ **809/526-2244.** Fax 809/526-3141. www.coralhotels.com. 535 units. Year-round US$160–US$210 double; US$220–US$300 suite. Children 2–12 US$20 extra. AE, DC, MC, V. Free parking. **Amenities:** 3 restaurants; 3 bars; 4 pools; nearby golf; tennis court; health club; spa; watersports equipment; children's center; salon; limited room service; laundry service; dry cleaning; casino; disco; Internet center; nightly entertainment; 24-hour medical service. *In room:* A/C, TV, fridge, hair dryer, safe.

Decameron Beach and Casino Resort 🛝 *Kids*   This is a mammoth all-inclusive right on the golden sands at Villas de Mar and enveloped by luxuriant vegetation. It sits next to the Talanquera Beach Resort & Casino. If you wake up in a room at any of these resorts, you wouldn't be able to tell which one you're in until you went outside.

Since there's not much difference in price, ask for one of the "superior" bedrooms, each with sea views. Otherwise, you'll find all the bedrooms fairly standard and comfortable, furnished with decorative tropical flavor. Although this resort is old (1985) in terms of upstart Juan Dolio, it has been renovated frequently and kept fairly up-to-date. Most rooms are midsize, with a small bathroom with tub/shower combination.

Most guests find the attractions, entertainment, and dining on-site so comprehensive that they don't feel the need to leave the resort at night. The food is good and international in scope, with the rare Brazilian cuisine a feature along with Mexican and Italian specialties, combined with the usual barbecue stands and pizza. A wide range of sports is offered, including everything from kayaking to archery. Kids are especially catered to with their own play area and pool. A "nanny" can also be provided.

Playa de Villas del Mar, San Pedro de Macoris, Dominican Republic. ℂ **809/339-2009.** Fax 809/526-1430. www.oceanarc.com. 440 units. Year-round US$36–US$72 per person double. Children 2–12 US$30–US$50 extra. AE, DC, MC, V. Free parking. **Amenities:** 4 restaurants; 2 bars; 3 pools; 2 tennis courts; health club; watersports equipment; salon; massage; babysitting; laundry service; basketball court; casino; children's playground; nightly entertainment. *In room:* A/C, TV, hair dryer, safe.

Grand Caribe 🛝 *Kids*   Lying on one of the best beachfront areas in the southwestern part of the island, this is a rather massive all-inclusive in a tropical setting of palm trees and landscaping. Rooms are spread over three different buildings, each opening onto the water. The furnishings of the midsize bedrooms are airy and tropical, very Caribbean, each with a modern bathroom with tub/shower combination. Many of the rooms are geared toward accommodating families with small children at reduced rates. Each room is designed to accommodate up to four guests in reasonable comfort. A wide range of restaurants from casual to elegant await your choice,

since you will most likely take all your meals here. You dine on every cuisine from Mexican to Italian, even enjoying an outdoor barbecue or seafood on a grill by the beach.

There's entertainment at night, even a karaoke pub bar. The program of outdoor activities is extensive, embracing water aerobics, water polo, kayaking, windsurfing, canoeing, snorkeling, scuba diving and, yes, even biking and archery. The fitness center with a sauna and steam room complements the Jacuzzis and beauty salon, and an Internet room is open 24 hours for those who need a daily e-mail fix.

Playa de Villas del Mar, San Pedro de Macoris, Dominican Republic. (C) 809/526-1521. Fax 809/526-2194. www.grandcaribe.com.do. 260 units. Year-round US$75–US$100 double. Children 2–11 50% discount. AE, DC, DISC, MC, V. Free parking. **Amenities:** 4 restaurants; 4 bars; pool; 2 tennis courts; health club; watersports equipment; salon; babysitting; laundry service; nightly entertainment. *In room:* A/C, TV, hair dryer, safe.

Plaza Real Beach Resort *(Kids)*   Lying directly on the beach, this is a hotel that just grew and grew, opening first in 1987, with the last building added in 1997. Close to the center of Juan Dolio, it is separated by palm trees from golden sands. The place is almost a cliché of a Caribbean beach resort surrounded by well-landscaped gardens and palm trees. The standard rooms here are midsize and comfortably furnished, each with a shower-and-tub combo.

Even better is a room in the on-site Club Playa Real, like a hotel within a hotel, offering more personalized attention and such extra features as a private Jacuzzi. The food is of an acceptable international standard, but hardly the reason to stay here. For variety and as a break from those endless buffets, Italian and Mexican restaurants are a possibility as well.

The hotel is very activity-oriented, featuring everything from horseback riding to scuba diving. The Occidental Fun Club organizes a variety of activities during the day, everything from aerobics to merengue lessons.

Calle Villas del Mar, San Pedro de Macoris, Dominican Republic. (C) 809/526-1114. Fax 809/526-1623. www.amhsamarina.com. 391 units. Year Round US$120 double. Children 4–12 US$60 extra. Extra adult US$96. AE, MC, V. Free parking. **Amenities:** 5 restaurants; 4 bars; 2 pools; tennis court; watersports equipment; children's center; room service; babysitting; laundry service; aerobics; disco; horseback riding. *In room:* A/C, TV, safe.

INEXPENSIVE

Hotel Fior di Loto *(Finds)*   In business for some 2 decades, this is a hip, most affordable, and friendly oasis for those who wish to escape from the curse of the megaresorts. A three-story villa, this gay-friendly and laid-back guesthouse offers simply furnished but comfortable guests rooms. Although small, they are cozy, often with Indian accents. Each of the small units comes with a tidily maintained little bathroom with shower. Your hostess, Mara Sandri, is surely the most worldly in the area, even teaching yoga and meditation classes. She can do everything for you—from setting you up with an acupuncturist to having a "therapeutic sacred dance" performed for you by a troupe nearby. She's also a font of information about this part of the island.

Calle Central 517, Guayanes, Dominican Republic. © **809/526-1146.** Fax 809/526-3332. www.fiordilotohotel.com. 24 units. Year-round US$20–US$40 double. MC, V. Free parking. **Amenities:** 24-hr. Restaurant/bar; laundry service. *In room:* TV, ceiling fan.

BEACHES, DIVING & OTHER OUTDOOR PURSUITS

BEACHES   There are three major beaches spread along the Caribbean Sea, beginning with **Playa Guayacanes** in the west, with **Playa Juan Dolio** in the center and **Playa Real** in the east. These beaches are often referred to collectively as Playa de Villas del Mar. Our favorite of these is Playa Guayacanes, which is one of the most beautiful beaches in the area and home to a little community of locals called Guayacanes.

As you move east from Guayacanes, the sands are better than the water, the latter filled with wide expanses of dead coral, making the swimming less than desirable. Many of the best sandy beaches are maintained zealously by the all-inclusives.

Frankly, if wide, sandy beaches are important to your holiday, the beaches of Punta Cana and Bávaro (see chapter 6) are better. The chief advantages of the resorts at Boca Chica and Juan Dolio are their accessibility to Santo Domingo, only a 1-hour bus ride away on a *guagua* (midsize bus).

GOLF   An 18-hole championship golf course, **Guavaberry Golf Course,** Km 55, Autovía del Este, Juan Dolio (© **809/333-4653**), opened in 2002 and accepts players daily from 7am to 7pm. Reservations are recommended for this par 72 course of 7,092 yards. The cost is RD$2,772 ($99) for 18 holes or RD$1,960 ($70) for 9 holes, including cart fees.

An older course, also 18 holes, from 1995 is **Los Marlins Golf Course,** Metro Country Club, Las Américas Highway, Juan Dolio (© **809/526-3315**), designed by Charles Ankrom. Reservations are recommended at this par 72 course of 6,396 yards. Greens fees are RD$1,652 ($59) for 18 holes or RD$840 ($30) for 9 holes (includes cart fees). Carts, clubs, and caddies are available at both courses, which also have a clubhouse and lockers.

SCUBA DIVING & SNORKELING   There are more than 15 dive sites in Juan Dolio, and new ones are being discovered yearly. Depth ranges are from 9m to 30m (30 ft.–100 ft.). A lot of underwater photographers come here to view the deep channels and ravines offshore and the diversity of soft and hard corals along with the rainbow-hued fish.

One of the best dive centers in southwestern Dominican Republic is the **Neptuno Dive Center,** in the Barceló Colonia Tropical, Playa de Villas del Mar, San Pedro de Macoris (© **809/526-1473;** www.neptunodive.com. Here a one-tank dive costs RD$1,008 ($36) and a three-tank dive RD$2,772 ($99), with a night dive an additional RD$784 ($20). Complete equipment, including snorkel fins, can also be rented. A snorkel course is also offered for RD$980 ($35). This is a complete PADI diving facility with all the equipment, offering dive courses. Even nondivers can ask about their 1-day cruise from Juan Dolio to the Catalina Island offshore, costing RD$2,100 ($75) per person, including lunch.

JUAN DOLIO AFTER DARK
ROLLING THE DICE   One of the older casinos is found at **Barceló Decameron Beach & Casino Resort,** Playa de Villas del Mar, San Pedro de Macoris (© **809/339-2009**), which is open daily from 11pm to 4am. Slots get the most attention, but you can also play roulette, blackjack, poker, and other games of chance.

Coral Costa Caribe Beach Resort, Calle San Pedro de Macoris (© **809/526-3318**), contains one of the best casinos in the southern part of the country. Elegantly decorated, it aggressively pursues the gringo dollar with its games of chance, such as blackjack, poker, and roulette, along with plenty of slot machines. Open daily from 8pm to 4am.

3 La Romana & Altos de Chavón
114km (71 miles) E of Santo Domingo, 37km (23 miles) E of San Pedro de Macoris

On the southeast coast of the Dominican Republic, La Romana was once a sleepy sugar-cane town that specialized in cattle raising. Visitors didn't come near the place, but when Gulf + Western Industries opened a luxurious tropical paradise resort, the Casa de Campo, about 1.6km (1 mile) east of town, La Romana soon began drawing the jet set. It's the finest resort in the Dominican Republic, and especially popular among golfers.

Just east of Casa de Campo is Altos de Chavón, a charming and whimsical copy of what might have been a fortified medieval village in Spain, southern France, or Italy. It's the country's leading sight-seeing attraction.

ESSENTIALS

VISITOR INFORMATION The government maintains **La Romana Tourist Office** at Teniente Amado García 22 (© **809/ 550-6922**), open Monday to Friday 8am to 6pm. Don't expect to come away with a wealth of information, however.

GETTING THERE By Plane **American Airlines** (© **800/ 433-7300** in the U.S.; www.aa.com) offers one daily flight to Casa de Campo from Miami, with a travel time of about 2½ hours each way. (Yes, it's a slow plane.) **American Eagle** (same phone number) operates at least two (and in busy seasons, at least three) daily non-stop flights to Casa de Campo/La Romana airport from San Juan, Puerto Rico. The flight takes about 45 minutes, and it departs late enough in the day to permit transfers from other flights.

By Car You can drive here in about an hour and 20 minutes from the international airport, along Las Américas Highway. (Allow another hour if you're in the center of the city.) Of course, everything depends on traffic conditions. (Watch for speed traps—low-paid police officers openly solicit bribes, whether you're speeding or not.)

GETTING AROUND Most visitors don't rent a car but rely on local transportation, which is very haphazard and operated by inde-pendent drivers. You'll find both taxis and *motoconchos* (motorized scooters) at the northeast corner of Parque Central in the heart of La Romana. A typical ride almost anywhere within town costs less than RD$60 ($2.15), with the average taxi ride costing less than RD$120 ($4.30). Prices are always to be negotiated, of course.

You can also rent a car at the airport. Your best bet is **Budget,** La Romana Airport (© **809/813-9111**), open Monday to Saturday 9am to 5pm. A competitor is **Honda Rent a Car,** Calle Santa Rosa 84 (© **809/556-3835**), in La Romana, open Monday to Friday 8am to 6pm, Saturday and Sunday 8am to 4pm.

FAST FACTS

To exchange money, go to **Scotiabank,** a bank at Calle Trinitaría 59 (© **809/556-5151**), open Monday to Friday from 8:30am to 4:30pm. There's an ATM out front. Long-distance calls can be made at **Verizon,** the phone company at Calle Trinitaría 51 (© **809/220-7927**), open Monday to Friday 8am to 6pm, Saturday

La Romana & Altos de Chavón

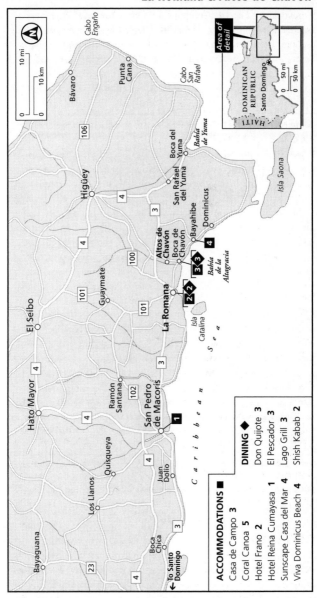

Area of detail

DOMINICAN REPUBLIC

Santo Domingo

HAITI

0   50 mi
0   50 km

Cabo
Engaño

Punta
Cana

Bávaro

Cabo
San Rafael

10 mi

10 km

106

Boca del
Yuma

Bahía
de Yuma

Higüey

San Rafael
del Yuma

4

3

Isla Saona

**Altos de
Chavón**
Boca de
Chavón

Bayahibe

Dominicus

4

100

3 ◄ 3

Bahía de la
Altagracia

4

4

101

Guaymate

101

2 ► 2

La Romana

El Seíbo

3

Isla
Catalina

C   a   r   i   b   b   e   a   n   S   e   a

102

Ramón
Santana

Hato Mayor

4

San Pedro
de Macorís

1

4

Quisqueya

Juan
Dolio

Los Llanos

Boca
Chica

4

Bayaguana

23

3

◄ To Santo
Domingo

ACCOMMODATIONS ■

Casa de Campo **3**
Coral Canoa **5**
Hotel Frano **2**
Hotel Reina Cumayasa **1**
Sunscape Casa del Mar **4**
Viva Dominicus Beach **4**

DINING ◆

Don Quijote **3**
El Pescador **3**
Lago Grill **3**
Shish Kabab **2**

97

9am to 1pm. The **La Romana Post Office** lies on Calle Francisco del Castillo Marquéz (© **809/556-2265**), 2 blocks north of Parque Central. For Internet access, head to the **Casa de Campo** resort (see below). The **business center** here (© **809/523-3333**) is open Monday to Saturday 8am to 7pm, and Sunday 8am to 2pm. Use of a computer costs RD$65 ($2.32) for 15 minutes or RD$260 ($9.28) for 1 hour.

WHERE TO STAY
THE MEGARESORTS

Casa de Campo ⭐⭐⭐   Translated as "country house," Casa de Campo, on its own beach, is the leading resort in the Dominican Republic. In the 1960s, the former Gulf + Western corporation took a vast hunk of coastal land, more than 2,800 hectares (6,916 acres) in all, and carved out this chic resort. Tiles, Dominican crafts, mahogany furniture, louvered doors, and flamboyant fabrics decorate the interior of both the public areas and the accommodations.

Rooms are divided into red-roofed, two-story casitas, each with four units, radiating out from the main building, and more upscale villas that dot the edges of the golf courses, the gardens near the tennis courts, and the shoreline. (Ask for one near the water if you plan to spend most of your time on the beach, or one near the links if you're an avid golfer, since the grounds are massive.) Nineteen of the villas each have their own private pool. Some are clustered in a semiprivate hilltop compound with views overlooking the meadows, the sugar cane, and the fairways down to the distant sea. Accommodations have either a shower only or a shower/tub combination.

La Romana, Dominican Republic. © **800/877-3643** or 809/523-8698. Fax 809/523-8548. www.casadecampo.cc. 279 units. Winter US$190–US$299 casita for 2, US$580 suite; off season US$183–US$214 casita for 2, US$312 suite. Rates are all-inclusive. AE, DC, MC, V. **Amenities:** 8 restaurants; 5 bars; 8 outdoor pools; 3 18-hole golf courses; 13 tennis courts (10 lit); health club; sauna; watersports equipment; bikes; children's center (ages 3–12); limited room service; massage; babysitting; laundry service; aerobics; horseback riding; polo; theater. *In room:* A/C, TV, dataport, minibar, hair dryer, iron/ironing board, safe.

Coral Canoa ⭐⭐   When you come here and see the thatch roof huts, you'll think you've arrived south of Pago Pago. The hotel's architecture has a real tropical ambience, with many small villas reproduced in the style of the island's native thatch houses, called *clavos*. Some of the architecture uses such island materials as stone, jute, and canna, along with some symbolic architectural details of the Taíno Indians, the original inhabitants. Bedrooms come in a

range of styles, from midsize to spacious, although each has a tiled
bathroom with tub/shower combination. Much use is made of rattan, the furnishings placed against creamy walls given added color
by the flamboyant fabrics.

Many outdoor enthusiasts like its location on the border of Parque Nacional del Este (see description later this chapter).

The resort's most outstanding feature is its spa, with an array of
treatments and classes, everything from yoga to shiatsu massages
and hydrotherapy along with beauty treatments. The food is plentiful and fresh, and prepared more or less well without arriving at the
sublime. Caribbean and Italian favorite dishes are served, along with
a selection of international specialties, including pizza and pastas.

Bayahibe Beach, La Romana, Dominican Republic. © 809/682-2662. Fax 809/
688-5799. www.coralhotels.com. 532 units. Year-round US$190–US$290 double;
US$280–US$330 junior suite. Children 2–12 US$60 extra. Rates are all-inclusive.
AE, DC, DISC, MC, V. Free parking. **Amenities:** 4 restaurants; 4 bars; 2 pools; health
club; spa; sauna; children's center; 24-hr.room service; babysitting; laundry service;
dry cleaning; nightly entertainment. *In room:* A/C, TV, kitchenettes in suites, minibar,
hair dryer, safe.

Sunscape Casa del Mar ✦   Casa de Campo dominates the
southeast coast, but this contender on a spectacular beach is giving
the grand dame a run for her money. The golf and tennis facilities
here aren't as elaborate as those at Casa de Campo, and there are no
polo grounds, but the resort, dating from 1997, is beautifully landscaped, and the beach is palm fringed.

Accommodations are within seven three-story buildings with yellow walls and blue-tiled roofs. Decor inside features lots of tile, var-
nished hardwood, wicker, and rattan, plus a neatly appointed
shower-only bathroom. There's an overall cheerfulness about the
place and lots of emphasis on merengue music that helps keep the
good times rolling. Everything served in all of the resort's restaurants
is covered by the all-inclusive price. Michelangelo serves Italian
food, Chinese is on the menu at Asia, and Saona does beachfront
barbecues and grills, Dominican style. There's also a buffet restaurant and a disco.

Bayahibe Beach, La Romana, Dominican Republic. © 866/786-7227 in the U.S., or
809/221-8880. Fax 809/221-2776. www.sunscaperesorts.com. 563 units. Winter
US$150–US$167 per person double, US$184 per person suite; off season
US$60–US$95 per person double, US$72–US$120 per person suite. Rates are all-
inclusive. AE, MC, V. **Amenities:** 4 restaurants; 6 bars; 2 outdoor pools; 4 tennis
courts; health club; Jacuzzi; sauna; watersports equipment; bikes; children's programs; limited room service; babysitting; disco; horseback riding. *In room:* A/C, TV,
dataport, minibar, hair dryer, iron/ironing board, safe.

Viva Dominicus Beach ⓐ   This is a megaresort that lies 5km (3 miles) east of Bayahibe, opening onto a magnificent golden sandy beach with a swimmable surf. Dating from the '80s, it is like a small village of buildings four or less floors each. This is a sort of all-purpose resort that's a destination unto itself. Many patrons confess that they hardly leave the premises until the end of their vacation.

The midsize bedrooms feature decorative accents of the island and are comfortable and tasteful, with a variety of places to lay your head at night. The least desirable rooms are rated "standard." Since there is so little price difference, it's better to ask for a superior room. Even better might be to request one of the thatch-roof bungalows opening onto the ocean or tropical gardens. Each unit comes with a well-maintained private bathroom with tub and shower.

Even if the food is not always "get *Gourmet* magazine on the phone," it is plentiful and generous, prepared with fresh ingredients. Menus are eclectic, inspired by international recipes, especially those of the Caribbean, Mexico, and Europe, with plenty of American dishes as well. Buffets are big here, and there's also a grill restaurant and a pizzeria. On our latest rounds, we spotted guests still eating at 2:30am.

Although no great competition for Casa de Campo, the resort aggressively features activities around the block, from complimentary land and nonmotorized watersports to musical cabaret shows often staged by the staff as performers.

Bayahibe Beach, La Romana, Dominican Republic. ℂ **809/686-5658.** Fax 809/ 687-8383. www.vivaresorts.com. 530 units. Year-round US$160–US$170 double. Rates are all-inclusive. AE, DC, DISC, MC, V. Free parking. **Amenities:** 4 restaurants; 4 bars; 3 outdoor pools; 4 tennis courts; health club; spa; Jacuzzi; sauna; watersports equipment; babysitting; laundry service; dry cleaning; basketball court; disco; Internet center; nightly entertainment; soccer field. *In room:* A/C, TV, hair dryer, iron/ironing board, safe.

MODERATE

Hotel Reina Cumayasa ⓐ *Finds*   Most chain properties are megaresorts, except this one lying at the mouth of the Cumayasa River with a small private beach of golden sands. The property is far more intimate than the bigger resorts and is surrounded by the wild flora and fauna of this part of the D.R. The complex appears like a large, overscaled villa you might encounter on the Mediterranean. Furnishings are traditional, with lots of cedar wood and mahogany. The tallest of the structures is three floors, and there are no elevators. All bedrooms are midsize and rather tastefully most comfortably furnished, with tiled bathrooms, each with a shower. Children are not welcome at this hotel. Daytime activities include an array of activities ranging from horseback riding to hiking, canoeing to snorkeling, and even water-skiing.

Km 12, Carretera San Pedro de Macorís, La Romana, Dominican Republic. ✆ 809/ 550-7506. Fax 809/550-8105. 50 units. Year-round US$170–US$270 double; US$150–US$300 junior suite. Rates are all-inclusive. AC, DC, MC, V. Free parking. **Amenities:** Restaurant; 2 bars; outdoor pool; 2 tennis courts; watersports equipment; laundry service; horseback riding; Internet center. *In room:* A/C, TV, minibar, coffeemaker, hair dryer, safe.

INEXPENSIVE

Hotel Frano   This is for frugal travelers who shun the megaresorts, preferring more of a guest house–type accommodation. The prices are so affordable that many traveling Dominican salesmen often book in here. The midsize bedrooms are simply but tastefully decorated and quite comfortable, each with a small tiled bathroom with tub and shower. The three-story building is from the early '90s and has been kept up-to-date since then. Within the little town of La Romana itself, these are the best guest rooms, though you'll have to travel nearby for a good beach.

Calle Padre Abreu 9, La Romana, Dominican Republic. ✆ 809/550-4744. 41 units. Year-round US$43 double. AE, DC, MC, V. Free parking. **Amenities:** Restaurant. *In room:* A/C, TV.

WHERE TO DINE

Café del Sol   ITALIAN   The pizzas at this stone-floored indoor/outdoor cafe, which is positioned one flight above the medieval-looking piazza outside, are the best on the south coast. The favorite seems to be *quattro stagioni,* topped with mushrooms, artichoke hearts, cooked ham, and olives. The chef makes a soothing minestrone served with freshly made bread. To reach the cafe, climb a flight of stone steps to the rooftop of a building whose ground floor houses a jewelry shop.

Altos de Chavón. ✆ 809/523-3333, ext. 5346. Pizzas RD$255–RD$480 ($9.10–$17); salads RD$180 ($6.45). AE, MC, V. Daily noon–11pm.

Casa del Río   FRENCH/CARIBBEAN   The most romantic restaurant at Altos de Chavón occupies the basement of an Iberian-style 16th-century castle whose towers, turrets, tiles, and massive stairs are entwined with strands of bougainvillea. Inside, brick arches support oversized chandeliers, suspended racing sculls, and wine racks. Amid this bucolic atmosphere, you can indulge in some of the best seafood dishes on the south coast. Although the food has a slight French flair, and often a few Thai twists, everything tastes and looks firmly West Indian. Any of the seafood dishes, such as lobster lasagna, is worthy of attention. Lobster might also appear glazed with vanilla vinaigrette, which tastes a lot better than it sounds. You'll encounter innovative taste sensations here, especially in dishes involving lemon grass or coriander. Some favorites include warm goat cheese with a tossed almond-and-arugula salad; Provençal-style snails au gratin; and sautéed tenderloin of beef with Roquefort cheese and almonds.

Altos de Chavón. ℂ **809/523-3333**, ext. 3260. Reservations required. Main courses RD$256–RD$576 ($9.20–$21). AE, MC, V. Daily 6–11pm. Closed Feb–Oct.

Don Quijote ⭐ *Finds* INTERNATIONAL/SEAFOOD   Outside Casa de Campo, you get some of your best seafood here. The menu offers few exciting surprises, and the dishes are all very familiar to those who dine here, but everything is nicely served and tastes good. Their seafood paella is the best we've sampled in the area, and we are especially fond of lobster Creole style. The chicken breast is beautifully sautéed and flavored, and a tender and well-flavored chateaubriand comes with shrimp in a coconut sauce, a combination that's a bit jarring to our palate but which receives praise from the regular diners. If you have no room for dessert, finish off with a strong Dominican coffee.

Calle Diego Avila 42. ℂ **809/556-2827**. Main courses RD$175–RD$900 ($6.30–$32). AE, DC, MC, V. Mon–Fri 11am–4pm; Sat–Sun 11am–11pm.

El Pescador ⭐⭐ SEAFOOD   The best and the freshest seafood in the area is served at one of the restaurants inside the Casa de Campo, which is not only the finest place to stay along the southern coast, but serves the grandest cuisine. In an elegant setting, you can dine inside or out on the alfresco terrace. The atmosphere is informal, but the service is first rate. The freshest fish, based on the catch of the day, is brought here for the chefs to concoct into a number of delectable dishes, including perfectly grilled fish, the preferred method of cooking for most diners. A justifiably favorite dish is the deep-fry mix of calamari, shrimp, and the "catch of the day." For lunch many visitors prefer the fish salad with tropical fruit, or fish sandwiches, which are among the best in the area.

In Casa de Campo. ℂ **809/523-3333**. Reservations recommended. Main courses: lunch RD$335–RD$605 ($12–$22), dinner RD$650–RD$1,500 ($23–$54). AE, DC, MC, V. Daily noon–4pm and 7–11pm.

El Sombrero MEXICAN   In this thick-walled, colonial-style building, the jutting timbers and roughly textured plaster evoke a corner of Old Mexico. There's a scattering of rattan furniture and an occasional example of Mexican weaving, but the main draw is the spicy cuisine. Red snapper in garlic sauce is usually very good as are the beef and chicken fajitas. Most guests dine outside on the covered patio, within earshot of a group of wandering minstrels. Chances are you've had better versions of the standard nachos, enchiladas, black-bean soup, pork chops, grilled steaks, and brochettes served here, but a margarita or two will make it a fun night out anyway.

Altos de Chavón. 📞 **809/523-3333**. Reservations recommended. Main courses RD$570–RD$780 ($20–$28). AE, MC, V. Daily 6pm–midnight.

Giacosa ITALIAN/INTERNATIONAL   This is the only restaurant within Altos de Chavón that's not owned and operated by Casa de Campo. As such, its owners and staff tend to try a bit harder. It's a branch of a success story based in Coral Gables, Florida. Within a two-story stone Tuscan-style building you can try Mediterranean dishes like seafood soup studded with lobster and shrimp, risotto with shrimp and sun-dried tomatoes, or savory imported mussels with olive oil, garlic, white wine, parsley, and fresh tomatoes. Another superb dish is red snapper filet with fresh tomatoes, baked in a paper bag to seal in its aromatic flavors.

Altos de Chavón. 📞 **809/523-8466**. Reservations recommended. Main courses RD$500–RD$1,000 ($18–$36). AE, MC, V. Daily noon–midnight.

Lago Grill CARIBBEAN/AMERICAN   With one of the best-stocked morning buffets in the country, Lago Grill is ideal for break-fast. At the fresh-juice bar, an employee in colonial costume will extract juices in any combination you prefer from 25 different tropical fruits. Then you can select your ingredients for an omelet, and another staff member will whip it up while you wait. The lunchtime buffet includes sandwiches, burgers, *sancocho* (the famous Dominican stew), and fresh conch chowder. There's also an abundant salad bar.

In Casa de Campo. 📞 **809/523-3333**. Breakfast buffet RD$750 ($27); buffet RD$1,500 ($54). AE, DC, MC, V. Mon–Sat 7–11am and noon–3pm; Sun 6:30–11am and noon–4pm.

Shish Kabab MIDDLE EASTERN/INTERNATIONAL/ DOMINICAN   Very close to the center of town, this is an informal restaurant that's a real change of pace from Dominican fare. Naturally, the chefs specialize in kabobs, but there are many other Middle Eastern specialties as well, notably *baba ghanoush*, with mashed eggplant studded with fresh parsley, fresh garlic, lemon juice, olive oil, and sesame paste. The beef kabobs are perfectly grilled. There's even a shish kabob pizza. Skewered grouper is yet another worthy specialty. You can also order substantial meals such as broiled lobster, deep fried chicken, or stuffed grape leaves.

Calle Francisco del Castillo Marquez 32. © **809/556-2737.** Main courses RD$600 ($22). DC, MC, V. Tues–Sun 10am–11pm.

HITTING THE BEACH

La Minitas, Casa de Campo's main beach and site of a series of bars and restaurants all its own, is a small but immaculate beach and lagoon that requires a 10-minute shuttle-bus ride from the resort's central core. Transportation is provided by bus, or you can rent an electric golf cart. A bit farther afield (a 30-min. bus ride, but only a 20-min. boat ride), **Bayahibe** is a large, palm-fringed sandy crescent on a point jutting out from the shoreline. Finally, **Catalina** is a fine beach on a deserted island, surrounded by turquoise waters; it's just 45 minutes away by motorboat. Unfortunately, many other visitors from Casa de Campo have learned of the glories of this latter retreat, so you're not likely to have the sands to yourself.

SPORTS & OTHER OUTDOOR PURSUITS

Casa de Campo is headquarters for just about any sporting activity or outdoor pursuit in the area. Call the resort's guest services staff at © **809/523-3333** for more information. Casa del Mar weighs in with a heavy array of outdoor activities ranging from horseback riding to banana boating. Call © **809/221-8880** for more details.

FISHING You can arrange **freshwater river–fishing trips** through Casa de Campo. Some of the biggest snook ever recorded have been caught around here. A 3-hour tour costs RD$868 ($31) per person, and includes tackle, bait, and soft drinks. A 4-hour deep-sea fishing trip costs RD$15,372 to RD$20,496 ($549–$732) per boat, with 8 hours going for RD$22,204 to RD$30,744 ($793–$1,098).

GOLF *Golf* magazine declared Casa de Campo (© **809/523-3333,** ext. 3187) "the finest golf resort in the world." The **Teeth of the Dog** course has been called "a thing of almighty beauty," and it is. The ruggedly natural terrain has seven holes skirting the ocean. Opened in 1977, **The Links** is an inland course modeled after some of the seaside courses of Scotland. In the late 1990s, the resort added a third golf course to its repertoire, **La Romana Country Club,** which tends to be used almost exclusively by residents of the surrounding countryside rather than by guests of Casa de Campo.

The cost for 18 holes of golf is RD$4,480 ($160) at the Links and RD$5,544 ($198) at Teeth of the Dog or the La Romana Country Club. (Some golf privileges may be included in packages to Casa de Campo.) You can also buy a 3-day membership, which lets you play all courses for RD$7,056 ($252) per person (for Casa de Campo guests only). A 7-day membership costs RD$14,056 ($502). You can hire caddies for RD$700 ($25); electric golf-cart rentals cost RD$560 ($20) per person per round. Each course is open 7:30am to 5:30pm daily. Call far in advance to reserve a tee time if you're not staying at the resort.

HORSEBACK RIDING   Trail rides at Casa de Campo or Casa del Mar cost RD$700 ($25) per person for 1 hour, RD$1,120 ($40) for 2 hours. The stables shelter 250 horses, although only about 40 of them are available for trail rides. For more information, call **Casa del Campo** at © **809/523-3333,** ext. 5249, or **Casa del Mar** at © **809/221-8880.**

SNORKELING   Casa de Campo has one of the most complete watersports facilities in the Dominican Republic. You can charter a boat for snorkeling. The resort maintains eight charter vessels, with a minimum of eight people. Full-day snorkeling trips to Isla Catalina cost RD$980 ($35) per snorkeler. Rental of fins and masks cost RD$140 ($5) per day, although they probably won't clock your time with a stopwatch; guests on all-inclusive plans use gear for free. Snorkeling is also included in the all-inclusive rates at **Casa del Mar** (© **809/221-8880**).

TENNIS   Casa de Campo's 13 clay courts are available from 7am to 9pm (they're lit at night). Charges are RD$672 ($24) per court per hour during the day or RD$840 ($30) at night. Lessons are RD$1,708 ($61) per hour with a tennis pro, and RD$1,372 ($49) with an assistant pro. Call far in advance to reserve a court if you're not staying at the resort. The four courts at **Casa del Mar** (© **809/ 221-8880**) are reserved for the resort's all-inclusive guests.

PARQUE NACIONAL DEL ESTE ⍟

The National Park of the East, its English name, lies in the south-eastern part of the island, comprising some 310 sq. km (121 sq. miles) of dry forest, one of the largest such forests in the Caribbean. The park is home to 112 known species of birds, a total of eight endemic to the Dominican Republic.

This is a most interesting park to explore as it is the site of trails, cliffs, caves, mangrove estuaries, sandy beaches, and even Taíno

Altos de Chavón: An Artists' Colony

In 1976, a plateau 161km (100 miles) east of Santo Domingo was selected by Charles G. Bluhdorn, then chairman of Gulf + Western Industries, as the site for a remarkable project. Dominican stonecutters, woodworkers, and ironsmiths began the task that would produce **Altos de Chavón,** a flourishing Caribbean art center set above the canyon of the Río Chavón and the Caribbean Sea.

A walk down one of the cobblestone paths of Altos de Chavón reveals architecture reminiscent of another era at every turn. Coral block and terra-cotta brick buildings house artists' studios, craft workshops, galleries, stores, and restaurants. The **Church of St. Stanislaus** is the central attraction on the main plaza, with its fountain of the four lions, colonnade of obelisks, and panoramic views. Masses are conducted at this church every Saturday and Sunday at 5pm.

The **galleries** (© 809/523-8470) at Altos de Chavón offer an engaging mix of exhibits. In three distinct spaces—the Principal Gallery, the Rincón Gallery, and the Loggia—the work of well-known and emerging Dominican and international artists is showcased. The gallery has a consignment space where finely crafted silk-screen and other multiple works are available for sale. Exhibits change about every month.

Altos de Chavón's *talleres* are craft ateliers, where local artisans have been trained to produce ceramic, silk-screen, and woven-fiber products. From the clay apothecary jars with carnival devil lids to the colored tapestries of Dominican houses, the rich island folklore is much in evidence. The

Indian ruins. Traversing the park is hell, however, as no roads lead into its luxuriant interior. The usual method of exploring it is to hire a boat in Bayahibe and travel along the highlights at the water's edge. Often you'll see trails where you can hike into the interior.

The road leading into town ends at a car park, often filled with tour buses. If you're not part of a group, you can negotiate with one of the captains for a tour of the park, going as far as Peñón Gordo on the park's western coast. A 2-hour trip usually costs RD$500 ($18) per person.

posters, note cards, and printed T-shirts that come from the silk-screen workshops are among the most sophisticated in the Caribbean. All the products of Altos de Chavón's *talleres* are sold at **La Tienda** (© 809/523-3333, ext. 5398), the foundation village store.

The Altos de Chavón **Regional Museum of Archaeology** (© 809/523-8554) houses the objects of Samuel Pion, an amateur archaeologist and collector of treasures from the vanished Taíno tribes, the island's first settlers. The timeless quality of some of the museum's objects makes them seem strangely contemporary in design—one discovers sculptural forms that recall the work of Brancusi or Arp. The museum is open Tuesday to Sunday from 9am to 8pm. Entrance is free.

At the heart of the village's performing-arts complex is the 5,000-seat open-air **amphitheater.** Since its inauguration over a decade ago by Carlos Santana and the late Frank Sinatra, the amphitheater has hosted renowned concerts, symphonies, theater, and festivals, including concerts by Julio Iglesias and Gloria Estefan. The annual Heineken Jazz Festival has brought together such diverse talents as Dizzy Gillespie, Toots Thielmans, Randy Brecker, Shakira, Carlos Ponce, Carlo Vives, and Jon Secada.

The creations at **Everett Designs** (© 809/523-8331) are so original that many visitors mistake this place for a museum. Each piece of jewelry is handcrafted by Bill Everett in a minifactory at the rear of the shop.

SHOPPING

An artisans market, **El Artístico** (© 809/556-2273), lies on the northern side of Carretera Romana, Km 3.5, at a point 1km (½ mile) east of Yina Bambu Shop (see below). This is set up almost exclusively for tourists and offers a limited selection of arts and crafts. It's mainly for souvenirs, most of which are of dubious quality. The market is open daily from 7:30am to 7pm.

For more substantial shopping, head to **Yina Bambu Shop,** Km 4.5, Carretera Romana (© 809/550-8322), open daily 7:30am to

7pm. Lying on the south side of the main road into town, this is the best showcase in the area for Dominican handicrafts and furnishings, even amber necklaces and bracelets. The merchandise dims when compared with what's available in the Colonial Zone of Santo Domingo, but you may not be going there to shop.

If you're a true shopper, seeking some quality items, we suggest you head to Altos de Chavón (see above).

LA ROMANA AFTER DARK

The best entertainment is at the hotels, where programs can change weekly based on their house count (or lack of guests thereof). One popular place is **El Pirata,** Km 12, Carretera San Pedro, Hotel Santana Beach Resort (© **809/412-5342**). Since this is an all-inclusive, you can purchase a night pass for RD$600 ($22) entitling you to dinner and drinks. There's are shows on Wednesday and Fridays at 9pm, followed by dancing from 10:30pm to 2am when a deejay plays salsa, merengue, and pop. On-site is a casino, open daily from 8pm to 4am, where the usual games of chance, such as blackjack, are offered.

At the previously recommended Viva Dominicus Beach in Bayahibe (© **809/686-5658**), **La Locura,** a dance club, is the scene of much of the local action. Deejays play the latest international hits along with a selection of salsa, merengue, and pop. You have to call the management during the day and arrange for a night pass since this is an all-inclusive resort. The cost of RD$560 ($20) entitles you to dinner, drinks, and any entertainment being presented that night. The club is usually open from 11:30pm or 12:30am to about 4am, though it may close earlier on less busy nights.

Many nonguests, willing to purchase night passes, can also go to the previously recommended **Coral Canoa (The Cocuyo Disco),** in Bayahibe (© **809/682-2662**). There are two types of night passes sold here, the regular pass costing RD$1,120 to RD$1,260 ($40–$45) for adults. This entitles you to a buffet and "national drinks" of the Dominican Republic, and it's good daily from 6 to 11pm. Night owls might want to purchase the "Disco Pass" for RD$560 to RD$700 ($20–$25), including admission to the disco and unlimited home-brewed libations. This pass is valid nightly from 11pm to 2am. No live entertainment is presented, but there's usually a "hot" deejay.

At Casa de Campo (see previous recommendation) **The Pot Bunker Sports Bar** (© **809/523-3333**) is a popular gathering spot at night, especially for male guests. Important sports events are broadcast live via satellite transmission on large screen TV sets while visitors cheer their home teams. From 5 to 11pm, a light menu, costing from RD$280 to RD$560 ($9.95–$20), is available, although the bar itself, with its table games and pool table, remains open daily from 3pm to midnight.

6

Punta Cana & Bávaro

On the easternmost tip of the island, 211km (131 miles) east of Santo Domingo is Punta Cana, the site of major vacation developments, including the Barceló and Meliá properties, with more scheduled to arrive in the near future. Known for its 32km (20 miles) of white-sand beaches and clear waters, Punta Cana and Bávaro are an escapist's retreat. Set against a backdrop of swaying palm trees, these beaches are unrivaled in the Caribbean, and that's the chief and perhaps only reason to come here. Within some of the most arid landscapes in the Caribbean—it rarely rains during daylight hours—Punta Cana and Bávaro have been recognized throughout Europe (especially Spain) and the Americas for their climate.

Both Punta Cana and Bávaro, two resort areas at either end of a long curve of beach lined with coconut palms, are virtual towns within themselves. The beach is so mammoth there is rarely overcrowding even with masses of visitors every month of the year. Bávaro and Punta Cana combine to form what is nicknamed La Costa del Coco, or the Coconut Coast, land of the all-inclusive resorts. Don't expect a town or city. From Punta Cana in the south all the way to Playa del Macao in the north, there's only one small community, El Cortecito. Everything else is nothing but all-inclusives and beaches.

Capitalizing on cheap land and the virtually insatiable desire of Americans, Canadians, and Europeans for sunny holidays during the depths of winter, a half-dozen European hotel chains participated in something akin to a land rush, acquiring large tracts of sugar-cane plantations and pastureland. Today, at least a dozen megahotels, most with no fewer than 500 rooms, some with even more, attract a clientele that's about 70% European or Latin American. The hotel designs here range from the not particularly inspired to low-rise megacomplexes designed by the most prominent Spanish architects.

Some of them, particularly the Barceló Bávaro complex (see below), boast some of the most lavish beach and pool facilities in the Caribbean, spectacular gardens, and relatively new concepts in architecture (focusing on postmodern interplays between indoor and outdoor spaces).

Don't expect a real town here. Although the mailing addresses for most hotels is defined as the dusty and distinctly unmemorable Higüey, very few guests at any of these hotels ever spend time there. Most remain on the premises of their hotels, as part of all-inclusive holidays, where it's very tempting to never leave the confines of your resort.

If you choose to vacation in Punta Cana, you won't be alone, as increasing numbers of Latino celebrities are already making inroads there, usually renting private villas within private compounds. Julio Iglesias has been a fixture here for a while. And one of the most widely publicized feuds in the Dominican Republic swirled a few years ago around celebrity designer Oscar de la Renta, who abandoned his familiar haunts at Casa de Campo for palm-studded new digs at Punta Cana.

Above all, don't expect a particularly North American vacation. The Europeans were here first, and many of them still have a sense of possessiveness about their secret hideaway. For the most part, the ambience is Europe in the tropics, as seen through a Dominican filter. You'll find, for example, more formal dress codes, greater interest in soccer matches than in the big football game, and red wine rather than scotch and soda at dinner. Hotels are aware of the cultural differences between their North American and European guests, and sometimes strain to soften the differences that arise between them.

1 Essentials

VISITOR INFORMATION   Amazingly, with the largest concentration of visitors in the entire Caribbean Basin, and with visitors numbering at least 750,000 a year (no one knows for sure), the Dominican Republic government, in their infinite wisdom, has yet to open a tourist office.

GETTING THERE   **American Eagle** (© 800/433-7300 in the U.S.; www.aa.com) offers two to six daily nonstop flights to Punta Cana from San Juan, Puerto Rico; flying time is about an hour. You can also opt for one of American Eagle's two or three (depending on the season) daily flights from San Juan to La Romana and then make the 90-minute drive to Punta Cana.

In addition, **Takeoff Destination Service S.A.,** Plaza Brisas de Bávaro #8, (© 809/552-1611 or 809/522-1333; www.takeoffweb. com) also flies in from Santo Domingo in 55 minutes; frequency of flights depends on demand, with more in the busier winter months.

A typical fare—say, from Santo Domingo to Punta Cana's airport—costs RD$1,876 ($67) one way with no discount for flying round-trip. You can also fly from San Juan's airport to Punta Cana.

Lying adjacent to the Punta Cana Resort and Club, the **International Airport of Punta Cana** (② **809/959-2376**) is the world's first privately owned international airport, or so it is believed. Flights, mainly from North America and Europe, wing into this airport at the rate of 100 per week in summer. In winter, the volume of flights increases to approximately 250 per week. Private buses from the all-inclusives are waiting to shuttle arriving passengers to their respective resorts. When your vacation is over, you're placed in a private van and hauled back to the airport. The location of the airport is about 5km (3 miles) from where the Higüey–Punta Cana main highway reaches the coast.

Motorists driving across the southern tier of the Dominican Republic along Highway 104 reach the rural city of Higüey before continuing to the northeast to the Coconut Coast. Highway 104 runs along the entire length of the Punta Cana/Bávaro resorts before coming to an end at the port city of Miches on the Bahía de Samaná.

THE LAY OF THE LAND

One of the most remarkable real-estate developments in the Caribbean, Punta Cana grew out of the perceived need for a mass-market vacation destination, capable of receiving visitors from Europe and North America, that was near a worthy set of beaches, on land that was cheap, plentiful, and undeveloped. The result is Punta Cana and Bávaro, two resorts completely dependent upon an international airport (which they have), a string of sandy beaches (which they have), and a maze of tarmac-covered roads that wind in a labyrinth through land that used to be (and which to some degree still is) covered with sugar cane.

Don't expect a burgeoning downtown settlement, because there really isn't one, and don't expect a coherent set of roads with names, because most of them are unnamed. Look instead for signs with arrows that point the way to the individual hotels, each of which were designed like cities unto themselves. Each resort—especially the all-inclusives—has enough amenities to keep visitors happily sequestered on site for the duration of their holidays. And to our surprise, even the employees of the individual resorts rarely, if ever, meander through to visit competing resorts. The result is a necklace of self-contained communities, each with drugstores, food markets, coin-operated laundromats, and all-inclusive food services, draped along the waterfront of the peninsula.

Whereas the policy of self-containment (which is encouraged by the architecture and the closed-off, fenced-in nature of each resort) suits the hoteliers just fine, many small start-up businesses, including restaurants, must rely almost exclusively on local Dominican business for their livelihood, having been cut off from the masses of foreign visitors who tend to remain within their individual hotels. And since the hotels do everything they can to increase their allures in-house, there simply aren't a lot of independently operated Dominican businesses, outside the big resorts, in this newly built community.

Every large resort maintains at least one beachfront kiosk loaded with staff and watersports equipment. They tend to be operated by the same central organization, charge all the same prices, and even move their staff from one kiosk to another, regardless of whose beachfront they're sitting on. And it's entirely likely that the scuba or snorkeling trip you sign up for at the kiosk of your hotel might combine your outing with clients of several other hotels along the same beachfront.

GETTING AROUND   Most **taxi fares,** including those connecting the airport with most of the major hotels, range from RD$700 ($25) for up to four passengers. Your hotel can summon a cab for you. If you want to tour along the coast, you can **rent a car** on site at the car-rental desks of all the major resorts.

Guaguas also run up and down the coastal road during the day, but not at night. Most of these motorized vans charge RD$30 ($1.10) for the average ride. The price, of course, depends on the distance traveled.

Should you wish, you can also rent a car for the duration of your stay, although most visitors manage to forego this luxury since they are so resortbound at their all-inclusive. There is little need to get about. If you're interested, **National Car Rental,** Cruce de Coco Loco (© **809/221-0286**), rents cars, as does **Avis Car Rental,** Carretera Arena Gorda (© **809/688-1354**). Rates at both companies are subject to wild fluctuations, even in the same season, even week from week. **Europcar,** Calle Friusa Fiesta (© **809/686-2861**), also rents vehicles. Just as a general guideline, the same economy car can begin as little as RD$760 ($27) a day, going up to RD$1,700 ($61) a day.

FAST FACTS: PUNTA CANA & BAVARO

To call the **police** in an emergency, dial **911**. Otherwise, use ✆ **809/554-1340**. For Internet access, go to **Business Center,** Punta Cana Resort and Club, Carretera Punta Cana (✆ **809/959-2262**), open daily 8am to 9:45pm, charging RD$70 ($2.50) for 15 minutes. The office of **Western Union** is found at Plaza Bávaro (✆ **809/532-7381**), open Monday to Friday 8am to 10pm, Saturday 8am to 6pm, Sunday 8am to 5pm. Many hotels have offices that will sell you routine drugstore items, and some actually have full pharmacies. Otherwise you'll have to go to the inland city of Higüey, where you'll find that the most central pharmacy is **D'Hidarnis Farmacia,** Av. Trejo 26 (✆ **809/554-2719**), open Monday to Saturday 8am to 10pm, Sunday 8am to 1pm.

2 Where to Stay & Dine

The rates given below are only for your general guidance. In all candor, we must confess that no one actually pays these so-called rack rates. Guests book into the all-inclusives on some sort of deal, package or otherwise. The prices given below can change within the week, if management, even in the dead of high season (winter), decides that business is slow and they want to lure more business by slicing prices.

In other words, prices along La Costa del Coco, unlike anywhere else in the Caribbean, virtually change week from week. Prices, incidentally, are always lower when purchased from an agent overseas. If you show up without a reservation seeking a room, you'll be charged about twice as much.

THE ALL-INCLUSIVES

Barceló Bávaro Beach, Golf & Casino Resort ✿   This huge complex of low-rise luxury hotels opens onto one of the most desirable of the many white-sand beaches along the 32km (20-mile) coast known as Bávaro Beach. This is the most ambitious resort colony in the Dominican Republic, a project whose scope hasn't been equaled since the early days of Casa de Campo, a resort Barcelo Bávaro strives to outdo but doesn't. Built in postmodern Spanish style, it occupies almost 12 sq. km (4¾ sq. miles) of land, including some of the best seafront property on the island. Developed by the Barcelos Group, a group of Spanish hotel investors, it consists of five separate hotels: Bávaro Beach Hotel, Bávaro Caribe Hotel, Bávaro

Punta Cana & Bávaro

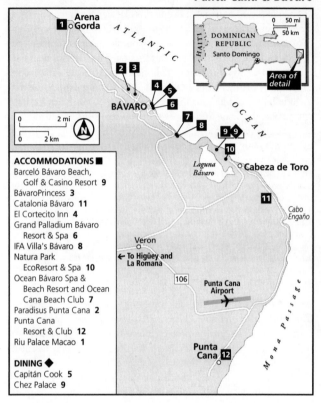

ACCOMMODATIONS ■

Barceló Bávaro Beach,
    Golf & Casino Resort **9**
BávaroPrincess **3**
Catalonia Bávaro **11**
El Cortecito Inn **4**
Grand Palladium Bávaro
    Resort & Spa **6**
IFA Villa's Bávaro **8**
Natura Park
    EcoResort & Spa **10**
Ocean Bávaro Spa &
    Beach Resort and Ocean
    Cana Beach Club **7**
Paradisus Punta Cana **2**
Punta Cana
    Resort & Club **12**
Riu Palace Macao **1**

DINING ◆

Capitán Cook **5**
Chez Palace **9**

Golf Hotel, Bávaro Casino Hotel, and the latest contender, the Bávaro Palace Hotel. Arranged within a massive park, and connected via a labyrinth of roadways and bike trails, all but one parallel the beachfront (the Bávaro Casino Hotel faces the golf course). Neither the decor nor the gardens are as well-conceived and stylish as those within the Meliá Caribe Tropical, but the effect is nonetheless comfortable and pleasant. Accommodations in all five hotels are roughly equivalent and are outfitted in tropical furniture, with private verandas or terraces, plus an attractively tiled bathroom with tub and shower. (The Bávaro Palace's rooms are bigger and somewhat more comfortable than the others.) Bedrooms have tile floors, Dominican-made furniture, and colorful upholsteries and fabrics.

Each of the 15 restaurants within this megahotel is interconnected by minivan service, and each will cheerfully accept diners from even the most far-flung corners of the compound. The most upscale and "gastronomic" of the lot is Chez Palace, serving French cuisine, some of whose main dishes require that all-inclusive guests pay a reasonable supplement for their meal. Other, slightly less pretentious eateries include Bohio and La Piña for Dominican food, Los Piños for Italian cuisine, the Coral Steakhouse for two-fisted slabs of grilled beef, chicken, and veal; Mexico Lindo, for Mexican food; and an absolutely vast buffet setup within the open-to-the-breezes Ambar.

Apdo. Postal 3177, Punta Cana, Higüey, Dominican Republic. ℂ 800/227-2356 in the U.S., or 809/686-5797. Fax 809/656-5859. www.barcelo.com. 1,921 units. Winter US$250 per person double in Palace, rooms in any of the other 4 hotels US$190 per person; off season US$154 per person double in Palace, doubles in any of the other 4 hotels US$95 per person. Prices are all-inclusive. Discounts of 45%–65% for children 2–12 staying parent's room. AE, DC, MC, V. **Amenities:** 12 restaurants; 13 bars; 6 outdoor pools; 18-hole golf course; 9 tennis courts; health club; whirlpools big enough for 30 people; watersports equipment; salon; limited room service; massage; babysitting; laundry service; dry cleaning; nonsmoking rooms; limited mobility rooms; aerobics; casino; 3 discos; horseback riding; 3 theaters. *In room:* A/C, TV, dataport, minibar, hair dryer, iron/ironing board, safe.

Bávaro Princess 🏊 Drawing some of its architectural inspiration from Bali, this hotel opens onto a 2km-long (1¼-mile) white-sand private beach. The Spanish-born architect Alvaro Sanz retained most of the palms and mangrove clusters on the property and installed freshwater reservoirs, creating an oasis not only for vacationers, but also for the many species of birds that call the resort home.

All accommodations lie within 86 low-slung bungalows. The split-level suites contain refrigerators and king-size or twin beds, each fitted with comfortable furnishings. The small bathrooms have combination shower/tubs and marble counters.

Playa Arena Gorda, Punta Cana, Higüey, Dominican Republic. ℂ 809/221-2311. Fax 809/686-5427. www.princesshotelsandresorts.com. 935 units. Year-round US$170–US$200 double. Rates all-inclusive. AE, MC, V. **Amenities:** 7 restaurants; 6 bars; 2 outdoor pools; 4 lit tennis courts; health club; watersports equipment; scooter rental; concierge; car rental desk; shopping arcade; 24-hr. room service; babysitting; laundry service; dry cleaning; disco; horseback riding. *In room:* A/C, ceiling fans, TV, minibar, hair dryer, iron/ironing board, safe, dataport.

Catalonia Bávaro 🏊 *Kids* Constructed right at the close of the 20th century, this resort is like a large village of three-story villas, with two dozen rental units per building. It lies in the very heart of Playa Bávaro's resort sprawl. Run by a Spanish chain, it is a large U-shaped complex of buildings constructed around a mammoth free-form pool.

The beachfront in front of Catalonia is one of the finest strips of white sand along the Coconut Coast. The open-air pavilions sheltering the public areas evoke Bali, with walkways bridging lotus ponds.

Bedrooms are more spacious than many of this resort's competitors, and they come with tiled bathrooms with tub and shower. Standard rooms are junior suites (there are no doubles), and they are as large as suites in most hotels. Rattan furnishings, plus colorful draperies, spreads and fabrics, and local island art create a tropical ambience for doing nothing. When the house count is up, the maids seem overwhelmed.

There are so many restaurants here you're sure to find something you like. When you tire of those endless buffets you can seek out specialty dining such as Italian, French, Japanese, American, or Tex-Mex. Kids are likely to be found at the creperie-ice cream bar. The kids' club is one of the best along the coast. Like the dining options, activities prevail ranging from golf to watersports.

Playa Bávaro, Punta Cana, Dominican Republic. ℰ 809/412-0000. Fax 809/412-0001. www.cataloniabavaro.com. 711 units. Year-round US$160–US$250 junior suite. Children 2–12 pay 50% of adult rate. AE, MC, V. Free parking. **Amenities:** 6 restaurants; 5 bars; 2 pools (1 for children); 9-hole golf course; 2 tennis courts; health club; spa; sauna; watersports equipment; bikes; babysitting; laundry service; dry cleaning; nonsmoking rooms; limited mobility rooms; aerobics; archery; casino; nightly entertainment;. *In room:* A/C, TV, minibar, hair dryer, safe.

Grand Palladium Bávaro Resort & Spa 𝒶𝒶   Right at the front-line action at Playa Bávaro, with some of the best white sandy beachfront on the coast, this is a megaresort with government-rated five-star facilities. Set in well-landscaped gardens of towering palms, the resort grew up on what had once been a coconut palm plantation. A special feature is the coral reef right offshore, where diving, sailing, and other watersports are avidly pursued.

There's a wide range of accommodations here, all of them comfortably and tastefully furnished, including two-floor bungalows, four two-floor villas, and standard doubles which give you a choice of a king-size bed or two queens. Built in 1992, the resort receives yearly refurbishing and stays up-to-date. Junior suites, Romance suites and Superior rooms have been totally renovated.

There are many outdoor pursuits, from water aerobics to windsurfing, but not enough to overwhelm you. The chefs do much to provide you with a variety of foodstuff, everything from a Mediterranean cuisine to Tex-Mex specialties. For the munchies, there is even a late-night pizzeria. Two of the dining rooms are on the beach. The international cuisine buffet is one of the better "showcase" ones.

Playa Bávaro, Punta Cana, Dominican Republic. © **809/221-8149.** Fax 809/221-8150. www.fiestahotelgroup.com. 636 units. Year-round US$260–US$280 double; US$300–US$320 junior suite. Children 2–12 pay 50% of adult rate. AE, MC, V. Free parking. **Amenities:** 7 restaurants; 5 bars; 2 pools; 2 tennis courts; health club; 2 spas (1 on the beach); Jacuzzi; sauna; salon; room service; massage; babysitting; laundry service; dry cleaning; basketball; disco; Internet center; mini-golf; nightly entertainment; pharmacy; photo shop; steam baths; supermarket; 24-hr medical service. *In room:* A/C, TV, minibar, coffeemaker, hair dryer, iron/ironing board, safe.

IFA Villas Bávaro 𝄐 *Kids*　This midsize resort from 1998 is one of the most fun-loving along the coast. It's not the most tasteful—certainly not the most elegant—but those who like a party day and night check in here and often don't want to go home. Obviously the focus is on plenty of activities and lots of entertainment.

The balconied rooms are midsize and spread over 23 villa-style houses, each with 10 rental units. Walls are white or cream, with the fabrics and draperies providing the tropical color accents. The food is only ordinary but the settings are amusing, including a margarita snack bar by one of the pools, or food and drinks at the beach club. There is more formal dining with wine and excellent service as well. Parties, dancing, live shows with carnival themes, and a "Jungle Disco" are just some of the amusements provided.

Playa Bávaro, Punta Cana, Dominican Republic. © **809/221-8555.** Fax 809/221-8556. www.ifahotels.com. 262 units. Year-round US$164–US$190 double. Children 2–12 US$21 extra. AE, DC, MC, V. Free parking. **Amenities:** 5 restaurants; 5 bars; 3 pools (1 for kids); tennis courts; health club; watersports equipment; bike rentals; salon; 24-hr. room service; massage; babysitting; laundry service; dry cleaning; beach club; dance classes; nightly entertainment. *In room:* A/C, TV, fridge, hair dryer, safe, ceiling fan.

Natural Park EcoResort & Spa 𝄐𝄐　It's "Me Tarzan, you Jane" time. At last a resort comes along that has originality escaping the peas-in-pod similarity of the Coconut Coast's string of imitative hotel sprawls. Set near a protected island estuary, the resort opens onto one of the coast's premier white sandy beaches. Nature lovers flock to its 32 hectares (79 acres) of park grounds, the setting evokes a *Jungle Book*. It doesn't quite rival Disney, but there's a fantasy aura about the place, where its various rooms are distributed across 13 two-story buildings painted in "blinding" white and surrounded by an oasis of coconut palms. This unusual vacation retreat burst onto the scene in 1997 and proved an instant hit, with its setting at a lagoon and a mangrove forest.

In general, accommodations are spacious and given homelike touches by the use of area rugs, comfy sitting areas, and king or paired double beds, the setting enhanced by tropical fabrics and the art of island artists.

The tiled bathrooms come with tub and shower and have sliding louvered doors that separate the dressing areas from the toilets. They are politically correct here regarding ecology, offering guests biodegradable soaps and recycling plastic whenever they can.

At the dramatic thatch-roofed main reception building, held up by large beams, you can learn the agenda of the day ranging from watersports to catamaran sailing or dancing lessons. Botanical walks are a big feature. Or else you can indulge yourself and make yourself even more beautiful than you are in the spa, getting health and beauty treatments.

Don't expect to dine in air-conditioned comfort, but in heat-wave conditions. Most dining is at a buffet but you can also enjoy a grill room and a seafood eatery where the quality of the cuisine is topnotch.

Is there a downside to nature's paradise? Yes, we found all the seaweed at the beach a bit disconcerting. Also, we detected a slight anti-American attitude. Yankees are accepted, of course, but, as one waiter privately confided to us, "We're much happier with our clients from Spain or Germany."

Cabeza de Toro, Punta Cana, Dominican Republic. © **809/221-2626.** Fax 809/221-6060. www.blau-hotels.com. 490 units. Year-round US$150–US$160 double. Children 2–12 50% discount. AE, DC, MC, V. Free parking. **Amenities:** 4 restaurants; 4 bars; 2 pools; 3 tennis courts; health club; spa; sauna; watersports equipment; bikes; children's center; salon; limited room service; botanical walks; disco; nightly entertainment; water aerobics. *In room:* A/C, TV, minibar, coffeemaker, hair dryer, safe.

Ocean Bávaro Spa & Beach Resort and Ocean Cana Beach Club ✿ *(Kids)* This two-in-one resort consists of government-rated four-star hotels, each is all inclusive, offering a mass of rooms. Spread across a beachfront of white sand, it somehow manages to rise above a mere dormitory factory, housing planeloads of visitors flying in for fun in the sun. Canals and lagoons cut across the landscaped grounds with a trip of pools, along with habitats for pink flamingos and ducks. Water sports are a strong attraction here as is the spa with its body treatments, Vichy showers, yoga classes, even tai-chi classes, and lots of other offerings.

Bedrooms are midsize to large, with a choice of beds (such as queen or king); each is tastefully decorated in a rather minimalist style with colorful fabrics. Accommodations open onto private balconies or terraces. Bathrooms come with tub and shower, and the larger and more expensive units have their own Jacuzzis. Family units come with two separate bedrooms and two different entrances along with two bathrooms and two closets. Activities range from kayaking to windsurfing, from horseback riding to archery. Unlike most all-inclusives, this resort breaks its kids' programs into ages 4 to 12 and 12 to 17, with different activities planned.

With eight restaurants, there is a wide array of different food choices. Three of the restaurants are a buffet style, the rest are a la carte, featuring both Dominican and international dishes. As night falls, there's everything from a disco to a beer house to keep you amused, even a live show in La Rumba Theater.

Playa Bávaro, Punta Cana, Dominican Republic. ☏ **1-888-403-2603** in U.S. and Canada or **809/683-1010.** Fax 809/683-2303. www.oceanhotels.net. 310 units. Year-round US$90–US$170 double. Children 4–12 US$50 extra. Rates are all-inclusive. AE, DC, MC, V. Free parking. **Amenities:** 8 restaurants; 7 bars; 3 pools; 2 tennis courts; health club; sauna; watersports equipment; bike rentals; children's center; salon; massage; babysitting; laundry service; dry cleaning; limited mobility rooms; archery; disco; beer house; children's playground; horseback riding; nightly entertainment; theater. *In room:* A/C, TV.

Paradisus Punta Cana ⟲ *Kids*   Lying on some choice white sands of Bávaro Beach, this all-inclusive has two important assets: Its staff is one of the friendliest and most helpful on the coast, and it offers a lot of facilities-per-guest ratio. Inaugurated in 1996, the resort has more style and flair than most. Oscar de la Renta didn't design it, but the decorators were obviously inspired by this Dominican's elegant flair.

Rooms have recently been refurbished, and the spacious studios are just as good as those at the Princess Bávaro next door. In many cases, elevated sleeping platforms overlook spacious living areas. Hand-thrown pots, Dominican island art, macramé wall hangings, red-tile floors, and lots of painted wicker give the place style. You are given a choice of a king or two double beds, and units open onto furnished balconies or patios. Most have garden views, although some choice units open onto the ocean. Each comes with a tiled bathroom with tub or shower.

One of the reasons to stay here is the food, as the resort offers almost more dining choices than any other along the coast—every cuisine from French to Chinese, from Mexican to Japanese, along with international, Dominican, and American food specialties. Grilled fish and barbecues are other notable culinary features. Entertainment is diverse, ranging from a karaoke disco to an aqua bar to bars that often serve Dominican cigars with their drinks. Theme parties are big here, and there are live shows nightly, along with casino action.

Playas de Bávaro, Higüey, Dominican Republic. ☏ **809/687-9923.** Fax 809/687-0752. www.solmelia.com. 542 units. Year-round US$275–US$440 double. Children 2–12 pay 50% of adult rate. AE, DC, MC, V. Rates are all-inclusive. Free parking. **Amenities:**

11 restaurants; 6 bars; 2 pools; 18-hole golf (across the road); 4 tennis courts; health club; spa; sauna; watersports equipment; children's center; 24-hr. room service; laundry service; dry cleaning; archery; bike and walking tours; casino; deep-sea fishing; horseback riding; karaoke disco; nightly entertainment. *In room:* A/C, TV, minibar, coffeemaker, hair dryer, iron/ironing board, safe.

Punta Cana Resort & Club *Kids*   Perhaps the most laidback of the all-inclusives, this one is a "golden oldie." Anything older than 20 years in Punta Cana qualifies as an "antique." One of the first hotels built along the Coconut Coast, it has kept abreast of the times and opens onto a beach of white sands that look cliché beautiful but is patchy with coral. The sprawling complex, set on 105 acres (42.4 h) site, is comprised of three- or four-story buildings, each decorated with tropical flair, with gabled balconies attached. The choice is for a studio, suite, or villa, each with tropical "Dorothy Lamour" fabrics, cool tile floors, and carved and painted headboards, along with compact bathrooms with a tub and shower combo. Even though the villas are provided with kitchenettes, one wonders why such an amenity even exists at an all-inclusive with a vast array of restaurants and snack bars. We prefer the Tortuga Beach Villas with interiors by Oscar de la Renta.

The food is superior to most resorts at this coastal sprawl, and many dining spots open directly onto the beach. Our vote goes for *El Cocoloba* with its Caribbean nouvelle cuisine.

Activities are of the usual type, although more golfers stay here because of the nearness of an oceanfront course. There's a kids' club, but the only thing different from most competitors are the ecological tours.

Carretera Punta Cana/Bávaro, Punta Cana, Dominican Republic. ✆ **809/959-2262.** Fax 809/959-3951. www.puntacana.com. 420 units. Year-round US$186–US$340 double. Rates are all-inclusive. Children 2–12 US$47-US$86 extra. AE, DC, MC, V. Free parking. **Amenities:** 8 restaurants; 5 bars; lounge; 2 outdoor pools; golf; 4 tennis courts; health club; watersports equipment; children's center; limited room service; babysitting; laundry service; horseback riding; mini-zoo for kids; nightly entertainment; 24-hr medical center; . *In room:* A/C, TV, kitchenette (in some), minibar, hair dryer, safe.

Riu Palace Macao   Built in 1994, and continually renovated, this member of the Riu chain attracts mostly German-speaking visitors to its precincts. A casino in its main building, a three-floor Colonial-style structure, is one of its chief attractions. We find this the best of the Riu's chain of hotels along the Coconut Coast. The architects wisely planned that this midrise hotel fan out along the beach for better views and greater access to the white sands.

Where to Dine in Punta Cana & Bávaro

Given the wealth of restaurants in the hotels listed above, many guests never leave the premises for meals. But the following are worth a special trip.

Capitán Cook *🌴* SEAFOOD Don't expect any elaborate food or fancy sauces; the allure here is the ultrafresh seafood that's simply but superbly grilled to order. A battery of smoldering outdoor grills lies near the entrance to a dining area whose tables are positioned beneath palm-frond gazebos overlooking a superb beach. Some guests don't bother to consult a menu, but order their meal based on whatever is sputtering over coals or displayed on ice as they enter. Platters of grilled fish or shellfish, chicken, pork chops, or steaks are accompanied by salad, baked potatoes, or french fries. As an alternative, try a heaping platter of paella. The shrimp and grilled calamari are superb. Beer is the perfect accompaniment for anything served here, perhaps preceded by a rum-based cocktail.

Playa El Cortecito, Marina El Cortecito. *📞* **809/552-0645.** Reservations recommended for dinner. Main courses US$12–US$45. AE, DC, MC, V. Daily noon–midnight.

Standing in well-landscaped and palm-studded gardens, this is one of the more luxuriously and elegantly decorated of the all-inclusives. As a startling surprise in the tropics, a top-hatted doorman directs you into the reception area.

Verde-iron chandeliers and ceiling fans evoking those Bogie and Sydney Greenstreet movies whirl over the granite floors and Asian rugs below.

Rooms are tastefully decorated with rich fabrics and reproductions of classic furnishings, each unit coming with some of the best bathrooms along the coast, complete with tub/shower combos, granite vanities, and even bidets. Another nice touch is the Dominican rocking chairs on the balconies, the type made famous when JFK was in the White House.

Tropical drinks and endless food flow here from the kitchens and bars. We especially like the on-the-spot cooking stations at both lunch and dinner, where you can order a meal cooked to order even at a buffet. Even better is a specialty restaurant serving a Mediterranean

Chez Palace *⚘* INTERNATIONAL   This is the showcase restaurant of one of the biggest resort complexes in the Dominican Republic. If you're not staying at one of the Barcelo hotels, you'll have to make reservations in advance. The decor is cool and stylish, as though it were imported from a chic resort in the south of Spain. A formally dressed staff serves superb dishes that include salmon mousse in a prawn sauce, tartar of tenderloin, grilled red snapper, grouper with mustard sauce, and filet mignon with truffles and foie gras. The set-price menu offers many different choices. In the same complex you can also dine at the **Buffet Caribe,** open daily 7am to 10:30pm, costing RD$560 ($20) per person for a buffet lunch or dinner.

In the Bávaro Palace Hotel, within the Barcelo Bávaro Beach, Golf & Casino Resort. © **809/686-5797.** Reservations required. Set-price dinner US$20. AE, DC, MC, V. Daily 7–11pm.

cuisine and a grill-steakhouse with some of the best cuts of beef along the coast. Theme buffets are also staged twice a week. Guests here seem more independent than the Club Med types, where everything is planned for them.

Playa Arena Gorda, Punta Cana, Dominican Republic. © **809/221-7171.** Fax 809/682-1645. www.riu.com. 356 units. Year-round US$285–US$480 double; US$515–US$620 suite. Children 2–12 pay 50% of adult rate. Rates are all-inclusive. AE, DC, MC, V. Free parking. **Amenities:** 4 restaurants; 4 bars; 2 pools (with children's pool); 4 tennis courts; health club; spa center with body and beauty treatments; Jacuzzi; watersports equipment; salon; babysitting; laundry service; dry cleaning; casino; disco; Internet center; pharmacy; photo shop; nightly entertainment. *In room:* A/C, TV, minibar, hair dryer, safe.

INEXPENSIVE

The all-inclusives, as we've just previewed, dominate the Coconut Coast. Because of the crazy and ever-changing rate structure, and because of all the deals and the decision of management to suddenly slash prices to get business, you might call any of the all-inclusives a budget deal if you get in on the right price.

This bargain-basement price slicing has severely limited truly charming little inns that might flourish here in a different economy. There are some low-rent dives, including boarding houses and even private homes for those wanting to escape the curse of the all-inclusive. Here is one of the better selections we've found.

El Cortecito Inn *Value*   It's definitely not on the A-list of megaresorts, but a certain independent and frugal traveler likes to stop off here. You get to enjoy the same glorious white sands of the all-inclusives, but life is a lot simpler. In a building from 2001, this three-level structure offers very simply, yet comfortably, furnished bedrooms that are midsize, each with small tiled bathrooms with tub/shower combinations. The decor, if it could be called that, is very Caribbean and rather minimalist, although maintenance is high. For a lot of your amenities, action, and facilities, you'll have to look elsewhere. The food is home-styled and generous in portions, much of it like that served in the home of a typical island family.

Av. Meliá Fiesta, Playa Bávaro Dominican Republic. © **809/552-0639.** Fax 809/552-0641. 75 units. Year-round US$68–US$90 double. Rates include breakfast. AE, MC, V. Free parking. **Amenities:** 2 restaurants; bar; pool. *In room:* A/C, TV, safe.

3 Beaches & Other Outdoor Pursuits

One of the Caribbean's great beaches stretches along the so-called Costa del Coco, or Coconut Coast, covering more than 32km (20 miles) of brilliant white sand—so there's room for everyone. Flanked by the all-inclusives, the major beaches here include Playa Macao, Playa Cortecito, Playa Bávaro, Playa Punta Cana, and Playa Punta Juanillo. The upmarket all-inclusives have staked out the best beachfront properties, so everything is done for you here, including unlimited access to food and drinks and watersports concessions at each hotel. For facilities, bars, and restaurants, you can use the hotel at which you are a guest.

This beachfront is the stuff of Sunday supplements in travel magazines, with perfect sand and zillions of coconut palms. Under an almost constant blue sky during the day, European, American, and Canadian guests frolic at the gin-clear waters.

The beaches here are wide, they're gorgeous, and it's safe to swim all year round. A cyclone fence runs along much of the coastal road, prohibiting access to the various beaches fronting the hotels. Entrances guarded by security forces prevent nonguests from entering, since once inside you're entitled to unlimited food and drink.

Activities abound, not only scuba diving but snorkeling, wind-surfing, kayaking, water biking, sailing, beach volleyball or soccer, even water polo, along with aqua aerobics and tons of children's activities.

Within Punta Cana, the guest services staff at your hotel can probably arrange horseback riding for you, but if they can't, consider an equestrian jaunt at the region's biggest stables. These are head-quartered at **Rancho RN-23,** Arena Gorda (© **809/747-7356** or 7538). It supervises as many as 125 horses that are stabled at three separate "ranches," each within a reasonable distance of one another. For RD$1,680 ($60) an hour, you'll be guided on equestrian tours through groves of coconut palms near the beach and, in most cases, onto the beach itself. To reach it, you'll follow some clearly marked signs 3km (2 miles) through some of the wildest terrain left in Punta Cana, down winding sandy paths to a series of palm groves, to the site of these stables.

The Bávaro Golf Course at **Barcelo Bávaro Beach, Golf & Casino Resort,** Bávaro Beach (© **809/686-5797**), isn't as great as the one at Casa de Campo, but it's the best on this end of the island. Greens fees are RD$970 ($35) for 18 holes, with cart rentals going for RD$1,050 ($37). Guests of the hotel pay only 50% of greens fees. Open daily 7am to 5pm.

Punta Cana Golf Club, near the Punta Cana Resort and Club (© **809/959-4653**), is a seaside golf club designed by P. B. Dye of the famous golfing family. Fourteen of its holes open onto panoramic views of the Caribbean Sea, and four play along the ocean itself. Dye is known for crafting each hole to present a unique challenge. For 18 holes, hotel guests pay RD$2,800 ($100), and nonguests are charged US$144. In summer, greens fees are reduced to RD$2,240 ($80) for hotel guests, RD$3,080 ()$110 for nonguests. The clubhouse is spectacular, with interiors by Oscar de la Renta.

MANATI PARK

This animal park, opening in 1997, is the most controversial in the Caribbean. It's your choice if you want to patronize it or not. The zoo-logical park features an array of sea lions, parrots, and even a danc-ing horse show, inspired by the traditional equestrian performances in the Spanish city of Jerez de la Frontera. There's even a crocodile cage and a parade of elegant pink flamingos.

What makes the park controversial is its policy of allowing people to swim with dolphins. Certain marine biologists have claimed that the tank holding the dolphins is too small and that the animals are forced into regular contact with humans. This, it is believed, upsets their natural bacteria levels. That, in turn, can lead to a breakdown in their immune systems. Already, four "stressed-out" dolphins have died since the park opened. Many countries, including Canada, have requested that the Dominican Republic cease its treatment of dolphins, calling the park's policy "inhumane."

If you must visit, the park is open daily from 9am to 6pm, charging adults RD$500 ($18) and children RD$300 ($11). To swim with the dolphins costs RD$1,400 ($50) with advance booking required.

SHOPPING

We'd not pursue this as a serious activity, although all the megaresorts feature gift shops for those inevitable souvenirs. If you like to look beyond your hotel, you'll find an upmarket shopping complex, **Plaza Bávaro,** lying between the Allegro Flamenco Bávaro Resort and Fiesta Palace Beach Resort.

There's another shopping complex, mainly for crafts, on the beach along the northern tier of this shopping complex reached along a dirt road labeled MERCADO, meaning "market." This leads to a bustling crafts market open daily anytime from 8am to sunset.

PUNTA CANA AFTER DARK

If you're staying at an all-inclusive, your nightly entertainment is already provided. You need not leave the grounds for action. Depending on the night of the week, many hotels present Las Vegas–type revues.

Bávaro Disco, on the grounds of the Bávaro Barcelo Beach, Golf & Casino Resort (© **809/686-5797**), has emerged as the hottest, most popular, and sexiest disco in Punta Cana, thanks to a superb sound system. The venue is more European than North American, thanks to a heavy concentration of clients from Italy, Spain, and Holland. If you've been tempted to dress provocatively but never had the courage, the permissive and sexually charged ambience at this enormous club will give you the confidence to try. Painted black, with simulated stars overhead and lots of mirrors, the place is open nightly from 11pm to 5am. Entrance is free for guests of the Barcelo Hotel complex; nonguests pay RD$1,260 ($45).

7

The Samaná Peninsula

A real offbeat destination where prices are still affordable, Samaná is an undeveloped 48km-long (30-mile) peninsula located in the northeastern corner of the country. It's about as Casablanca as the Caribbean gets. Hiding out here is an international expatriate enclave of rampant individualists. It also has some of the finest white sandy beaches in the Dominican Republic.

The best beach, **Las Terrenas,** lies on the north coast of the peninsula. At any minute you expect to encounter Robinson Crusoe here. Although the strand strip is narrow, it is filled with white sand set against a backdrop of palms. The beach is never crowded. About the only visitors you'll encounter are at sea: the several thousand humpback whales who swim in from the North Atlantic to birth their calves from January through March. The main town, **Samaná,** lies on the southern side of the peninsula, overlooking a bay. The north coast of the peninsula is more accessible by boat. The roads are a bit of a joke, better suited for donkeys than cars.

In 1824, the *Turtle Dove,* a sailing vessel, was blown ashore at Samaná. Dozens of American slaves from the Freeman Sisters' underground railroad escaped to these shores. They settled in Samaná, and today, their offspring are waiting to greet you. Although Spanish is the major language, you can still hear some form of 19th-century English, and you'll see villages with names such as Philadelphia or Bethesda.

Samaná peninsula is one of the fastest-developing tourist regions of the Dominican Republic, but so far the government has yet to open any visitor information offices here.

GETTING THERE The Peninsula of La Samaná lies in one of the more remote locations along coastal Dominican Republic, a lush strip of land in the far east of the country. Many visitors wing their way in because of the difficult approach roads to La Samaná.

It's best to drive southeast along the coast after a stopover on the Amber Coast, perhaps at Puerto Plata or Cabarete. Motorists can head southeast from Cabarete. After you approach the town of Sánchez, Route 5 continues east into the little town of Samaná.

If your ultimate goal is the resort of Las Galeras, continue east from Samaná on Route 5, following the signposts when they cut north into Las Galeras. Should you be going to Las Terrenas on the north coast of Samaná, leave the town of Sánchez and follow the secondary road northeast to the coast, cutting through some of the interior of the Peninsula of La Samaná.

Driving to Samaná is so difficult you'd anticipate an efficient air service. Not so. As of now, there is no regularly scheduled service to this tourist-trodden peninsula. You have to charter flights aboard **Takeoff Destination Service S.A.** (© **809/522-1333;** www.takeoffweb.com). A small plane can be chartered for RD$5,400 ($194) for 3 passengers or else RD$24,000 ($864) for 15 passengers, all one way. Arrangements to charter a craft should be made at least 2 days in advance.

If you want to land on the southern coast, the plane will fly you to Aeropuerto Internacional Arroyo Barril, lying a 30-minute drive west of the town of Samaná. The airport for destinations along the north coast is Aeropuerto Internacional El Portillo, which is in the little hamlet 6km (3¾ miles) east of Las Terrenas. Charters leave from the Herrera airport at Santo Domingo or from the Punta Cana airport. Flight time from Herrera takes 30 minutes, or 40 minutes from Punta Cana.

1 Samaná

245km (152 miles) NE of Santo Domingo

The town of Samaná lies on the southern coast, east of the airport at Arroyo Barril and opening onto the scenic Bahía de Samaná. Known for its safe harbor, it was the former stamping ground of some of the Caribbean's most notorious pirates, including such ne'er-do-wells as England's Jack Banister, whose men killed 125 British soldiers when they came to arrest him. Banister escaped, although 40 of his pirates were killed in the melee.

Samaná (more formally known as Santa Bárbara de Samaná), is the main town of the peninsula, fronting a bay of tiny islands, sometimes called Banister Cays in honor of that notorious pirate. Columbus arrived here on January 12, 1493. After battling the Ciguayos Indians, he named the bay Golfo de las Flechas, or "the Gulf of Arrows."

If you stand along the water looking south, the two islets you'll see in the bay are Cayos Linares and Vigia.

In an ill-conceived urban renewal plan under President Balaguer, much of the atmosphere of old Samaná, with its narrow streets and

ATLANTIC OCEAN

ACCOMMODATIONS ■

Casa del Mar **1**
Club Bonito **2**
Coco Plaza Hotel **1**
Guatapanal Bahia
   de Cosón **1**
Iguana Hotel **1**
Moorea Beach **2**
Occidental Gran
   Bahia Hotel **4**
Plaza Lusitania **2**
Residence Colibri **1**
Tropic Banana **1**
Tropical Lodge **3**
Villa Serena **2**

DINING ◆

Casa Boga **1**
Chez Denise **2**
Club Bonito
   Restaurant **2**
La Hacienda **3**
El Bambus **3**
El Martinique Resort
   Restaurant **2**
La Yuca Restaurant
   y Pizzeria **1**
Rancho Suizo **1**

wrought-iron balconies, was destroyed, giving way to ugly concrete buildings and wide asphalt-paved boulevards.

As you arrive in town, expect to be overpowered by hard-to-shake English-speaking local hustlers who will try to sell you virtually anything from a hotel room to themselves.

Most activity centers along the main road running along the bay front, Avenida La Marina (most often called Malecón, or "sea wall").

VISITOR INFORMATION   As mentioned, there is no local government-sponsored tourist office. However, the somewhat misleadingly named **Samaná Tourist Service,** Av. La Marina 6 (© **809/ 538-3322;** www.samana.net), is a font of information about the area and can take care of most of your travel needs (see below). Hours are Monday to Saturday 8:30am to 12:30pm and 2:30 to 6pm.

GETTING AROUND

Most visitors walk around Samaná, renting a car only if they prefer to take an independent tour of the peninsula. **Sama Rental Moto,** Avenida Malecón 5 (© **809/538-2380**), is your best bet, renting economy-sized cars beginning at RD$1,500 ($54) per day. This outfitter also rents bikes for RD$125 ($4.50) daily.

FAST FACTS: SAMANA

If you need to make calls (hotels impose huge surcharges), you can go to the main office of the phone company, **Verizon,** Calle Santa Bárbara (© **809/220-7841**), open from Monday to Saturday 8am to 8pm, Sunday 8am to 2pm. They also offer Internet access, charging RD$30 ($1.10) for 30 minutes, RD$50 ($1.80) for 1 hour. For a pharmacy, go to **Farmacia Bahía,** Francisco del Rosario Sánchez 1 (© **809/538-2236**), open daily 8am to 9pm or **Farmacia Giselle,** Calle Santa Bárbara 2 (© **809/538-2303**), open Monday to Saturday 8am to 10pm and Sunday 8am to 1pm.

For money exchanges or an ATM, go to **Banco Popular,** Av. Malecón 4 (© **809/538-3666**), open Monday to Friday 8am to 4pm and Saturday 8am to 1pm. The **Samaná Post Office** is at Calle Santa Bárbara (© **809/538-2414**), open Monday to Friday 8:30am to noon and 2 to 5pm, Saturday 8am to noon. Offering emergency medical service 24 hours a day is **Centro Médico San Vicente,** Francisco del Rosario Sánchez 2 (© **809/538-2535**). For Internet access, go to **CompuCenter Samaná,** Calle Lavandier (© **809/538-3146**), open Monday to Friday 9am to 12:30pm and 3 to 6pm. The cost is RD$25 (90¢) for 30 minutes or RD$50 ($1.80) for 1 hour. The **Western Union** office is at Francisco del Rosario Sánchez 15 (© **809/538-2195**).

WHERE TO STAY

Occidental Gran Bahía Hotel   This is our favorite nest on the peninsula, an ocean-fronting Victorian-inspired hotel that's an architectural network of fretwork, gables, and *Addams Family* gables and turrets. Bedrooms are spacious and tastefully and comfortably furnished with Caribbean flair, including island watercolors, cool tile floors, and flamboyant floral prints. The four-level building is painted in a startling lime and black, and the inn has been going strong since the early '90s. Every accommodation comes with a tiled bathroom with tub and shower. The hotel lies east of the center and is set on well-landscaped grounds with pools, watersports, and horse stables.

Carretera Samaná/Los Cacaos, Samaná, Dominican Republic. ② 809/538-3111. Fax 809/538-2764. www.occidentalhotels.com. 113 units. Year-round US$208–US$288 double; US$230–US$314 junior suite. Rates are all-inclusive. AE, MC, V. Free parking. **Amenities:** 2 restaurants; 2 bars; 2 outdoor pools; health club; watersports equipment; laundry service; horseback riding. *In room:* A/C, TV, kitchenette, safe, fan.

Tropical Lodge ⚿ *Finds*   Brigitte and Jean-Philippe Merand operate one of the best inns on the peninsula, and have been in business for some two decades. At the end of the Malecón, they are in the center but still set back from the bull's-eye core, with its noise and bustling atmosphere. Their bedrooms are a bit small but still comfortably and tastefully furnished, with small, shower-only bathrooms. The best accommodations open onto a private balcony. The hotel staff will help book you on many jaunts in the area; everything from Jeep safaris to horseback riding and waterfall visits, along with sailing, fishing, and biking trips. The kitchen staff is skilled at turning out both Dominican and continental fare, and, for more fast food, there is also a cafeteria and pizzeria. In the tropical garden is a pool with a Jacuzzi constructed on a hill fronting the bustling Malecón.

Av. La Marina, Samaná, Dominican Republic. ② 809/538-2480. Fax 809/538-2068. www.tropical-lodge.com. 17 units. Year-round US$40–US$70 double. Children 2–12 pay 50% of adult rate. Rates include breakfast. AE, MC, V. Free parking. **Amenities:** Restaurant; cafeteria; pizzeria; outdoor pool. *In room:* A/C, TV, fan.

WHERE TO DINE

El Bambus ⚿   DOMINICAN/INTERNATIONAL   By the beach, this is one of the best restaurants at this little port, lying along the seafront. All the tasty main dishes are served with side dishes, including freshly cooked vegetables. A peninsula favorite is the fresh catch of the day, which can be prepared several ways, including grilled. For real Caribbean flair, order it with coconut sauce. Fresh shrimp is garlic flavored, as are the pork chops, which are grilled. Deep-fried chicken is the favorite dish of the locals. Freshly made salads, and such eternal favorites as spaghetti and steaks are also served, along with one of the best arrays of seafood in town.

Av. La Marina 3, Samaná, Dominican Republic. ② 809/538-2495. Main courses RD$200–RD$350 ($7.20–$13). No credit cards. Daily 7am–11pm.

La Hacienda   DOMINICAN/INTERNATIONAL/FRENCH Of the many expat dives along the Malecón, this is a good choice for gourmet international dishes and some expertly prepared French selections such as a marvelous shellfish bouillabaisse, the main reason we visit the place. A selection of grilled seafood is set out nightly to entice you. The chefs also prepare octopus, which one satisfied diner recommended to us as "divine." Grilled loin of beefsteak is another favorite, along with fried Dominican chicken.

Av. La Marina 6, Samaná, Dominican Republic. ✆ 809/538-2383. Reservations recommended in winter. Main courses RD$190–RD$600 ($6.85–$22). No credit cards. Daily 5–11:30pm; Aug and Dec–Mar daily 11am–midnight. Closed Wed off-season.

BEACHES ALONG THE COAST

The beaches aren't in the town of Samaná itself, except for a stretch of sand at the foot of a steep road leading over to **Bahía Escondido.** To reach the best beaches, you have to go farther afield.

All the beaches either west or east of the town of Samaná can be reached by *guaguas* (small buses or vans) that run to the sands frequently throughout the day and can be hailed along the road.

Moments   Whale-Watching

Since untold millennia, humpback whales have used Bahía de Samaná as a breeding ground and nursery. Even Columbus encountered these mammoth mammals in 1493, as noted in his journal.

After cruising the North Atlantic, where they are often killed, the **whales** 𝖆𝖆𝖆 return to the sanctuary and warm waters of Samaná in December. The colony slowly grows until the end of January, when there are some 4,000 humpbacks in the bay.

It's an awesome sight watching these whales engage in their courting rituals, as the males track down compliant females. It's also enthralling to listen to whale songs—that is, a bizarre melody of chirps and moans. After a one-year gestation period, babies are born, weighing a ton.

For the best tours, go to the pioneer herself, Kim Beddal, a marine biologist from Canada. Her agency's whale-watching tours are the best and offered by **Victoria Marine,** Avenida La Marina (✆ 809/538-2494; www.whalesamana. com), in front of the port at Samaná. Tours, costing RD$1,372 ($49) per person, are offered from January 15 to March 20. Tours leave daily at 9am, returning at 1pm.

Samaná Tourist Service, Avenida La Marina 6 (✆ 809/538-3322; www.samana.net), also offers whale-watching jaunts from January to late March, costing RD$1,960 ($70) per person.

A series of good sandy beaches also lie east of Samaná on the road to Las Galeras (see below). A "secret" beach is **Playa El Valle,** which is isolated and cut off from the main Route 5 by steep mountains. It is reached by following a tortuous road for 11km (6¾ miles) north of Samaná.

A more approachable beach lies 5km (3 miles) east of Samaná. **Playa Las Flechas** is reached by going along Carretera Las Galeras. Historically, this beach was the site of the first battle between Native Americans and Europeans.

Near the mouth of Bahía de Samaná, **Cayo Levantado** ⋳⋳ lies 7km (4¼ miles) southeast of Samaná. Here in the midst of luxuriant tropical vegetation you will find a trio of lovely beaches of white sand. These beaches are on an island but can be easily reached by public transportation.

You can also travel independently to the island, as various boats leave daily from 8:30 to 11am, with the last return at 4pm. There is no central ferry service, and departures of these boats are from the Samaná Pier Marina. Since the boats are independently owned, fares can vary based on what each boatman charges, but expect to pay RD$135 ($4.85) round-trip.

Cayo Levantado was the original Bacardi Rum island photographed in a famous ad campaign that ran on TV in the '70s. Regrettably, the famous swaying palm featured in the ad was uprooted in a tropical storm. Yet hundreds of its siblings are still here to shade you when you're not racing across the white sands.

Once at Cayo Levantado, and should you tire of the beach, you can take one of the trails that crisscross the island; one leads to a promontory on the southern tier of the island, the lookout point opening onto panoramic views. Yet another trail cuts across to the western side of the island, with a beautiful beach on a secluded bay.

PARQUE NACIONAL LOS HAITISES ⋳⋳

On the southern tier of Samaná Peninsula, this sprawling mass is the country's second-most visited park, covering 202 sq. km (78 sq. miles) and spanning 24km (15 miles) west from Boca de Inferno and Bahía de San Lorenzo to the head of Río Barracote, that river at the western end of Bahía de Samaná. The park can only be visited by boat (see below).

The park, which is actually a mammoth expanse of mangrove swamp, is home to 112 bird species, nearly 100 plant species, a mammoth variety of marine life, and several Taíno caves once inhabited by the island's original settlers.

The interior of the park is almost impenetrable, the home of a dense rainforest that is eerily punctuated by the ruins of sugar plantations "gone with the wind." On the boat tours offered, you will get to view mangrove rivers with tiny islets and coastal caves that today are the habitat of rainbow-hued tropical birds, such as the jacana or the Hispaniolan parakeet.

The mangroves aren't necessarily green, but red or white in color. You'll think you're in an aviary with flocks of roseate terns, frigate birds, ruddy ducks, snow-white egrets, narrow-billed todies, white-cheeked pintails, grebes, and the Ridgway's hawk, along with double-breasted cormorants, coots, solenodons, hutias, and the stunning blue heron. Falcons fly overhead.

At least three caves contain pre-Columbian drawings. The best of these is the stunning Cueva San Gabriel because of its stalactites and stalagmites. Some of the most notorious pirates in the Caribbean were said to have hung out in these caves, including Jack Banister and John Rackham.

At the entrance to Cueva de la Línea you'll see a long row of rocks which are the remains of a railroad erected more than 50 years ago as part of a long-abandoned railway to ship sugar cane.

Near the entrance to Cueva Arena is a most unhelpful ranger station, with some bored attendants charging an entrance fee of RD$50 ($1.80).

Entrance to the park is at a port of entry, Cana Hondo, a small pier. Getting here is not easy, as you must endure a 19km (12-mile) passage along an often rough sea.

Samaná Tourist Service, Av. La Marina 6 (✆ **809/538-3322**), offers daily tours to Los Haïtises, costing RD$1,960 ($70) per person and including lunch and drinks. **Victoria Marine,** Avenida La Marina (✆ **809/538-2494**), runs tours to the park only Wednesday and Friday, leaving at 9:30am with a return at 4:30pm, costing RD$1,372 ($49) per person.

Transporte Marítimo Minadiel, Av. La Marina 3 (✆ **809/538-2556**), offers combined tours of the park as well as Cayo Levantado (see above). Tours leave around 9:30am daily, returning at 4pm and costing RD$700 ($25) without food or RD$980 ($35) with food and drink included. A tour just to the park costs RD$476 ($17), with a tour to Cayo Levantado going for RD$224 ($8). On the Cayo Levantado tour, you can also take a jaunt that includes food and drink for RD$420 ($15).

A final operator, **Colonial Tour and Travel,** Plaza Comercial Tío Billy 13 (© **809/240-6822;** www.colonialtours.com.do), offers combined tours to the Parque and Cayo Levantado on Monday to Friday 9am to 12:30pm and 2:30 to 5pm, costing RD2,240 ($80) with meals and drinks or RD$1,960 ($70) without.

SAMANA AFTER DARK

Many visitors head for one of the bars or outdoor restaurants along the Malecón and make an evening of it. Many of these are expat joints, and some of them come and go with such frequency that a guidebook can't keep up-to-date with places that change from season to season.

That doesn't matter. All you have to do is stroll along the waterfront and check out the current favorites. You'll be blasted away by blaring merengue. There is a trio of discos nearby that also change their stripes frequently.

If you're a woman traveling alone (or women in groups), expect a heavy dose of machismo if you patronize many of the waterfront bars. Men traveling alone can anticipate offers from prostitutes, both female and male.

2 Las Galeras

26km (16 miles) NE of Samaná

Lying northeast from the town of Samaná, Las Galeras practically didn't exist until the early '90s. At the end of a scenic road, you approach this quaint, little remote settlement known for its half-mile of white sandy beach, which is what put it on the map in the first place.

Being transported to La Samaná on a *guagua* in 1 hour is half the fun. Small beaches opening onto a crashing surf from the Bahía de Samaná, coconut plantations, secluded beaches, limestone outcrops, and exotic trees, such as the tamarind, are just some of the sites you'll see as you bump up and down along a bad (but paved) road that rises and falls across the hilly, undulating terrain.

Before foreign visitors discovered it, Las Galeras was a mere fishing village with seemingly hundreds of coconut palms with fronds blowing in the trade winds.

Learning the lay of the land in Las Galeras doesn't require a degree in geography. There's only one main artery, Calle A, running through the little resort. Calle A runs parallel to the beach.

In lieu of a tourist office, many of the local, English-speaking visitors seem friendly and only too willing to help a bewildered visitor. What's the downside to paradise? Las Galeras, in spite of its setting in an area of great natural beauty, is one hell of a humid and hot place, and U.S. and Canadian visitors used to summer air-conditioning might find it tough going here. The cheaper rentals, and even some of the better hotels and inns, aren't air-conditioned. Locals are used to the heat, but you may not be.

GETTING AROUND   Since Las Galeras lies in a luxuriant and remote part of the Dominican Republic, you might consider renting a Jeep or a small car if you don't mind potholed roads. The surrounding terrain is Jungle Jim country, and there are many beautiful but secluded beaches within a short distance of Las Galeras. Chances are, you might discover an isolated playa just for you and yours. **Samaná Rent-a-Motor,** Calle A (✆ **809/538-0208**), offers Hondas for RD$1,260 ($45) per day, with a sometimes much-needed 4WD Jeep going for RD$1,820 ($65) per day. You can also rent bikes and motorcycles here. Motorcycles, incidentally, cost RD$700 ($25) per day. Open Monday to Friday 9am to 1pm and 3 to 6pm, and Saturday and Sunday 9am to 1pm.

A competitor is **Caribe Fun Rentals,** Calle A (✆ **809/538-0109**), where most car rentals range from RD$1,680 to RD$2,100 ($60–$75) per day, depending on the make. It's open Monday to Saturday 9am to noon and 3 to 6:30pm, Sunday 9am to noon.

Both car-rental companies provide area maps, offering information about driving in this part of the country, and their employees speak English.

Without a car, you can rely on one of the *motoconchos* that run throughout the area all day. You might see an occasional independently operated taxi or two, but don't count on it.

WHERE TO STAY

Club Bonito 🏖🏖   This is one of the better resort hotels in this part of eastern Dominican Republic. The place is small and family owned, and the inn is known for its freshly prepared food based on some of the season's best ingredients. The staff is one of the most helpful in the area, often organizing beach barbecues or picnics. They always seem to have an ice-cold beer handy for you or a fruit-based tropical punch. The building, from the late '80s, opens onto a good beachfront, and rooms on the third floor get the best sea breezes, although Club Bonito is one of the few hotels in the area with much-needed air-conditioning. The bedrooms are spacious and most comfortable in this adobe structure, each with terraces or private balconies. More than a dozen of the bedrooms also come with sitting areas. Our favorites are three rooms with king-sized four-poster beds with canopies and Jacuzzi. Many other hotels envy Club Bonito's summer place, the best place to be on an August day.

Calle Principal, Las Galeras, Dominican Republic. © 809/538-0203. Fax 809/538-0061. www.club-bonito.com. 21 units. Year-round US$111–US$176 double. Children 4–12 50% of adult rate. Rates include American breakfast and dinner. AE, MC, V. Free parking. **Amenities:** Restaurant; 2 bars; outdoor pool; watersports equipment; bikes, salon; massage; laundry service; limited mobility rooms; badminton. *In room:* A/C in 18 units, safe, fan.

Moorea Beach   This is a well-run and affordable hotel built in a typical whitewashed Dominican style, with balconies, and everything lying under a tiled roof and shaded by coconut palms. Under Greek-German expat management, it is one of the town's favorites. In business since the mid '90s, this is a three-story building with vaguely colonial overtones. The midsize bedrooms are simply but comfortably decorated with Dominican wood furnishings, each coming with a small tiled bathroom with shower. Bedrooms are cooled by ceiling fans over a queen-size bed or two doubles. In summer this place can get awfully hot during the day. The hotel lies 148m (492 ft.) from a sandy beach.

Las Galeras, Dominican Republic. © 809/538-0007. Fax 809/538-0202. www.hotel moorea.com. 8 units. Year-round US$40–US$60 double; US$60–US$80 apt. Children 6–12 US$10 extra. Rates include breakfast. AE, MC, V. Free parking. **Amenities:** Pool. *In room:* Safe, fan.

Plaza Lusitania *(Value)*   This place is a bit rawboned but well maintained and a friendly oasis. It's recommended mainly because it charges prices known to travelers in the 1960s. Launched around the time of the millennium, it is a colonial-style complex of apartments. All are painted white and are midsize, each furnished with local island pieces resting on cool tiled floors. Each also comes equipped with a little kitchenette and a small bathroom with tub and shower. The bedrooms rest on the second floor above a grocery store and restaurant. Amazingly, for such a cheap rental in the area, air-conditioning is mercifully provided. There's many a muggy night here. The food is good, solid Dominican fare—nothing more.

Calle Principal, Las Galeras, Dominican Republic. © 809/538-0093. Fax 809/538-0066. www.plazalusitania.com. 10 units. Year-round US$53 double. AE, MC, V. Free parking. **Amenities:** Restaurant. *In room:* A/C, kitchenette.

Villa Serena 🍷🍷 This hotel was built in the early 1990s along the lines of a rambling, two-story Victorian house with a wrap-around balcony lying 100m (328 ft.) from the sea. Painted white with a blue-green roof and a large front garden, it sits above a rocky coastline, a 3-minute walk from a relatively uncrowded beach. Each accommodation has a private balcony and a decor that's different from its neighbors—yours might be Chinese, neoclassical gold-and-white, or Laura Ashley romantic. The more expensive rooms are air-conditioned; others have ceiling fans. The beds are most comfortable here, and the bathrooms, which have tub/shower combos, are tidily kept. Conceived for honeymooners, and anyone else who's looking for a place to escape urban life, the site is quiet, isolated, and low-key, with little to do other than swim in the oval-shaped pool, visit the beach, read, and chat with other guests. Many guests order lunch from operators of small charcoal grills set up on the beach (simple platters of pork or fish). The in-house restaurant, however, is the best of the three or four mainstream restaurants in Las Galeras, opening every day for breakfast, lunch, and dinner.

Las Galeras, Dominican Republic. ☎ **809/538-0000.** Fax 809/538-0009. www.villa serena.com. 21 units. Year-round US$130–US$150 double with A/C; US$120–US$140 double with fan. Children 2–12 50% adult rate. Rates include breakfast. MC, V. Free parking. **Amenities:** Restaurant; outdoor pool; bikes; kayaks. *In room:* A/C (in some units), fan.

WHERE TO DINE

We gravitate to that array of ramshackle Dominican fish shacks that are found by the entrance to Playa Las Galeras, the local beach. The fish is fresh and caught that day, and eating seafood on the beach is the way to go. On the negative side, when the vendors hear the sound of a foreign voice, they double the price of their tantalizing food.

Chez Denise FRENCH/INTERNATIONAL Denise Flahaire, the owner, operates what has been a local favorite with the expat community here for some two decades. This is a casual and informal restaurant, but the food coming out of the kitchen is most often delicious. The setting is Caribbean in style, a proper venue for dining on some good-tasting dishes prepared with fresh ingredients whenever possible. The local catch of the day is hauled in here and often appears on your plate cooked in coconut milk with potatoes and fresh vegetables. Such favorite dishes as beef stew or lasagna also appear with frequency, as does a shellfish-studded paella. The crepes are a specialty.

Carretera Samaná, Las Galeras, Dominican Republic. ☎ **809/538-0219.** Main courses RD$80–RD$300 ($2.90–$11). No credit cards. Daily Mon–Sat 8am–11pm.

Club Bonito Restaurant INTERNATIONAL/FRENCH/ DOMINICAN   In this previously recommended hotel, cooks turn out a cuisine hardly Nuevo Latino, relying on tried-and-true recipes for appeal. It is an unassuming and rather charmingly authentic place in a beautiful setting right by the sea. The food is both delicious and freshly prepared. The palate is won over by such dishes as the freshly caught fish of the day simmered in coconut milk. For a more elegant French touch, that same fish can be served in a white wine sauce. If you don't want fish, you'll find all sorts of succulent pastas, even a large T-bone steak, on the menu.

Calle Principal, Las Galeras, Dominican Republic. ✆ **809/538-0203.** Reservations not required. Main courses RD$120–RD$500 ($4.23–$17). AE, MC, V. Daily 7:30am– 10pm.

El Marinique Resort Restaurant 🍴 *Finds*   One visiting German woman from Düsseldorf helped us discover this place. "I was alone in a foreign country, and they practically adopted me," said Greta H. Keller. We agreed with her assessment of this undiscovered place, finding a choice of different main courses each day, fresh ingredients, flavorful preparation, good service, and generous portions.

Guests check in here for "barefoot vacations," and often come back the next year. In this open-air restaurant, in business for nearly 2 decades, you can feast on the offerings of the day. We recently sampled the fresh catch of the day sautéed in garlic butter, our companion opting for the delectable grilled tuna. For those who want it, the chefs will always throw a T-bone steak on the grill.

Av. Malecón 6, Las Galeras, Dominican Republic. ✆ **809/538-0262.** Reservations required. Main courses RD$150–RD$350 ($5.40–$13). MC, V. Daily 7:30am–7:30pm. Closed Easter–Oct.

BEACHES, SCUBA DIVING & WHALE WATCHING

Condé Nast Traveler called **Playa Rincón** 🍴🍴🍴 "one of the top 10 playas in the Caribbean," and we concur. It's reason enough to go to Las Galeras. In the background appear the cliffs of Cape Cabrón at 600m (2,000 ft.).

If you're a beach buff, this is the one best beach on the peninsula, and you'll often have its sands to yourself. It's a pity that it's so inaccessible. A rocky road leads to it from Las Galeras, taking 40 minutes by Jeep along a rough track. A much easier way to go is to take a ferry departing daily from Dive Samaná, Calle las Galeras, and costing RD$100 ($3.60) for the 20-minute ride.

Coconut Cannons

You've heard of the dessert "death by chocolate." In the Dominican Republic, there's a twist on this: "death by coconut." The whole area is filled with coconut palms, which are remarkable for their beauty but can be lethal. Falling coconuts not only dent the hoods of cars but also shatter the windshields. These plummeting fruits can also be deadly missiles. People are killed every year on the island by coconuts falling from the sky. In a tropical storm, run for cover, as high winds can send a coconut shooting through the air like ammunition blasted from a cannon.

Many families from Santo Domingo come to Playa Rincón to camp out for the night as a base opening onto Bahía Rincón. The beach is tranquil, its waters calm, as it is protected by two large capes at each end. During the day the waters are a bright turquoise and are gin clear. This beach with interruptions stretches along a 7km (4¼-mile) stretch of diamond-white sands set against the backdrop of a coconut forest.

One daytime thrill from the southern tier of Playa Rincón is to take a 1km (½-mile) trail north to Río Frío. The waters of this river are freezing cold even in summer, but locals like to go here to wash off the sand and salt from Playa Rincón. In our view, there's no better place in the Dominican Republic for cooling off on a hot day. Facilities along this beach, other than a fish hut here or there, are very few. There's talk of big development, but right now you can wander like Robinson Crusoe, sometimes walking for a mile (1.6 km) before encountering another beach bum.

Of course, if you don't want to make that trek to Playa Rincón, all you have to do is walk out your door to discover the sands of **Playa Las Galeras** ⊛ itself. This half-mile beach of white sands lies in a tranquil and beautiful setting at the eastern end of Samaná Peninsula. Many foreign visitors practically never leave the beach all day, taking lunch at one of the fish huts that line parts of the beach. A small, palm-tree island lies out in the bay.

The adjoining beach of **Cala Blanca** is even more spectacular, a cliché of Caribbean charm with its tranquil turquoise waters and swaying palms. The offshore reef breaks the waves, so the waters are very gentle here, which makes this beach a particular favorite of families with young children.

Other beaches in the area, also lovely and filled with white sand, are more difficult to reach. To the immediate east is the beautiful beach, **Playa Madama,** ridged by crags and rocks and set against a cave-studded backdrop where some Taíno Indian petroglyphs have been discovered. The water is excellent for snorkeling here.

The adjoining **Playa Colorado** is another beautiful stretch of sand set against a backdrop of tropical planting, including coconut palms.

3 Las Terrenas

17km (11 miles) NE of Sánchez, 249km (155 miles) NE of Santo Domingo

On the La Samaná's north coast, this former fishing village has grown greatly since its discovery by expats, often from Switzerland and France, in the late '70s. Las Terrenas stands as one of the newest and emerging resorts of the Caribbean.

In an attempt to end urban slums in Santo Domingo, the dictator Trujillo began exporting people here in the 1940s, instructing them to make their living fishing and farming the land.

Of course, it was its beaches (see below) that put Las Terrenas on the tourist map, and these strips of golden or white sand remain its major attraction. Otherwise, there is very little to see and do here except hang out on the beach, eat seafood dinners at night, and frequent the beachfront merengue dives until the early hours.

If you ever tire of the beach, consider a day jaunt over to the El Limón waterfall. Otherwise, you'll find Las Terrenas one of the least formal and least structured resorts in the Dominican Republic.

GETTING AROUND   You don't need a car. *Motoconchos* and taxis will take you where you want to go—even to the airport at El Portillo where most rides there will cost RD$120 ($4.30) per person. Taxis and *motoconchos* are constantly traversing Las Terrenas, and all you have to do is hail one.

FAST FACTS: LAS TERRENAS

In lieu of a government tourist office, you can go to the offices of **Sunshine Services,** Calle del Carmen 151 (© **809/240-6164**), a travel agent. The staff here is very helpful and will provide information about the area and assist you in your travel needs. There's a TOURIST INFORMATION sign posted outside. Of course, this is a profit-making organization, and the English-speaking staff hopes to make some money off you by helping you in your travel arrangements. Hours are Monday to Saturday 9am to noon and 4 to 7pm.

A **Western Union** office is at Calle Principal 165 (© **809/240-6551**), open Monday to Saturday 8am to 6pm, Sunday 8am to noon. For the local phone company, head for **Verizon,** Calle Principal S/N (© **809/220-7412**), open daily 8am to 10pm. Internet access is also possible here, costing RD$21 (75¢) for 30 minutes or RD$42 ($1.50) for 1 hour.

For a police, fire, or medical emergency, dial **911.**

The most central pharmacies are **Farmacia De La Plaza,** Calle Principal 6 (© **809/240-5708**), open Monday to Saturday 8am to 7pm, and also **Farmacia R y R,** Ramon Matia Mella 8 (© **809/240-6135**), open Monday to Thursday 8am to 7pm, Friday 8am to 6pm, Saturday 7am to 10pm, and Sunday 8am to 10pm.

To exchange money, go to **Banco del Progreso,** Calle Duarte at Plaza El Paseo de la Costanera (© **809/240-6409**), open Monday to Friday 9am to 3:30pm and Saturday 9am to 1pm.

WHERE TO STAY

Casa del Mar ⭐ Katherine Chately, who bought Casa del Mar in 2004, welcomes you to this series of bungalows that lie only 25m (82 ft.) from the golden sands. The little inn offers good value in its series of pleasantly furnished and comfortable bungalow rooms, with terraces and a tropical garden setting. Accommodations are midsize and well organized, each with a tiled bathroom with a shower. In business since 1997, the hotel doesn't have air-conditioning. Mosquito netting protects the beds. A continental breakfast is served, and there is a restaurant next to the hotel operated under separate management.

Calle del Portillo 1, Las Terrenas-Samaná, Dominican Republic. © **809/360-2748.** Fax 809/240-6070. 8 units. Year-round US$45–US$50 double. Rates include breakfast. No credit cards. Free parking. **Amenities:** Breakfast served in garden setting. *In room:* Safe, fan.

Coco Plaza Hotel ⭐ *Kids* Lying southeast of the center, this hotel opens on a good beach, Playa Las Ballenas. This is a Mediterranean-styled building also close to the much-frequented Playa Cacao. Run by Italian expats, the building rents midsize bedrooms that are tastefully and comfortably decorated, each with a tiled bathroom with a tub/shower combination. Families often stay here for two reasons: Management is very family friendly, and meals can be prepared in the small kitchens in some units (the studios and apartments), cutting down on food costs. The most luxurious way to stay here is to request a spacious penthouse apartment, one of the best accommodations at this resort.

Calle Chicago Boss 2, Las Terrenas-Samaná, Dominican Republic. © **809/240-6172.** jesuscanpelo@hotmail.com. 20 units. Year-round US$42–US$70 double; US$60– US$100 suite; US$70–US$140 apts. AE, MC, V. Free parking. **Amenities:** Breakfast room. *In room:* A/C, TV, kitchenette, safe, ceiling fan.

Guatapanal Bahía de Cosón ♠   This is the first government-rated four-star hotel to open on Samaná, and it's the best place to stay on the peninsula, opening onto a white, sandy beach. The trip along the unpaved road doesn't look too promising, but when you come to the end at this first-class place, and are greeted with a waterfall, the hotel looks like Eden in the tropics. In well-landscaped grounds underneath the sheltering palms, the hotel became an immediate hit when it opened its door.

Comfortably furnished standard bedrooms open onto private terraces or balconies, most of them with views of the ocean. Each comes with a private bathroom, coated in tile and furnished with shower and tub. The English-speaking hotel staff is helpful in arranging excursions, including everything from whale-watching expeditions to treks through National Park Los Haïtises.

The food is plentiful, varied, and made, for the most part, with market-fresh ingredients. Dominican theme dinners are a regular feature, and there is also a pasta and pizzeria dining selection. The location is 12.8km (8 miles) from the airport at El Portillo and 8km (5 miles) from the village of Las Terrenas.

Playa Cosón, Las Terrenas-Samaná, Dominican Republic. © **809/240-5050.** Fax 809/ 240-5536. www.guatapanal.com.do. 208 units. Winter US$77; US$84 suite; US$151 villa. Off-season US$68 double; US$75; US$96 villa. Rates are per person daily and all-inclusive. AE, MC, V. **Amenities:** 3 restaurants; 4 bars; outdoor pool; watersports equipment; car-rental desk; disco; dive shop. *In room:* A/C, TV, hair dryer, safe.

Iguana Hotel ♠ *(Kids)*   A real discovery, this series of bungalows rented out by French expats lies 720m (2,362 ft.) from a beautiful sandy beach protected by a barrier of corals. A tranquil, secluded hotel, reached by a sandy path, it offers bungalows spread across its grounds that house two to four persons comfortably. As such, this is a good choice for families. Decorations are in a simple Caribbean style, and the bedrooms are small, each with a private bathroom with shower. The bungalows lie in parklike grounds, far removed from the traffic, especially those noisy mopeds.

Playa Las Vallenas, Las Terrenas-Samaná, Dominican Republic. © **809/249-4066.** Fax 809/240-6070. www.iguana-hotel.com. 10 units. Year-round US$50–US$70 double; US$100–US$120 3–4 persons. Rates include American breakfast. No credit cards. Free parking. **Amenities:** Bar; babysitting; barbecue grill; children's beds; kitchen for clients. *In room:* Safe, fan.

Residence Colibrí 🐦 *Kids*   Launched in 2000, these are a series of fairly elegant apartments for the area, spread across palm-studded grounds in three-story buildings overlooking the beach, one of the best strips of sand at the resort. Close to the center of Las Terrenas, but somewhat protected from the noise, the apartments are very modern and spacious, each comfortably furnished with tropical furnishings painted in pastels. Each unit comes with a small tiled bathroom with shower. Families like to stay here because the apartments have fully equipped kitchenettes, each opening onto a balcony with a view, often of the swimming and Jacuzzi. The complex takes its name, *colibrí,* from the hummingbirds seen picking nectar from the red hibiscus bushes in the flower beds. Included in the rates are linens and bath towels along with maid service twice a week. On request, a full-time maid can be provided, as can a private cook. On site is a restaurant and bar run by different people and definitely not recommended.

Calle Francisco Tamayo, Las Terrenas-Samaná, Dominican Republic. © **809/240-6434.** Fax 809/240-6917. www.playacolibri.com. 45 units. Year-round US$50–US$75 double; US$80–US$110 for 4. MC, V. Free parking. **Amenities:** Outdoor pool; babysitting. *In room:* Kitchenette, safe, fan.

Tropic Banana 🐦   In a tropical park of 2.8 hectares (7 acres), this hotel opens onto a beach of golden sands, lying a 15-minute ride from the Portillo airstrip. It is set against a backdrop of rolling hills and mountains and is a real escapist retreat. Bedrooms are pleasantly and comfortably furnished, ranging from small to midsize, each with a tiled bathroom with shower. Newly renovated rooms are spread across two buildings on two levels, the hotel dating from the late '70s. The top-floor rooms open onto a private balcony, the lower floor units onto a terrace. A French-run tropical hotel, the inn offers a restaurant serving an excellent French and international cuisine. Every Friday is devoted to sushi prepared from the freshest of the day's catch. The on-site bar is rather exotic and worth a visit on your night-time prowl. Filled with rattan furnishings, it opens onto a sea view.

Calle Francisco Alberto Camaño, Las Terrenas-Samaná, Dominican Republic. © **809/240-6110.** www.las-terrenas-hotels.com. 21 units. Year-round US$70–US$110 double; US$145–US$170 triple. Children 2–12 US$10 extra. Rates include breakfast. MC, V. Free parking. **Amenities:** Restaurant; bar; outdoor pool; billiards; library; gift shop; TV room. *In room:* A/C, safe, fan.

WHERE TO DINE

To eat as the islanders do, head west of the mouth of Río Las Terrenas to a series of fishermen's huts, which become virtual sea-bordering restaurants under a thatch roof. With a Presidente beer resting beside your plate, dig into the catch of the day, which is most often served fried. If it's raining (highly unlikely), you'll find that a few of these shacks have tables under roofs. Otherwise, you dine outside under the stars.

Casa Boga ⋆ *Finds* BASQUE/SEAFOOD   Launched right before the beginning of the millennium, this restaurant has become an enduring fixture on the local dining scene, lying in front of Paseo de la Costanera. Light and satisfying meals prepared with fresh ingredients put this place on the map, where it looks like it's around to stay. Some of the dishes are Basque inspired, and many savvy Spanish diners consider that cuisine the finest in their country.

Begin, perhaps, with an inspired tuna carpaccio, and then select from a wide variety of fish, the individual offerings depending on the catch of the day. The fish can be grilled almost to your specifications, and platters are always served with mixed, freshly made salads and fried yucca. Various white fish can also be sautéed in garlic and onion, and tuna fish is fried with green peppers and onions. For true Basque flavor, order the fresh mussels in a garlic-laced green sauce made with fresh herbs. The chefs also prepare the resort's best kettle of fish soup.

Playa de Las Terrenas. ℂ **809/240-6321.** Reservations recommended. Main courses RD$300–RD$750 ($11–$27). MC, V. Mon–Sat 12:30–11pm.

La Yuca Restaurant y Pizzeria ⋆ SPANISH   In front of Paseo de la Costanera, this restaurant, established in 2002, serves some of the resort's finest Spanish cuisine with a certain Dominican flavor. The local cooks here score points with budget-minded but ever-curious foreign gastronomes. The owners secure the best catch from the local fishermen, and then proceed to concoct a number of savory dishes from this sea harvest.

By the beach, the local dive serves the most savory seafood paella in Las Terrenas. Some diners, however, prefer the *parrillada mixta,* a medley of grilled seafood that often features octopus and fresh shrimp among other choice delicacies. Locally caught fish is herb flavored and then grilled on both sides to your specifications. Nothing on the menu costs a king's ransom, especially that savory kettle of seafood stew that was so succulently delicious that it immediately won our hearts. The pizzeria has 15 different toppings available for pizzas, and prices range from RD$170 to RD$340 ($6.10–$12).

Calle Libertad 6. ℂ **809/240-6634.** Main courses RD$75–RD$660 ($2.70–$24). AE, MC, V. Daily 11am–11:30pm.

Rancho Suizo *Value* STEAKHOUSE A "Swiss Ranch" sounds like an oxymoron, but this eatery, dating from the late '90s, serves the best cuts and the tenderest steaks along the northern coast of Samaná peninsula. The reason behind the unusual name is a Swiss expat, named Christian Wiedmer, who formerly owned the restaurant. The new owner, Patrik Muller, who is also Swiss, brings incredibly affordable dining to Las Terrenas, especially if you order one of the fixed-price meals.

Most savvy diners opt for a big platter containing the perfectly cooked T-bone steak with potatoes. More delicate is the entrecôte in a peppery sauce. If you don't want steak, you can order such eternal favorites as spaghetti in a Bolognese sauce made with fresh tomatoes, cheese fondue, barbecue, or raclette.

Carretera Portillo 45. ⓒ **809/240-6162.** Main courses RD$180–RD$600 ($6.50–$22). MC, V. Daily 8am–midnight.

BEACHES & OUTDOOR PURSUITS

The aptly named **Playa Bonita** *ⓕⓕ*, or "beautiful beach," at Punta Bonita lies only a 10-minute ride by *motoconcho* west from the heart of Las Terrenas.

Once here, you'll find a kilometer (½ mile) of golden sand set against the backdrop of coconut palms and a surf of clean waters. In the distance you can see several palm-studded islets. Humpbacked whales can be spotted off the coast in season.

The beach at Playa Bonita is far less discovered than the beach at Las Terrenas, and we prefer it for this reason. If you don't want transport to this beach, you can walk here along a coastal road that's often dirty, muddy, and rather steep. Some beach buffs walk along the water from Las Terrenas to Punta Bonita, but it's a tricky trek through marshlands.

Punta Bonita, beginning west of a lesser beach, Playa Las Ballenas, offers 13km (8 miles) of uninterrupted powdery white sand. With its tranquil waters, this is a great beach for snorkelers.

Back in Las Terrenas, you can enjoy some good beaches as well, including **Playa Cacao,** although these sands are more crowded, especially in winter. The beachfront at Las Terrenas stretches for 1.9km (1¼ miles) both east and west from the center. The waters are generally tranquil here, suitable for swimming. Projecting out is a coral reef at 98m (328 ft.) that is ideal for some excellent snorkeling.

Scuba divers wanting to explore the northern shore of La Samaná peninsula head for one of the peninsula's best dive outfitters, **Stellina Dive Center,** Playa Cacao (© **809/868-4415** or 809/240-6149), the office open daily from 9am to 1pm and 3 to 5pm. The staff here offers diving for all levels from beginner to advanced. A 1-day dive costs RD$840 ($30) with equipment provided, RD$700 ($25) without equipment. Night dives go for RD$1,120 ($40) per person, with equipment, RD$840 ($30) without equipment.

LAS TERRENAS AFTER DARK

The entire waterfront of Las Terrenas becomes festive at night, especially at the **Night Market,** on Friday, Saturday, and Sunday. This is a real happening experience where locals descend on the waterfront to sell Dominican food and liquor (most often rum) from stalls. Hastily assembled island bands play music, and the party goes on until early morning.

The hottest dance club at the resort is **Discoteca Nuevo Mundo,** Calle Duarte 250 (© **809/240-6414**), lying on the main road 197m (656 ft.) south of the local cemetery. Both locals and visitors of all ages frequent this dance club, with its recorded music, mainly merengue, salsa, house, and Latin rock. Three or four times a month they bring in a local or international band to amuse the masses, and on these nights, the joint is packed. Normally there's no cover, but such a charge is likely to be imposed on nights of live performances. It is open Sunday to Friday 9pm to 4:30am and Saturday 9pm to 6am.

8

Puerto Plata & the Amber Coast

Columbus wanted to establish a city at Puerto Plata and name it La Isabela. Unfortunately, a tempest detained him, so it wasn't until 1502 that Nicolás de Ovando founded Puerto Plata ("port of silver"). The port became the last stop for ships going back to Europe, their holds laden with treasures taken from the New World.

Puerto Plata appeals to a mass-market crowd that prefers less expensive, all-inclusive resorts. More accommodations of this kind continue to pop up on this coast, and yet many are still booked solid almost year-round. Surprisingly, it's estimated that 95% of all visitors to the north coast stay at an all-inclusive, usually in the Playa Dorada complex, and limit their exploration of the coast to a ride from the airport to their resort and back again. An unfortunate byproduct of the all-inclusive trend is that several excellent restaurants have been forced to close; in fact, the most popular dining choice along the coast now is Pizza Hut.

Most of the hotels are not actually in Puerto Plata itself but in a tourist zone called Playa Dorada, which consists of major hotels, a scattering of secluded condominiums and villas, a Robert Trent Jones Jr.–designed golf course, and a riding stable. Playa Dorada is in fact the largest all-inclusive resort complex on earth.

The northern coastline of the Dominican Republic, 299km (186 miles) of prime waterfront property, is known by some as the "Silver Coast." But today more and more people are referring to it as the "Amber Coast" because of the rich deposits of amber found here.

You need not confine your visit just to the resorts in and around Puerto Plata and Playa Dorada. To the east lie the emerging resort towns of Sosúa, once a prime center for those seeking sex in the sun, or Cabarete, the windsurfing capital of the Americas.

1 Puerto Plata & Playa Dorada

209km (130 miles) NW of Santo Domingo

The sun reflected so brilliantly off the sea that an explorer once likened it to silver coins.

The town of Puerto Plata has few tourist attractions and, although the center of the area, it must simply watch as most of the tourist business heads elsewhere, notably to Playa Dorada.

Even if you don't stay in Puerto Plata, consider it for a morning or afternoon visit, walking along its ocean-bordering promenade called the Malecón. Sometimes you can see dolphins frolicking at play, or a humpback whale in winter.

Puerto Plata also contains the Dominican Republic's most interesting amber museums. You can also take a cable car for the most dramatic view of the north coast from the top of Pico Isabel de Torres.

Playa Dorada, beginning only 1km (½ mile) east of Puerto Plata, is one of the greatest concentrations of hotels in all the Caribbean. It's reached along the coastal road from Puerto Plata. Its gorgeous beach of golden sand puts it on the tourist maps of the world. It's also the site of an 18-hole golf course and some casinos.

Some savvy visitors are bypassing Playa Dorada with its mass appeal and heading instead to **Playa Cofresi,** 5km (3 miles) east of Puerto Plata. This ocean-bordering resort also opens onto a beautiful beach of golden sands and has a few all-inclusives, although nothing to compare with the mammoth facilities of Playa Dorada. On Sundays, islanders themselves pour into Playa Cofresi, turning the beach into a giant house party, with the eating, drinking, picnicking, barbecues, and merengue lasting well into the night.

You can also find more hotels, plus a gorgeous golden sand beach, at the town of Luperón, lying to the west of Puerto Plata, an hour's drive.

ESSENTIALS

GETTING THERE   The international airport is east of Playa Dorado on the road to Sosúa. **American Eagle** (✆ **800/433-7300** in the U.S.; www.aa.com) has daily flights from San Juan, Puerto Rico, to Puerto Plata. The 2-hour flight costs between RD$5,600 and RD$11,760 ($200–$420) round-trip. Most of the Puerto Plata resorts are about a 40-minute drive from the airport.

Canadians reach Puerto Plata from such cities as Toronto or Montreal, a typical flight lasting 4 hours. From the west coast of Canada, most charter flights take 7 hours. See your travel agent for details. There are no regularly scheduled flights from Canada to Puerto Plata. Likewise, travel agents in Europe send customers on weekly charter flights, most of which are of 7-hour duration.

American Airlines (© 800/443-7300) also flies in daily from Miami (2 hr., 10 min.) and from New York (3½ hr.).

Takeoff Destination Service S.A. (© 809/522-1333; www.takeoffweb.com) no longer offers regularly scheduled flights from such Dominican destinations as Santo Domingo or Punta Cana. Today, it's necessary to call and make arrangements for flights, which can be chartered and shared with others to cut costs.

It's a rough ride if you take a bus to reach Puerto Plata, and you might share the ride with some chickens. **Caribe Express,** corner of José Eugenio Conjas, Plaza Caribe (© 809/586-6796), offers service to Santiago and on to Santo Domingo. Travel time is 1 hour to "second city" Santiago and 1½ hours to Santo Domingo. Buses run back and forth between the two cities daily from 6am to 7pm (last departures). **Metro Buses,** Calle 16 de Agosto, corner of Calle Beller (© 809/586-6062), also runs buses from Santo Domingo and Santiago to Puerto Plata (or vice versa) daily at the same times. A one-way fare from Santo Domingo to Puerto Plata costs RD$215 ($7.75).

From Santo Domingo, the 3½-hour drive directly north on Autopista Duarte passes through the lush Cibao Valley, home of the tobacco industry and Bermudez rum, and through Santiago de los Caballeros, the second-largest city in the country, 145km (90 miles) north of Santo Domingo.

GETTING AROUND   **Avis** (© 800/331-1212 in the U.S., or 809/586-0214; www.avis.com), **Budget** (© 800/472-3325 in the U.S., or 809/586-0284; www.budget.com), and **Hertz** (© 800/654-3131 in the U.S., or 809/586-0200; www.hertz.com) all have offices at the airport.

You probably won't need to rent a car, however, if you're staying at one of the all-inclusive resorts. You might just like to get around Puerto Plata by **motor scooter,** although the roads are potholed. You can rent a scooter at the guest services kiosk at just about any large hotel in Puerto Plata.

Minivans are another means of transport, especially if you're traveling outside town. They leave from Puerto Plata's Central Park and will take you all the way to Sosúa. Determine the fare before getting

Puerto Plata

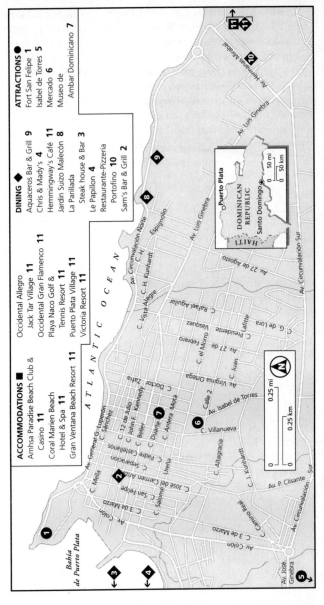

ACCOMMODATIONS ■
Amhsa Paradise Beach Club & Casino **11**
Coral Marien Beach Hotel & Spa **11**
Gran Ventana Beach Resort **11**
Occidental Allegro Jack Tar Village **11**
Occidental Gran Flamenco **11**
Playa Naco Golf & Tennis Resort **11**
Puerto Plata Village **11**
Victoria Resort **11**

DINING ◆
Aquaceros Bar & Grill **9**
Chris & Mady's **4**
Hemmingway's Café **11**
Jardin Suizo Malecón **8**
La Parillada Steak house & Bar **3**
Le Papillon **4**
Restaurante-Pizzeria Portofino **10**
Sam's Bar & Grill **2**

ATTRACTIONS ●
Fort San Felipe **1**
Isabel de Torres **5**
Mercado **6**
Museo de Ambar Dominicano **7**

ATLANTIC OCEAN

Bahia de Puerto Plata

DOMINICAN REPUBLIC
HAITI
Puerto Plata
Santo Domingo
0   50 mi
0   50 km

0   0.25 mi
0   0.25 km

151

in. Usually a shared ride between Puerto Plata and Sosúa costs RD$42 to RD$56($1.50–$2) per person. Service is daily from 6am to 9pm.

If you take a **taxi,** agree with the driver on the fare before your trip starts, as cabs are not metered. You'll find taxis on Central Park in Puerto Plata. At night, it's wise to rent your cab for a round-trip. If you go in the daytime by taxi to any of the other beach resorts or villages, check on reserving a vehicle for your return trip. A taxi from Puerto Plata to Sosúa will cost around RD$560 ($20) each way (for up to four occupants).

VISITOR INFORMATION   There's an **Office of Tourism** on Playa Long Beach (© **809/586-3676**). Hours are Monday to Friday 8:30am to 3:30pm.

FAST FACTS   Round-the-clock **drugstore** service is offered by **Farmacia Deleyte,** Calle John F. Kennedy 89 (© **809/586-2583**). Emergency medical service is provided by **Clínica Dr. Brugal,** Calle José del Carmen Ariza 15 (© **809/586-2519**). Medical services are also provided at Hospital Clínica Dr. José Regorio Gregora Hernández, 27 de Febrero 21 (© **809/586-1166**), maintaining 24-hour emergency service. The **Clínica Dental** is at Av. Juan Pablo Duarte 80, Galerías Las Bromelias 33 (© **809/971-5689**). To summon the **police** in Puerto Plata, Calle Luis Ginêbra, call © **809/586-2331.** If you need to visit in person, the address is Avenida Luis Ginêbra 14. The office of the local **Western Union** is at Playa Plaza Dorada (© **809/320-2501**), open daily from 8am to 9:45pm.

Because so many Canadian visitors descend on Puerto Plata annually, that country has opened a consulate at Virginia e Ortea, Edificio Isabel de Torres (Suite 311-C) at Puerto Plata (© **809/586-5761**), Monday to Friday 9am to 1pm.

The **U.K. Consulate** is at Beller 51 (© **809/586-4244**), open Monday to Friday 8:15am to 12:30pm The **U.S. Consulate** is at César Nicolas Penson (© **809/221-2171**), open Monday to Friday 7:30am to 4pm.

For Internet access, go to **SR Systems,** Carretera Puerto Plata and Maimon (© **809/320-1603**), where the charge is RD$196 ($7) per half hour or RD$364 ($13) for 1 hour. **Interconnect Service** is at Calle Rafael Aguilar 11 (© **809/586-2227**), charging RD$15 (55¢) per half hour or RD$30 ($1.10) per hour.

For money exchange or banks with ATMs, head for **Banco BHD,** Calle San Felipe (© **809/320-7919**), Monday to Friday 8am to 4pm; **Banco del Progreso,** Calle Beller 33 (© **809/320-0504**), open Monday to Friday 8:30am to 3pm, Saturday 9am to 1pm.

WHERE TO STAY
THE PLAYA DORADA ALL-INCLUSIVES

Note: Virtually no one checks in on the rates given below. Travel agents can book people in on some discounted package deal virtually any time of the year, even in the high season of winter.

AMHSA Paradise Beach Club & Casino *(R) (Kids)* This all-inclusive resort at the beach is the best-positioned of all the Playa Dorada hotels, with superior amenities and a well-trained staff. It also boasts an eco-friendly design: a cluster of Caribbean-Victorian low-rises with white-tile roofs and lattice-laced balconies. Brick paths cut through the well-manicured, tropical grounds, and kids have room to romp. Accommodations are neatly furnished with tile floors, twin or queen-size beds, refrigerators (in most cases), large closets, and tiled bathrooms with shower/tub combinations. Most rooms have French doors leading to private patios or balconies. Only the suites have views opening onto the water.

The resort has four restaurants, some of which are buffet style. The management also hosts poolside barbecues and weekly shows with singing and dancing acts.

Playa Dorada (Apdo. Postal 337), Puerto Plata, Dominican Republic. **© 800/752-9236** in the U.S., or 809/320-3663. Fax 809/320-4858. www.amhsamarina.com. 437 units. Year-round US$147–US$187 double, US$221–US$236 suite. Rates are all-inclusive. AE, MC, V. **Amenities:** 4 restaurants; 5 bars; 4 outdoor pools; lit tennis courts; whirlpool; watersports equipment; children's center; 24-hr. room service; babysitting; laundry service; dry cleaning; nonsmoking rooms; aerobics; casino; disco; horseback riding. *In room:* A/C, TV, dataport, safe.

Coral Marien Beach Hotel & Spa *(R) (Kids)* Couples seeking privacy at this all-inclusive resort will find it here, but those wanting around-the-clock activities will also be rewarded. Set against green mountains and the sea, the resort, consisting of three-story pastel-colored buildings with no elevators, opens onto a white sandy beach.

A complex of thatch-roofed structures is clustered around a huge free-form pool. A tobacco theme predominates, including broad leaves inlaid in ceramic tiles, upholstery fabric, art work, and even in the handmade iron headboards in the bedrooms. A special feature is a 750-seat theater for the presentation of "cultural extravaganzas."

The bedrooms are midsize to spacious, each well furnished and containing a balcony or ground-floor patio. A tropical decor prevails, with terra-cotta tile floors and sand-colored walls. Bathrooms are beautifully maintained with tub/shower combinations. Restaurants are colorful enough, and the food is varied enough, so that you shouldn't become bored with the full-board arrangement. All-you-can-eat dinners, Caribbean seafood, Mexican specialties, barbecue nights, and Dominican specialties are some of the choices awaiting you.

Costa Dorada, Puerto Plata, Dominican Republic. © **800/HILTONS** or 809/320-1515. Fax 809/320-1414. www.coralbyhilton.com. 332 units. Year-round $232–$476 double. Rates are all-inclusive. AE, DC, MC, V. **Amenities:** 4 restaurants; 5 bars; outdoor pool (also children's pool); health club; sauna; spa; children's center; 24-hr. room service; babysitting; limited mobility rooms; nonsmoking rooms. *In room:* A/C, TV, dataport, hair dryer, safe.

Gran Ventana Beach Resort *Kids*   Come here for the opulent style and glamour on the beach, everything set against a backdrop of 100 landscaped hectares (247 acres). If you like a hotel with some theatrical pizzazz, this is your baby. The three-story buildings are trimmed with ornate, Victorian-inspired gingerbread; each unit offers mahogany furniture, ceiling fans, a balcony or patio, and, in all but a few rooms, views of the sea. Bedrooms are compact but efficiently designed. Bathrooms are a bit small but have up-to-date plumbing with tub/shower combos. The gardens and lawns surrounding the site are dotted with gazebos, flowering shrubs, and tropical plants and palms.

The all-inclusive plan limits a guest to 1 hour per day for each of the following: snorkeling, windsurfing, sailing, horseback riding, kayaks, and scuba diving. It limits dining at the exclusive Octopus (the best cuisine at the resort) to once a week. Nightly entertainment is included.

Playa Dorada (Apdo. Postal 22), Puerto Plata, Dominican Republic. © **809/320-2111.** Fax 809/320-4017. www.vhhr.com. 506 units. Year-round US$90–US$130 double; US$150–US$190 suite. Rates are all-inclusive. AE, DC, MC, V. **Amenities:** 3 restaurants; 7 bars; 3 outdoor pools; tennis court; health club; sauna; watersports equipment; children's center; salon; limited room service; massage; babysitting; laundry service; dry cleaning; 1 limited mobility room; horseback riding. *In room:* A/C, TV, dataport, minibar (in suites), hair dryer, safe.

Occidental Allegro Jack Tar Village *Kids*   Launched in 1983, but frequently renovated, this is a series of 73 villas built in a vague colonial style and painted in Caribbean pastels. This was the first resort to open in Playa Dorada, and it is still the leader of the pack, having kept abreast of the times. The complex is spread across 39 hectares (98 acres) of well-landscaped and palm-tree-studded grounds. The beach is just a short walk from the pools, and the hotel is another all-inclusive that abuts the Robert Trent Jones Jr.–designed

18-hole golf course. Rooms are midsize for the most part, filled with pine furnishings and Dominican paintings, and come with screened windows, purified water, bathrooms with tubs, private balconies, or patios. Sofa beds are installed in the living rooms. The superior accommodations are placed closer to the sands. Honeymooners often check in here, enjoying the tranquillity, and the staff seems more attuned than any other in Playa Dorada in catering specifically to Americans (many of them speak English).

The cuisine is the best served at Playa Dorada all-inclusives, and there is a trio of specialty restaurants to choose from. The hotel now has a kids' club, a pool for kids, and babysitting services available.

Playa Dorada, Puerto Plata, Dominican Republic. (Ⓒ 809/320-3800. Fax 809/320-4161. www.occidental-hoteles.com. 290 units. Year-round US$110–US$150 double. Children 11 and younger stay free in parent's room. Rates are all-inclusive. AE, MC, V. Free parking. **Amenities:** 4 restaurants; 5 bars; 2 outdoor pools (including 1 kids' pool); golf course; 3 tennis courts; health club; sauna; watersports equipment; babysitting; laundry service; dry cleaning; casino; disco; horseback riding; nightly entertainment. *In room:* A/C, TV, dataport, minibar, hair dryer, safe, ceiling fan.

Occidental Gran Flamenco 🐾 *Kids*   Opening onto a tranquil stretch of Las Papas Beach, this is one of the most upscale and consistently reliable hotels in Puerto Plata. The Occidental exudes a low-key classiness that some of its competitors lack. Operated by the Spain-based Occidental chain, it has a tasteful, discreetly elegant lobby outfitted with bouquets of flowers and reproductions of Taíno statues. Accommodations are set within clusters of three-story buildings with white walls and red terra-cotta roofs. Throughout the accommodations there's a sense of Iberian dignity, with strong contrasts of dark paneling with white walls, blue-and-white tile work, and plenty of space. More expensive rooms, in the Club Miguel Ange, are somewhat larger and have upgraded amenities and round-the-clock access to a concierge. Each bathroom has a tub/shower combo.

Dining options range from hot dogs, burgers, and pizza, to an array of international cuisine including seafood and a sampling of Mediterranean dishes. Our favorite is the grill restaurant, Las Reses.

Complejo Playa Dorada (P.O. Box 547), Puerto Plata, Dominican Republic. (Ⓒ **809/320-5084.** Fax 809/320-6319. www.occidental-hoteles.com. 582 units. Year-round US$130–US$150 double. Rates are all-inclusive. AE, MC, V. **Amenities:** 8 restaurants; 6 bars; 2 outdoor pools; golf course; tennis courts; Jacuzzi; watersports equipment; children's center; travel agency; salon; babysitting; laundry service; aerobics; disco; horseback riding. *In room:* A/C, TV, dataport, minibar (in suite), safe.

Playa Naco Golf & Tennis Resort (Kids)   Standing in lush tropical gardens, this recently renovated resort opens onto the golden sands of Playa Dorada. From snacks to activities to national drinks, everything is included. There are even facilities for weddings. The grounds extend to the shore but are not as attractively landscaped as some. Most of the land is devoted to more than a dozen three-floor buildings hawked as timeshares. When the house is full, the hotel's facilities and staff are a bit overwhelmed.

Rooms are a bit minimalist but offer reasonable comfort, and you can request beds in various configurations to suit your needs. Most accommodations are midsize, with rather basic bathrooms with a shower/tub combo. Frankly, we prefer its neighbor, Occidental Gran Flamenco, but that hotel may be fully booked in season.

If not the greatest taste, the restaurants at least provide a wide variety of food, everything from Caribbean grills to a steak house, even a deli, a French cafe, and a coffee shop—but most often buffets at which long lines form. If it's your wish, you can be kept busy with the usual array of activities such as horseback riding and watersports.

Playa Dorada, Puerto Plata, Dominican Republic. © **809/320-6226.** Fax 809/320-6225. www.naco.com.do. 414 units. Year-round US$110–US$240 double; US$140–US$420 suite. Children 2–12 US$35 extra. Rates are all-inclusive. AE, DC, DISC, MC, V. Free parking. **Amenities:** 4 restaurants; 5 bars; outdoor pool; 18-hole golf course; 4 tennis courts; health club; spa; sauna; watersports equipment; children's center; massage; babysitting; laundry service; dry cleaning; disco; exchange bank; horseback riding; nightly entertainment; pharmacy. *In room:* A/C, TV, fridge, hair dryer, safe.

Puerto Plata Village (Kids)   This is the first hotel you approach as you enter the massive Playa Dorada resort development. As such, it's also one of the farthest from the sands. To its credit, the hotel staff hauls its guests to the beach every 15 minutes during the day, and it's only 5 minutes to the water, where the hotel has staked out its own part of the beach and has installed a grill that also offers drinks.

The resort's claim to fame is that its architects, inspired no doubt by Disney, designed the resort as a replica of the old village of Puerto Plata that existed before the present tourist invasion. With all its generous space, activities, and entertainment, the village draws a lot of family trade. The property is virtually enveloped by an 18-hole golf course.

On landscaped and palm-studded grounds, Victorian-inspired buildings are painted in candy-box colors. Rooms are jazzed up with colorful spreads and draperies, the usual rattan pieces, tile floors, and two double beds, each of these midsize choices coming with a bathroom with tub and shower. Some of the superior doubles and all of the suites open onto private balconies or terraces with a garden view.

The restaurants don't send us rushing to phone the editors of *Gourmet* magazine, but the food is fresh and most satisfactory. There's certainly a lot of it, ranging from plentiful buffets to international dishes, even Mexican or Italian. We appreciate that so many of the activities, such as banana-boat rides, are geared to families. At night a variety of spectacles and international shows is presented.

Playa Dorada, Puerto Plata, Dominican Republic. ℭ **809/320-4012.** Fax 809/320-5113. www.puertoplatavillage.com. 386 units. Year-round US$110–US$135 double; US$125–US$160 suites. Children 4–8 US$13–US$23 extra. Rates are all-inclusive. AE, MC, V. Free parking. **Amenities:** 3 restaurants; 4 bars; 2 outdoor pools; golf course; 2 tennis courts; watersports equipment; laundry service; disco; nightly entertainment. *In room:* A/C, TV, iron/ironing board, safe.

Victoria Resort 𝕲𝕲   It's a 10-minute walk to the beach, but this Playa Dorada complex, set on 99 hectares (247 acres) has been a favorite since it opened in 1989. Recently renovated, this is the best resort here that does not directly open onto the beachfront. If you don't want to stroll to the sands, a shuttle awaits you. You're welcomed into a reception area of marble floors, carnival masks, and peppermint-green walls. Set in the midst of palm tree–studded landscaping, this hotel, with its gingerbread fretwork, offers beautifully decorated bedrooms, mostly midsize, with terraces or balconies opening onto greenery. Each unit comes with a well-equipped private bathroom with a tub/shower combination. Designers brightened up the rooms with colorful fabrics, and cool tile floors, wicker, and two queen-sized beds make the accommodations especially inviting.

An excellent international cuisine is served here, making use of island-grown produce whenever available. Since the hotel isn't on the beach, we wish the architects had planned a bigger pool. There is less focus on around-the-clock activities here than in some neighboring resorts, but that may come as a blessing to some guests just wanting some R&R.

Playa Dorada, Puerto Plata, Dominican Republic. ℭ **809/320-1200.** Fax 809/320-4862. 190 units. Year-round US$125–US$240 double; US$225–US$420 suite. Children 2–12 pay US$60. Rates are all-inclusive. AE, DC, DISC, MC, V. Free parking. **Amenities:** 3 restaurants; 4 bars; 2 outdoor pools; 18-hole golf course; tennis court; health club; sauna; watersports equipment; room service; laundry service; nightclub. *In room:* A/C, TV, minibar, hair dryer, safe.

WHERE TO DINE
IN & AROUND PUERTO PLATA

Aquaceros Bar & Grill INTERNATIONAL/MEXICAN   This is one of our favorite restaurants on the Malecón, just across the busy boulevard from the sea. The menu lists such tempting food items as Creole-style conch, two different preparations of lobster, burgers, barbecued fish, burritos, quesadillas, and fajitas. Of special note is the house version of Monterrey chicken, made with chicken breast, ham, salsa, sour cream, and cheese. Rum punch and banana mamas give diners a buzz. Adobe walls, a fountain, and merengue music complete the picture.

Malecón 32, Puerto Plata, Dominican Republic. ℭ **809/586-2796.** Reservations recommended. Main courses RD$145–RD$365 ($5.20–$13). AE, MC, V. Daily 10am–2am.

Jardín Suizo Malecón INTERNATIONAL   This Swiss-run restaurant, a tradition here since 1990, resembles a European trattoria with its tiles, cloth-draped tables, and use of wood. Sliding windows are pulled back to take in views of the ocean. The food is fresh and well prepared, although some of the dishes might be a little heavy for the Tropics. You can order such dishes as filet of pork in a mushroom sauce, or three different medallions of meat in a wine sauce. The best item we recently enjoyed on the menu is the freshly caught fish filet of the day in garlic sauce. Many famous international dishes are offered as well, including tasty shish kabob, chicken curries, and a thick beef stroganoff.

Ave. Circunvalación Norte 13A. ℭ **809/586-9564.** Main courses RD$200–RD$475 ($7.15–$17). AE, DC, MC, V. Mon–Sat 11am–11pm. Closed 3 weeks in July.

La Parrillada Steak House & Bar STEAK/SEAFOOD   Come here for some of the best steaks in the area. Both imported and Dominican steaks are served, and they can be cooked pretty much as you desire them. This place often attracts a lively gringo crowd, plus some employees who work at the Playa Dorada complex. The drinks are well priced, and the food is enticing, especially the finest cut served here, the chateaubriand. If you're not a meat aficionado, you can also order such dishes as a savory prawns casserole. You can also order grilled fish based on the catch of the day.

Av. Manolo Tavares, Justo 15. ℭ **809/556-1401** or 809/261-2211. Reservations recommended. Main courses RD$295–RD$890 ($11–$32). AE, DC, MC, V. Daily 4pm–midnight.

Le Papillon CARIBBEAN/CONTINENTAL   This is an unusual but charming restaurant set on a hillside in a residential neighborhood about 5km (3 miles) south of Puerto Plata. The expatriate German owner, Thomas Ackermann, manages to combine aspects of the Black Forest with merengue music. The best way to start a meal here is with a *caipirinha* (a Brazilian cocktail) at the bar beneath the cane-frond ceiling. Later, within an open-sided pavilion overlooking a forest, you'll be presented with a menu that's divided into categories that feature different preparations of pork, chicken, beef, seafood, rabbit, and even vegetarian offerings. Enduring favorites include fettuccine with lobster; "pirate" kabobs with shrimp, tenderloin of beef, and vegetables; an especially worthy chicken stuffed with shrimp and served with saffron sauce; and a four-fisted version of chateaubriand that's only prepared for two.

Villas Cofresi. ⓒ 809/970-7640. Reservations recommended. Main courses RD$364–RD$560 ($13–$20). AE, MC, V. Tues–Sun 6–10:30pm. From the center of Puerto Plata, drive 5km (3 miles) south, following the signs to Santiago. Turn left at the signs to Villas Cofresi.

Restaurante-Pizzería Portofino INTERNATIONAL/ITALIAN
In this guesthouse, the town's best pizzas and pastas are served, along with a selection of well-chosen meat dishes, mostly Italian inspired, and some fresh fish, usually grilled. It's a safe haven, and its kitchen is well maintained. It has the look of an Italian trattoria with tables draped in checked cloth sitting under a thatched roof. You can expect generous helpings of such dishes as Parmesan breast of chicken, eggplant Parmesan, ravioli, and such regional dishes as *arroz con pollo* (chicken with rice). Chicken breast stuffed with ham and cheese is one of the more delightful offerings. Locals and visitors mingle freely here. It's a casual place to dine wearing casual dress.

Av. Hermanas Mirabal. ⓒ 809/261-2423. Reservations recommended. Main courses RD$70–RD$320 ($2.50–$12). MC, V. Daily 8am–midnight.

Sam's Bar & Grill STEAKHOUSE   The *gringo* and *gringa* expats have made Sam's their favorite dive since way back in 1970, when it was first established. In the center of town, only a block and a half from the central park and the Malecón, it lies in a Victorian building from 1896. Marilyn Monroe photographs and caricatures by local artists form the decor. Here is where you can order a plate of meatloaf like your mama made, or that eternal favorite, steak and eggs. The cook does a tasty filet of beefsteak or something more ambitious, like chicken cordon bleu. Come here for the memories, the good times, and, of course, the good-tasting food. You can start your day with fluffy pancakes, or later enjoy freshly made soups, salads, and sandwiches for lunch along with hot dishes.

Calle José del Carmen Ariza 34, Castilla Hotel. ✆ **809/586-7267**. Main courses RD$180–RD$250 ($6.45–$8.95). No credit cards. Daily 8am–11pm.

AT PLAYA DORADA

Hemingway's Café INTERNATIONAL/MEXICAN The rough-hewn character of this place stands in stark contrast to the manicured exterior of the shopping center that contains it. Inside, you'll find a dark and shadowy plank-sheathed bar and grill, dotted with accessories you might have found on a pier in Key West. We can just imagine Papa himself digging into the succulent pastas, fajitas, quesadillas, meal-size salads, burgers, and huge New York steaks, while downing one of the "Floridita" cocktails. After around 9pm, a karaoke machine cranks out romantic or rock 'n' roll favorites.

Playa Dorada Plaza. ✆ **809/320-2230**. Sandwiches, salads, and pastas RD$340–RD$400 ($12–$14); main-course platters RD$330–RD$1,050 ($12–$37). AE, MC, V. Daily noon–2am.

AT PLAYA COFRESI

Chris & Mady's ✿ *Finds* SEAFOOD/INTERNATIONAL This eatery is reason enough to drive over to Playa Cofresi if you aren't staying here. Since 1995, a Canadian man and his island wife have been attracting customers here for some of the best and freshest seafood along this part of the north shore. The price of freshly caught lobster changes daily based on market quotations, but it is among the most affordable in the area. We also like to come here to feast on Dominican crayfish (called *langostinos*). Guests sit at wood tables under a thatch roof, feasting on fettuccine with shrimp, chicken breast deep fried and served with a zesty tomato sauce, or fat shrimp cooked and flavored only with fresh garlic and olive oil. If you're stopping in for lunch, you'll find freshly made salads and sandwiches, along with regular hot food. A number of Dominican beef and chicken dishes are also served.

Playa Cofresi. ✆ **809/970-7502**. Reservations recommended only Dec–Apr. Main courses RD$160–RD$450 ($5.75–$16). AE, MC, V. Daily 8am–11pm.

BEACHES & WATERSPORTS

Although they face the sometimes turbulent waters of the Atlantic, and it rains a lot in winter, beaches put the north coast on the tourist map. The beaches at **Playa Dorada** are known collectively as the "Amber Coast" for all the deposits of amber that have been discovered here. Playa Dorada has one of the highest concentrations of hotels on the north coast, so the beaches here, though good, are likely to be crowded at any time of the year, both with visitors and locals. The beaches have lovely white or powdery beige sand. The Atlantic waters here are very popular for water-skiing and windsurfing. Many concession stands along the beach rent watersports equipment.

Don't expect Robinson Crusoe–style isolation at Playa Dorada; you'll never be alone on a stretch of beach in Puerto Plata, since the beach is shared with the residents at all of the all-inclusives, each jostling for position. However, if you enjoy beige sand that's rarely too hot to walk on, and a never-ending array of watersports kiosks, chaises lounges, and loudspeakers projecting merengue music, you'll be happy here. If you want more guaranteed sun and less rain, go to Punta Cana or the beaches on the southern coast.

Lying 5km (3 miles) west of Puerto Plata is a gorgeous beach set against a backdrop of all-inclusive hotels and some vacation villas that started to be built here in the 1990s. Although you can find plenty of space on this beach on weekdays, it comes alive on Sunday when several hundred local Dominican families descend from the hinterlands for fun, food, and sun.

Another good choice in the area, **Playa Luperón** lies about a 60-minute drive to the west of Puerto Plata. This is a wide beach of powdery white sand, set amid palm trees that provide wonderful shade when the noonday sun grows too fierce. It's more ideal for windsurfing, scuba diving, and snorkeling than for general swimming. Various watersports concessions can be found here, along with several snack bars.

Your watersports options in Puerto Plata are numerous. Most of the kiosks on the beach here are ultimately run by the same company, and prices don't vary among them. If there isn't one close to your hotel, try **Playa NACO Centro de Deportes Acuaticos (© 809/320-2567)**, a rustic clapboard-sided hut on the beachfront of the Dorado NACO Hotel. Prices are as follows: banana-boat rides, RD$280 ($10) for a 10- to 12-minute ride; water-skiing, RD$560 ($20) for a 10- to 15-minute ride; sea kayak and Sunfish sailboat rental, RD$560 ($20) per hour; sailboards, RD$560 ($20) a day; and paragliding, RD$1,400 ($50) for a 10-minute ride.

There are watersports kiosks about every 100m (328 ft.) along the beach, any of which will rent you snorkeling gear and tell you the best spots for seeing fish. Puerto Plata isn't great for snorkeling, but you can take a boat trip to some decent sites.

SPORTS

GOLF   Robert Trent Jones Jr. designed the 18-hole **Playa Dorada** championship golf course ((*C*) **809/320-4262**), which surrounds the resorts and runs along the coast. Even nongolfers can stop at the clubhouse for a drink or a snack and enjoy the views. Greens fees are RD$1,820 ($65) for 18 holes; RD$1,260 ($45) for 9 holes; a caddy costs RD$336 ($12). It's best to make arrangements at the activities desk of your hotel.

The 4,888-yard (4,469m) **Playa Grande Golf Course** at Playa Grande, Km 9, Carretera Rio San Juan-Cabrera ((*C*) **800/858-2258** or 809/582-0860), is generating a lot of excitement. Some pros have already hailed it as one of the best courses in the Caribbean. Its design consultant was Robert Trent Jones Jr. Ten of its holes border the Atlantic, and many of these are also set atop dramatic cliffs overlooking the turbulent waters of Playa Grande Beach. Greens fees are RD$3,360 ($120) in winter, RD$1,400 to RD$1,820 ($50–$65) off season.

TENNIS   Nearly all the major resort hotels have tennis courts.

SEEING THE SIGHTS

Most visitors don't have a car. Those who don't want to spend all their time on the beach might consider at least one organized tour along the north shore. The best tours are offered by **Tropical Sun Safari,** Playa Dorada Plaza ((*C*) **809/254-1390**). The staff here also offers the most varied tours, with an emphasis on sports. A Jeep Safari ride along the highlights of the north coast costs RD$1,120 ($40) per person. You can also book golfing trips to Playa Grande, costing RD$4,620 ($165) for the entire day, with lunch included. A half day of horseback riding goes for RD$980 ($35) per person, a full day is RD$15,540 ($55). Deep-sea fishing can be arranged for RD$1,680 ($60) per person if you are fishing, RD$1,120 ($40) if you are just enjoying the ride. One of the best jaunts is a catamaran ride to the port of Luperón in the west, costing between RD$1,680 and RD$1,960 ($60–$70) per person. A new trip is to Paradise Island. The trip is a full-day excursion and costs RD$1,820 ($65). Full-day trips include lunch and drinks, half-day trips do not.

A rival tour operator also stages several tours as well, many quite different. **Cafemba Tours,** Calle Separación 12 ((*C*) **809/586-2177**), features more extensive Jeep Safaris, costing RD$2,520 ($90) per person, including lunch. It also presents day trips to the Peninsula of Samaná for RD$1,652 ($59), including breakfast and lunch. Some trips go to the Colonial Zone of Santo Domingo for RD$1,820 ($65) per person, including lunch.

Fort San Felipe, the oldest fort in the New World, is a popular attraction. Philip II of Spain ordered its construction in 1564, a task that took 33 years to complete. Built with 2m-thick (6½-ft.) walls, the fort was virtually impenetrable, and the moat surrounding it was treacherous—the Spaniards sharpened swords and embedded them in coral below the surface of the water. The doors of the fort are only 1m (3¼-ft.) high, another deterrent to swift passage. During Trujillo's rule, Fort San Felipe was used as a prison. Standing at the end of the Malecón, the fort was restored in the early 1970s. Admission is RD$15 (55¢) (© **809/261-6043**). Open daily 9am to 5pm, free for children under 12.

Isabel de Torres (© **809/970-0501**), an observation tower that was heavily fortified during the reign of Trujillo, affords a panoramic view of the Amber Coast from a point near the top, 779m (2,555 ft.) above sea level. You reach the observation point by cable car *(teleférico),* a 10-minute ascent. Once here, you're also treated to 3 hectares (7½ acres) of botanical gardens. The round-trip costs RD$200 ($7.15) for adults, RD$100 ($3.55) for children age 12 and under. The aerial ride runs Thursday to Tuesday from 8:30am to 5pm. There's often a long wait in line for the cable car, and at certain times it's closed for repairs, so check at your hotel before you head out.

You can see a collection of rare amber specimens at the **Museo de Ambar Dominicano (Museum of Dominican Amber),** Calle Duarte 61 (© **809/586-2848**), near Puerto Plata's Central Park. It's open Monday to Friday 8am to 6pm, Saturday 9am to 5pm. Guided tours in English are offered. Admission is RD$40 ($1.45) for adults, RD$7 (25¢) for children.

Rum drinkers might want to head out for the **Brugal Rum Bottling Plant,** Carretera Luperón, Km 3.5 (© **809/586-2531;** www.brugal.com.do), on the outskirts of Puerto Plata, 1km (½ mile) from Puerto Plata. Admission is free, and it is open Monday to Friday 8:30am to 4pm. Some 350,000 bottles—maybe a lot more—of rum are filled and boxed annually for shipment. On a guided tour, visitors are taken through the plant to see how rum is bottled. At the end of the tour, you're treated to a fruit daiquiri and can purchase Brugal hats and other gifts or souvenirs if you wish.

One of the most visited attractions in the Dominican Republic is **Parque Nacional La Isabela** (© **809/472-4204**), open daily from 8am to 3pm, charging RD$70 ($2.50) for admission. In spite of its fame, there isn't a lot to see once you're here. Nevertheless, this park contains what's left of Columbus's second settlement on Hispaniola.

At the park, excavations have revealed the outlines of what may have been the explorer's house, the church where the first mass in the New World was conducted, and an observation tower where Columbus used to gaze at the stars.

The buildings were constructed of mud and limestone. The settlement established by the sailor of Genoa was ill-fated, one-third of the population falling sick within 4 or 5 days.

The ruins of La Isabela are reached along a paved road lying 15km (9¼ miles) west of the town of Luperón. It was declared a national park in 1998. The government has messed with the site and added more to the ruins, so its original remains have been tainted. A little museum displays artifacts believed to have been owned by these early settlers from Europe.

Getting to the park isn't easy. The most direct route is to go by one of the *guaguas* leaving from the center of Puerto Plata heading for Imbert. At Imbert you must take yet another minivan to Luperón. From here, *motoconchos* go to La Isabela. All this takes 2 hours or so. Alternatively, you can drive here by rented car, or ask at one of the tour operators (see above) if any tours to La Isabela are being organized during the time of your stay.

SHOPPING

The neoclassical house sheltering the Museum of Dominican Amber (see above) also contains the densest collection of **boutiques** in Puerto Plata. Many of the paintings here are from neighboring Haiti, but the amber, larimar, and mahogany wood carvings are local.

Although the marketplace at Puerto Plata hardly resembles the greater one at Santo Domingo in the Zona Colonial, the **Mercado** at Puerto Plata merits a visit. It lies at the corner of Avenida Isabel de Torres and Calle 2, and is open Monday to Saturday 8am to 5pm (it starts winding down after 3pm, however). Everything is sold here from both Dominican and Haitian art (loads of it) to handicrafts, along with the inevitable T-shirts, as well as luscious fruits and vegetables. It's a photo op.

Plaza Turisol Complex, the largest shopping center on the north coast, has about 80 different outlets. You may want to make this your first stop so you can get an idea of the merchandise available in Puerto Plata. This complex also has the most upscale and tasteful merchandise. You might want to stop in here if you don't have time to visit all the shopping centers. It's about 5 minutes from Puerto Plata and Playa Dorada, on the main road heading east. Nearby is a smaller shopping center, **Playa Dorada Plaza,** with about 80 shops, selling handicrafts, clothing, souvenirs, and gifts. Both it and the Plaza Turisol are open daily from 9am to 9pm. The **Amber Shop,** in the Playa Dorada Plaza (✆ 809/320-2215), is associated with the Amber Museum. This shop sells the best collection of Dominican amber in town, artfully displayed on racks and on shelves. It features necklaces, pendants, bracelets, and rings crafted from amber ranging in color from oil-clear yellow to dark blue. A competitor, **Galería de Ambar,** Calle 12 de Julio (✆ 809/586-2101), is both a museum and shop. On the ground floor, both amber and larimar are sold along with Dominican and Haitian art and crafts and with bottles of rum. Upstairs, a museum displays rare samples of Dominican amber, often with prehistoric insects imbedded inside. It is open Monday to Friday 8:30am to 6pm, Saturday 9am to 5:30pm, charging an admission of RD$25 (90¢). **Tobacco Shop,** in the Playa Dorada Plaza (✆ 809/320-2216), is the best shop selling cigars around Puerto Plata. Don't overlook the benefits of cigars rolled in the Dominican Republic from tobacco grown with Cuban seeds. They're a lot less expensive than most of the Cubans, and many of them are surprisingly good. Plus, you can take them into the U.S.

   Plaza Isabela, in Playa Dorada about 455m (1,492 ft.) from the entrance to the Playa Dorada Hotel complex, is a collection of small specialty shops constructed in Victorian gingerbread style, although much of its inventory has a Spanish inspiration or flair. Here you'll find the main branch of the Dominican Republic's premier jeweler, **Harrison's** (✆ 809/586-3933), a specialist in platinum work. Madonna, Michael Jackson, and Keith Richards have all been spotted wearing Harrison's jewelry. The store has a special clearance area; tours are available. There's another branch in the Centro Comercial Playa Dorada (✆ 809/320-2219) in the Playa Dorada Hotel complex.

   Back in Puerto Plata, you can also patronize **Cuevas y Hermanos Fabricantes de Cigarros,** Tan Tan Café, Malecón 6 (✆ 809/837-8866), open Tuesday to Sunday 1pm to midnight. This is the best outlet at which to purchase Dominican cigars, which some aficionados prefer to Cuban cigars. Those considering purchasing a box of cigars can smoke one for free.

PUERTO PLATA & PLAYA DORADO AFTER DARK

AMHSA Paradise Beach Casino (✆ 809/586-3663) has the most appealing design of Puerto Plata's three casinos. It is decorated in shades of hot pink, with a soaring ceiling and lots of mahogany trim and louvers. It's open daily 4pm to 4am. **Occidental Allegro Jack Tar Village,** Playa Dorada (✆ 809/320-3800), has a casino as well as a disco, a European-style restaurant, and five bars. These facilities are only for guests of the hotel. It's built in Spanish-Mediterranean-colonial style with a terra-cotta roof. **Playa Dorada Casino,** in the Occidental Allegro Playa Dorada (© 809/320-3988), has mahogany gaming tables reflected in the silver ceiling. If you have time to visit only one casino, make it this one. No shorts are permitted inside the premises after 7pm, and beach attire is usually discouraged. Access to the slot machines is at 4pm, with full casino action after 6pm.

The Playa Dorada Hotel complex contains about 20 hotels, five of which have **discos** that welcome anyone, guest or not, into their confines. These after-dark diversions tend to be filled mainly with foreign visitors, although it occasionally attracts locals looking to hook up with tourists. None charge a cover, and the almost-universal drink of choice, Presidente Beer, costs RD$150 ($5.35) a bottle. **Crazy Moon,** adjacent to the lobby of the AMHSA Paradise Hotel (© 809/320-3663), is the hottest, hippest, and most sought-after nightclub in Puerto Plata. Fronted by an artful re-creation of a clapboard-sided Creole cottage, it's open Monday to Saturday 11pm to 4am. Admission charges start at RD$50 ($1.80).

La Barrica, Avenida Manolo Tavares Justo 106 (© 809/586-6660), lies behind an ochre-colored Spanish colonial facade on the dusty highway leading from Puerto Plata to Santiago, about 2km (1¼ mile) south of the town center. It's mobbed with locals every night after 11pm. They talk, smoke, drink, flirt, and often make out on any of the thousands of folding chairs. If you enjoy active, sometimes aggressive merengue bars where a man will positively never need to be alone, you might find it fascinating. Women should not come here alone. Entrance is free, and you might be frisked for weapons before you enter. Open Monday to Thursday 6pm to 6am, Friday and Saturday 2pm to 6am.

2 Sosúa

24km (15 miles) E of Puerto Plata

This emerging resort boasts one of the finest beaches in the Dominican Republic, **Sosúa Beach.** A strip of white sand more than .8km (½ mile) wide, it's tucked in a cove sheltered by coral cliffs. The beach connects two strikingly disparate communities, which together make up the town known as Sosúa. As increasing numbers of visitors flock to Sosúa, mainly for its beach life, it is quickly becoming a rival of Puerto Plata. You don't come here for history, but oh, those soft, white sands and crystal-clear waters, all to be enjoyed when many northern climes are buried under snow. Sosúa also has a well-deserved reputation for resorts with much more reasonable rates than similar accommodations at Puerto Plata. You won't find the super-deluxe resorts that are commonplace in Puerto Plata, but prices in Sosúa are half what they are at the big resorts. And the beaches are just as lovely.

At one end of the beach is **El Batey,** an area with residential streets, gardens, restaurants, shops, and hotels. Real-estate transactions have been booming in El Batey and its environs, where many villas have been constructed, fronted by newly paved streets.

At the western end of Sosúa Beach lies the typical village community of **Los Charamicos,** a sharp contrast to El Batey. Here you'll find tin-roofed shacks, vegetable stands, chickens scrabbling in the rubbish, and warm, friendly people.

Sosúa was founded in 1940 by European Jews seeking refuge from Hitler. Trujillo invited 100,000 of them to settle in his country on a banana plantation, but only 600 or so Jews were actually allowed to immigrate, and of those, only about a dozen or so remained on the plantation. However, there are some 20 Jewish families living in Sosúa today, and for the most part they are engaged in the dairy and smoked-meat industries, which the refugees began during the war. Bi-weekly services are held in the local one-room synagogue. Many of the Jews intermarried with Dominicans, and the town has taken on an increasingly Spanish flavor; women of the town are often seen wearing both the Star of David and the Virgin de Altagracia. Nowadays many German expatriates are also found in the town.

To get here from Puerto Plata, take the autopista (Rte. 5) east for about 30 minutes. If you venture off the main highway, anticipate enormous potholes. Taxis, charter buses, and *públicos* from Puerto Plata and Playa Dorada let passengers off at the stairs leading down from the highway to Sosúa beach.

GETTING AROUND   Most visitors walk to where they want to go in Sosúa. Most of the taxis wait for passengers in the center of town at the intersection of Calle Pedro Clisante and Calle Arzeno. *Motoconchos* run up and down the town and all around all day long, most rides costing RD$60 ($2.15), which is about one-third the price of a typical cab. You might want to pay the added *dinero,* however, since these motorcycle drivers are wreckless and dangerous, speeding through traffic as if they didn't hold your life in their maniacal hands.

FAST FACTS: Sosúa

In lieu of a post office, you can go to **EPS Sosúa Business Services,** Calle Pedro Clisante 12, El Batey (📞 **809/571-3451**), open Monday to Friday from 9am to 5pm. A standard letter to the U.S. costs RD$82 ($2.95) or to Canada costs RD$91 ($3.30), and the business service promises delivery to your destination within 5 business days of mailing. For currency exchange or ATMs, go to **Banco del Progreso,** Calle Pedro Clisante 12 (📞 **809/ 571-2815**), open Monday to Friday 8:30am to 4pm and Saturday 9am to 1pm. Another choice is **Banco León,** Pedro Clisante 73, Plaza Perdomo (📞 **809/571-1204**), open Monday to Friday 8:30am to 5pm and Saturday 9am to 1pm.

For Internet access, go to **ALF Internet Café,** Calle Pedro Clisante 12 (📞 **809/571-1734**), open daily 9am to 10pm, charging RD$40 ($1.45) per half hour or RD$70 ($2.50) for 1 hour.

For a medical problem, there are two clinics open 24 hours: **Centro Médico Bella Vista,** Autopista Sosúa-Cabarete (📞 **809/571-3429**), and **Centro Médico Dr. Quiroz,** Calle Eugenio Kunhardt 57 (📞 **809/571-2060**). For an ambulance, dial **911.**

The best pharmacy is **Farmacia Sosúa,** Calle Pedro Clisante 10 (📞 **809/571-2350**), open Monday to Friday 8am to 9pm and Saturday 8am to 8pm. The local office of the **Western Union** is at Calle Duarte 2 (📞 **809/571-3800**), open Monday to Saturday 8am to 7pm. For the police, go to Calle Principal Cabarete (📞 **809/571-0810**).

WHERE TO STAY
THE ALL-INCLUSIVES
AMHSA Casa Marina Beach ℛ   This sprawling all-inclusive opens directly on a private beach set against a lush backdrop of vegetation. It is similar to its sibling (see below), but older, dating from the late 1980s. The bedrooms (almost too many of them) are stacked up against two big swimming pools. Each of the accommodations opens onto a small balcony with a view. Rooms are midsize for the most part and furnished in a typical Caribbean style, with rattan furnishings and vivid colors on the spreads and draperies. Each comes with a tiled bathroom with a tub and shower. A combination of Creole and international cuisine is featured in the hotel's dining venues, and it's quite creditable without ever rising to the sublime. To escape the curse of all those buffets, savvy guests book a table in one of the specialty

restaurants, featuring seafood or an Italian cuisine. The usual array of activities from windsurfing to sailing is offered, and management tries to keep its captive audience amused at night with bands or live shows.

Calle Dr. Rosendo, Sosúa, Dominican Republic. (℃ **809/571-3690**. Fax 809/571-3110. www.amhsamarina.com. 300 units. Year-round US$174–US$260 double. Children 4–12 US$44–US$65 extra. Rates are all-inclusive. AE, DC, MC, V. Free parking. **Amenities:** 5 restaurants; 5 bars; 2 outdoor pools; tennis court; watersports equipment; bikes; salon; massage; doctor on call; photo shop; nightly entertainment; 24-hr. medical services. *In room:* A/C, TV, safe.

AMHSA Casa Marina Reef 🐀🐀   Constructed right before the turn of the millennium, this all-inclusive is impressively built on a private reef. On palm-tree studded grounds, it's one of the best all-inclusives in town for a tropical hideaway vacation. Well-rounded facilities and affordable rates fill up its rooms all year. Each midsize guest room comes with charming tropical furnishings, mostly rattan, painted bright Dominican colors, and the use of local crafts throughout. Two full beds come with each bedroom, and all units contain a private bathroom with tub and shower. There's the invariable buffet restaurant, but such monotony is relieved by a series of specialty restaurants for which reservations are required. The by-now-familiar round of outdoor activities are featured here as well, including windsurfing and snorkeling.

Calle Dr. Rosendo, Sosúa, Dominican Republic. (℃ **809/571-3535**. Fax 809/571-3104. www.amhsamarina.com. 378 units. Year-round US$174–US$260 double. Children 4–12 US$44–US$65 extra. Rates are all-inclusive. AE, DC, MC, V. Free parking. **Amenities:** 5 restaurants; 5 bars; 3 outdoor pools; health club; watersports equipment; salon; massage; 24-hr. medical services. *In room:* A/C, TV, safe.

Sosúa Bay Hotel 🐀🐀   Launched in 2002, this is a handsome colonial-style, government-rated all-inclusive, opening onto the tranquil waters of Sosúa Bay. This is one of Sosúa's attempts to attract more upmarket clients who might normally patronize Playa Dorada. The pillared lobby is the most impressive at the resort. It's the pampered life here. As the management states, you can start your breakfast with a mimosa and be wined and dined throughout the day, staying up late dancing to the sound of merengue. The midsize bedrooms, scattered across a three-floor building, are decorated with colonial-style wood furnishings and colorful bedspreads and draperies. Each comes with a tiled bathroom with tub and shower. If available, opt for one of the superior doubles with ocean view; others open onto lushly planted gardens. Your choice is of one king-size bed or else two double beds; most accommodations come with private balconies.

The cuisine is varied and among the best at the resort. Breakfast and lunch buffets are lavish. At night you can dine more formally—and much better—at various venues that feature the likes of Italian or international cuisine. The resort also has some of the best entertainment at Sosúa, and offers one of the most diversified activities programs.

Dr. Alejo Martínez 1, Sosúa, Dominican Republic. ☎ 809/571-4000. Fax 809/571-4545. www.starzresorts.com. 243 units. Year-round US$95–US$180 per person, per night double. Children 4–11 50% discount. Rates are all-inclusive. AE, MC, V. Free parking. **Amenities:** 3 restaurants; 2 bars; 2 outdoor pools (1 for children); health club; watersports equipment; bikes; laundry service; dry cleaning; aerobics; yoga. *In room:* A/C, TV, fridge, safe.

INEXPENSIVE
La Puntilla de Piergiorgio ☆ *Value*   This hotel lies in a quiet residential neighborhood, within a 10-minute walk from the bustling commercial center of Sosúa. Built on a rocky promontory high above the beach, it has a neo-Victorian design that includes lots of enticing gingerbread, lattices, and whimsical grace. Accommodations are bright, large, very clean, and outfitted with white-tile floors, flowered chintz upholsteries, and a semicircular veranda with views of either the garden or the ocean. Each accommodation comes with a small but neatly arranged tiled private bathroom with shower stalls.

Calle La Puntilla 1, El Batey, Sosúa, Dominican Republic. ☎ **809/571-2215.** Fax 809/571-2786. 51 units. Year-round US$75–US$110 double. Rates include breakfast. AE, MC, V. **Amenities:** Restaurant; bar; outdoor pool; limited room service; babysitting; laundry service; dry cleaning. *In room:* A/C, TV, hair dryer, safe.

WHERE TO DINE
La Puntilla de Piergiorgio ☆ ITALIAN   A 10-minute walk west of Sosúa's center, this place serves the best Italian food in town, attracting an animated clientele of Europeans looking for a change from Creole and Dominican cuisine. The setting, located in the hotel of the same name, is a series of outdoor terraces, some of them covered, most of them open air, that cascade down to the edge of a sea cliff. There's enough space to allow conversational privacy for virtually any intimate dinner, and a pair of gazebo-style bars that provide an ongoing supply of mimosas and rum-based drinks. It's true we've had better versions of every dish served here, but for the area, it is outstanding, especially the different preparations of fresh fish caught off local waters, which you can even order barbecued. Sometimes the chef gets fancy, as when he flames the prawns with cognac, or goes continental with his filet steak in green-peppercorn sauce. The cannelloni Rossini (chopped meat and spinach) isn't bad at all.

Calle La Puntilla 1. ☎ **809/571-2215.** Main courses RD$186–RD$364 ($6.65–$13). AE, MC, V. Daily noon–midnight.

Morua Mai INTERNATIONAL   This is the most visible, and most deeply entrenched, restaurant in downtown Sosúa. Established by German entrepreneurs in the 1970s, and set at the town's busiest intersection, it incorporates the closest thing in town to a European cafe on the pavement in front. It was designed of timbers and palm thatch like an enormous Taíno teepee, under which ceiling fans slowly spin, and wicker and wooden furniture help create an ambience conducive to the leisurely consumption of tropical drinks and well-prepared food. Steaks and seafood are staples here. Depending on the arrival of fresh supplies that day, the menu might also include four different preparations of lobster; several kinds of shrimp, including a version with spicy tomato sauce and fresh vegetables; four different preparations of sea bass, including a version flavored with Chablis; orange-flavored chicken spiced with ginger; steak Diana, flavored with bacon; and pork in mustard-flavored cream sauce. An excellent version of paella contains chunks of lobster and fresh shrimp.

Pedro Clisante 5, El Batey. ℂ 809/571-2966. Breakfast RD$75–RD$85 ($2.70–$3.05); pizzas and pastas RD$175–RD$225 ($6.25–$8.05); main courses RD$100–RD$1,275 ($3.55–$46). AE, MC, V. Daily 8am–midnight.

On the Waterfront 𝒜𝒜 INTERNATIONAL/SEAFOOD   The memory of Marlon Brando's Oscar-winning 1954 movie, *On the Waterfront,* is perpetuated here. This informal yet elegant restaurant sits on a cliffside, serving the finest cuisine among the independent restaurants of Sosúa. As you peruse the menu, take in sweeping views before deciding on the best of the catch of the day, which might feature fresh lobster, sea bass, conch, calamari, or red snapper, the latter tasting delectable when perfectly grilled as it is here. If you don't want fish, opt for a tender steak in pepper sauce or some lamb chops grilled with aromatic herbs. Other menu highlights include filet of sole in a tangy orange sauce or fettuccine primavera.

Calle Dr. Rosendo 1. ℂ 809/571-2670. Reservations recommended. Main courses RD$540–RD$1,200 ($19–$43). AE, MC, V. Daily 7am–10pm.

SPORTS & OTHER OUTDOOR PURSUITS

There are watersports kiosks about every 90m (300 ft.) along the beach, any of which will rent you snorkeling gear and tell you the best spots for seeing fish. You can also rent sailboats, windsurfers, and other watersports gear at any of the kiosks.

Gipsy Ranch, Carretera Sosúa-Cabarete, opposite the Coconut Palm Resort (ℂ **809/571-1373**), is the region's largest and best-recommended **riding stable,** home to about 20 horses, which can be hired for equestrian treks of between 1 and 4 hours. You'll begin your experience at the stone corral about 7km (4½ miles) from Sosúa and 5km (3 miles) from Cabarete. A 1/2-hour jaunt goes for RD$448 ($16); a 4-hour excursion through forests and along beaches costs RD1,596 ($57). Reservations are strongly recommended.

Many divers are attracted to the waters off Sosúa. In town the best outfitter is **Northern Coast Diving,** Calle Pedro Clisante 8 (© 809/ 571-1028; www.northerncoastdiving.com). There are more than a dozen diving sites off the coast, including a wreck, a canyon dive, and a wall dive. Northern Coast offers PADI-certified divemasters or instructors, featuring a two-tank boat dive for RD$1,960 ($70) with equipment, RD$1,680 ($60) without. For RD$9,800 ($350) you get 3 days of diving and certification training. The outfitter also offers 3-hour snorkeling excursions for RD$1,120 ($40) per person.

Several adventure tours are offered by **El Tour Tours,** corner of Calle Dr. Alejo Martínez and Calle Duarte (© 809/571-4195; www.eltour.net), founded in 1999. River rafting is an exciting pastime costing RD$1,820 ($65). They can also arrange horseback riding for RD$896 ($32) and catamaran sailing for RD$2,100 ($75).

ORGANIZED TOURS

Since Sosúa itself is almost devoid of attractions except for its beach, visitors who want to explore some of the north coast can head over to **Melissa Tours,** Calle Duarte 2 (© 809/571-2567; www.melissatours. com), a travel agent that offers several tours of the area. Some of their tours include an excursion to Samaná peninsula on Monday, Wednesday, and Friday, costing RD$540 ($19) per person. A tour costing RD$380 ($14) departs Wednesday and Sunday, taking you to Río San Juan, where you board a boat to go through a mangrove tree forest with a crystal-clear water lagoon, taking in fauna, fish, and birdlife.

SHOPPING

Patrick's Silversmithy, Calle Pedro Clisante 3 (© 809/571-2121), was established by British expatriate Patrick Fagg in 1973 as a showcase for his unusual jewelry designs. At least half of the inventory here is made within his studios, and each incorporates such local stones as larimar, amber, and black coral. About 80% of the inventory is made from silver, making these one-of-a-kind creations affordable.

The best art gallery is **Viva,** Calle Dr. Alejo Martínez 10 (© 809/ 571-4222), which sells local art and giftware. An excellent selection of Dominican masters is on sale; the giftware includes beautifully crafted wood sculptures in mahogany and *guayacán* (ironwood). Many ceramic "faceless" dolls are also for sale.

Index

See also Accommodations and Restaurant indexes below.

ACCOMMODATIONS

RESTAURANTS

THE NEW TRAVELOCITY GUARANTEE

EVERYTHING YOU BOOK WILL BE RIGHT, OR WE'LL WORK WITH OUR TRAVEL PARTNERS TO MAKE IT RIGHT, RIGHT AWAY.

*To drive home the point,
we're going to use the word "right" in every single sentence.*

Let's get right to it. Right to the meat! Only Travelocity guarantees everything about your booking will be right, or we'll work with our travel partners to make it right, right away. Right on!

Here's a picture taken smack dab right in the middle of Antigua, where the guarantee also covers you.

The guarantee covers all but one of the items pictured to the right.

Now, you may be thinking, "Yeah, right, I'm so sure." That's OK; you have the right to remain skeptical. That is until we mention help is always right around the corner. Call us right off the bat, knowing that our customer service reps are there for you 24/7. Righting wrongs. Left and right.

For example, what if the ocean view you booked actually looks out at a downright ugly parking lot? You'd be right to call – we're there for you. And no one in their right mind would be pleased to learn the rental car place has closed and left them stranded. Call Travelocity and we'll help get you back on the right track.

Now if you're guessing there are some things we can't control, like the weather, well you're right. But we can help you with most things – to get all the details in righting,* visit **travelocity.com/guarantee**.

*Sorry, spelling things right is one of the few things not covered under the guarantee.

I'd give my right arm for a guarantee like this, although I'm glad I don't have to.

travelocity
You'll never roam alone.

IF YOU BOOK IT, IT SHOULD BE THERE.

Only Travelocity guarantees it will be, or we'll work with our travel partners to make it right, right away. So if you're missing a balcony or anything else you booked, just call us 24/7. **1-888-TRAVELOCITY.**

travelocity
You'll never roam alone.